TEACHER EVALUATION AS CULTURAL PRACTICE

D1526110

Moving beyond the expectations and processes of conventional teacher evaluation, this book provides a framework for teacher evaluation that better prepares educators to serve culturally and linguistically diverse (CLD) learners. Covering theory, research, and practice, María del Carmen Salazar and Jessica Lerner showcase a model to aid prospective and practicing teachers who are concerned with issues of equity, excellence, and evaluation. Introducing a comprehensive, five-tenet model, the book demonstrates how to place the needs of CLD learners at the center and offers concrete approaches to assess and promote cultural responsiveness, thereby providing critical insight into the role of teacher evaluation in confronting inequity. This book is intended to serve as a resource for those who are committed to the reconceptualization of teacher evaluation in order to better support CLD learners and their communities, while promoting cultural competence and critical consciousness for all learners.

María del Carmen Salazar is an Associate Professor of Curriculum and Instruction and Teacher Education at the University of Denver, USA.

Jessica Lerner is an Assistant Professor of the Practice and Director of the Teacher Education Program at the University of Denver, USA.

LANGUAGE, CULTURE, AND TEACHING

Sonia Nieto, Series Editor

Doing Youth Participatory Action Research
Transforming Inquiry with Researchers, Educators, and Students
Nicole Mirra, Antero Garcia, Ernest Morrell

Language and Power in Post-Colonial Schooling
Ideologies in Practice
Carolyn McKinney

Dialoguing across Cultures, Identities, and Learning
Crosscurrents and Complexities in Literacy Classrooms
Bob Fecho, Jennifer Clifton

Language, Culture, and Teaching
Critical Perspectives, 3rd Edition
Sonia Nieto

Teaching Culturally Sustaining and Inclusive Young Adult Literature
Critical Perspectives and Conversations
R. Joseph Rodríguez

Teacher Evaluation as Cultural Practice
A Framework for Equity and Excellence
María del Carmen Salazar, Jessica Lerner

For more information about this series, please visit: www.routledge.com/Language-Culture-and-Teaching-Series/book-series/LEALCTS

TEACHER EVALUATION AS CULTURAL PRACTICE

A Framework for Equity and Excellence

María del Carmen Salazar
Jessica Lerner

Routledge
Taylor & Francis Group

NEW YORK AND LONDON

First published 2019
by Routledge
52 Vanderbilt Avenue, New York, NY 10017

and by Routledge
2 Park Square, Milton Park, Abingdon, Oxon, OX14 4RN

Routledge is an imprint of the Taylor & Francis Group, an informa business

© 2019 Taylor & Francis

Library of Congress Cataloging-in-Publication Data
Names: Salazar, María del Carmen, author. | Lerner, Jessica, author.
Title: Teacher evaluation as cultural practice : a framework for equity and excellence / María del Carmen Salazar, Jessica Lerner.
Description: New York, NY : Routledge, 2019. |
Includes bibliographical references and index.
Identifiers: LCCN 2018043494 | ISBN 9781138333192 (hbk) |
ISBN 9781138333208 (pb.) | ISBN 9780429446108 (ebk)
Subjects: LCSH: Teachers–Rating of. | Culturally relevant pedagogy–Evaluation. | Education, Bilingual–Evaluation.
Classification: LCC LB2838 .S25 2019 | DDC 371.14/4–dc23
LC record available at https://lccn.loc.gov/2018043494

ISBN: 978-1-138-33319-2 (hbk)
ISBN: 978-1-138-33320-8 (pbk)
ISBN: 978-0-429-44610-8 (ebk)

Typeset in Bembo
by Newgen Publishing UK

CONTENTS

Preface   *vii*

Acknowledgements   *x*

PART I
Teacher Evaluation and Culture   **1**

1   Framing the Intersection between Teacher Evaluation
    and Culture   3

2   Examining Teacher Evaluation from the Cultural Lenses
    of the Developers   26

3   Unveiling Teacher Evaluation from the Center and
    Interrogating National Models   47

PART II
Culturally Responsive Teacher Evaluation   **71**

4   Proposing an Exemplar of Culturally Responsive
    Teacher Evaluation   73

5   Documenting Culturally Responsive Teacher Evaluation
    Through Teacher Narratives   95

6 Supporting Culturally Responsive Teacher Evaluation
   Through Scenarios   119

PART III
Moving Teacher Evaluation Beyond the Boundaries   **137**

7 Reframing Teacher Evaluation and Proposing a
   New Beginning and Way Forward   139

Author Bios   *151*
Appendices   *153*
Appendix A: FEET Equity-based Words   *154*
Appendix B: FEET Dimensions, Competencies, and Indicators   *155*
Appendix C: FEET Classroom Observation Instrument   *162*
Appendix D: FEET Supervisor Training Protocol   *170*
Appendix E: FEET Standards Matrix   *173*
Index   *180*

PREFACE

We remember feeling hope and despair when we were classroom teachers. Our hope emerged from our commitment to our students and their families. It was exhilarating when our students mastered the content. It was inspiring when they persisted, resisted, claimed their own humanity, and championed the humanity of the *others*. It was humbling to witness their parents' advocacy and love. Teaching culturally and linguistically diverse (CLD) learners, and learning from them, was a transformative experience. While we clung to hope, we also despaired over an educational system that is inequitable and marginalizes the most vulnerable students. We see the same hope and despair in the prospective and practicing teachers and school leaders we work with. They care about their students and have a deep desire to support their growth and development. At the same time, they recognize that the system is designed to leave certain children behind. How can we best support teachers and school leaders to meet the needs of all of our nation's children? Recent policy initiatives point to an answer – ensuring effective teachers for all learners through teacher evaluation.

Teacher evaluation is a formalized process used to rate teacher performance using instruments that define, assess, develop, and incentivize effective teaching. Teacher evaluation systems may include classroom observation tools, student test scores, student perception surveys, teacher-evaluator conferences, portfolios, instructional artifacts, and outcomes related to professional learning communities. We focus on one aspect of teacher evaluation – frameworks for teaching. These are teacher evaluation models that include classroom observation tools that provide a definition and common approach to develop and assess effective teaching. Teacher evaluation is more relevant than ever, given the current policy landscape, the growing number of CLD learners, and persistent opportunity gaps along color lines in K-12 classrooms.

We were motivated to write about this topic because we believe that the field has overlooked a vital issue: teacher evaluation is a cultural practice that privileges the dominant culture and excludes the resources of CLD learners. As a result, the dominant culture is positioned at the normative center of notions of effective teaching and CLD learners are relegated to the margins. Thus, in its current form, teacher evaluation fails to meet the needs of all learners. In contrast, we offer the construct of culturally responsive teacher evaluation (CRTE), which we assert better supports teachers to serve all of our nation's children. In this book, we introduce the concept of CRTE as a theoretical frame, and we share the Framework for Equitable and Excellent Teaching (FEET) as an exemplar of CRTE (see Appendix B: FEET Dimensions, Competencies, and Indicators). We encourage the design of models that align with the CRTE frame.

Our examination of the intersection between teacher evaluation and culture in this book is focused on race, ethnicity, and language in teaching and learning. We acknowledge that culture is a creation of the human imagination and is inclusive of many identities, including: abilities, gender, religion, sexual orientation, citizenship status, geographic region, age, etc. Thus, though we focus on race, ethnicity, and language, we believe that the ideas in this book can cross numerous social boundaries, in addition to these.

This book is intended to serve as a theoretical, research-based, and practical resource for those who are committed to advancing equity and excellence in teaching through teacher evaluation. It provides you with knowledge needed to be critical consumers and implementers of teacher evaluation models, and advocates for culturally responsive practices. This book is designed primarily for practicing and prospective teachers and school leaders; however, it is also useful for teacher and leader educators, instructional coaches, and policy makers. It is our hope that this book will help you reconceptualize teacher evaluation and advocate for CLD learners and their communities through culturally responsive approaches to teaching, leading, and evaluation. While our approach is focused on CLD learners, White students are not excluded; we build on the resources of the dominant culture, and we promote cultural competence and critical consciousness for all learners.

The book is organized into three parts. Each part begins with a brief description of the theme and overview of the supporting chapter(s). Each chapter begins with a brief overview, and ends with a summary and implications, critical questions, and supplementary resources. The critical questions are intended to extend your comprehension and help you relate the concepts to your own practice. The supplemental resources will spur your personal or professional reflection, application of the concepts in your own context, and community outreach efforts.

Part I, *Teacher Evaluation and Culture*, provides theoretical, experiential, and practical support for the assertion that teacher evaluation is a cultural practice. In Chapter 1, "Framing the Intersection between Teacher Evaluation and Culture," we explore the intersection between teacher evaluation and culturally responsive pedagogy, assessment, and evaluation. We propose a theoretical frame for culturally responsive teacher evaluation (CRTE). In Chapter 2, "Examining Teacher Evaluation from the Cultural Lenses of the Developers," the authors, a Latina and a White scholar, each share our lived experiences and interpretive frames, from the margins and the center, to describe how our cultural lenses impact our conceptualization of teacher evaluation. In Chapter 3, "Unveiling Teacher Evaluation from the Center and Interrogating National Models," we adopt critical race theory (CRT) to expose the dominant culture as the normative center of teacher evaluation and reveal the marginalization of CLD learners based on examples from nationally recognized teacher evaluation models.

Part II, *Culturally Responsive Teacher Evaluation*, provides practical examples and resources related to CRTE. In Chapter 4, "Proposing an Exemplar of Culturally Responsive Teacher Evaluation," we present the Salazar and Lerner Framework for Equitable and Excellent Teaching (FEET), an exemplar of a CRTE model. Appendices related to the FEET can be found at the end of the book. In Chapter 5, "Documenting Culturally Responsive Teacher Evaluation Through Teacher Narratives," we share narratives of the instructional practice of five teachers prepared through CRTE. In Chapter 6, "Supporting Culturally Responsive Teacher Evaluation Through Scenarios," we describe scenarios to guide practicing and prospective teachers and school leaders to advance CRTE.

Part III, *Moving Teacher Evaluation Beyond the Boundaries*, concludes by critically examining teacher evaluation as a system that has the power to liberate and oppress. In Chapter 7, "Reframing Teacher Evaluation and Proposing a New Beginning and Way Forward," we recap key points from the book, pose critical questions about teacher evaluation reproducing or interrupting inequity, and advocate for approaches that move beyond the boundaries.

ACKNOWLEDGEMENTS

I, María del Carmen Salazar, foremost acknowledge my parents who sacrificed so much for their children. No words can express the depth of my eternal gratitude and love for you. I am also blessed with my sisters, brothers, nephews, nieces, and extended family. Thank you for all of your loving support and encouragement. I would like to thank all of the teachers who helped me along my journey and believed in me. You made a difference. I am grateful to all of my mentors who have believed in me and invested in me and in my work. I wrote this book for my children. My love for you has no bounds; it stretches further than the human imagination can grasp, it is infinite. I believe in you, always and forever. I also wrote this book for the children who reside in the margins; their resources are brilliant, their power is vast, and their possibilities are cosmic.

I, Jessica Lerner, acknowledge all of the brilliant teachers I have worked with in my career. When I was a new teacher, my peers showed me, first, how to survive. Then, they inspired me every day to be a better teacher. I remember watching my colleagues engage their students with laughter and art and music. I saw how they connected with their students' families and advocated for them tirelessly. All these years later, I still use these examples of excellent teaching. Thank you, to all teachers, for the hard work you do on behalf of your students. We all benefit from your dedication.

We give thanks to the scholars who helped us to conceptualize and complete this book: Dr. Sonia Nieto, Dr. Kathy Green, Dr. Priyalatha Gvindasamy, Melissa Schneider, Rachel Goldberg, and Grant Goble. We also humbly thank the teachers who are highlighted in this book: Brian, Paulina, Sal, Aaron, and Jenny. You are our inspiration.

PART I

Teacher Evaluation and Culture

Part I presents theoretical, experiential, and practical assertions that illustrate the link between teacher evaluation and culture. Chapter 1 briefly describes the context of teacher evaluation reform, establishes the need for culturally responsive teacher evaluation (CRTE), and proposes a framework for CRTE. Chapter 2 describes how the cultural lenses of the authors of this book influence their conceptualizations of culture, teaching, and teacher evaluation. Chapter 3 reconceptualizes teacher evaluation through a critical race theoretical perspective to make the case that teacher evaluation is a cultural practice that positions the dominant culture at the normative center and marginalizes the *other*. This chapter includes concrete examples from nationally recognized teacher evaluation models to support this assertion.

1

FRAMING THE INTERSECTION BETWEEN TEACHER EVALUATION AND CULTURE

Chapter Overview: This chapter describes the need for teacher evaluation reform. Currently, teacher evaluation reform does not address the needs of culturally and linguistically diverse (CLD) learners. Thus, this chapter provides a framework that merges culture, pedagogy, assessment, and evaluation for the development of culturally responsive teacher evaluation (CRTE).

Students of Color currently comprise over 50% of public school enrollment and are expected to comprise 56% by 2024 (U.S. Department of Education, 2016). Educators struggle with how to best serve culturally and linguistically diverse (CLD) learners, who often face the starkest opportunity gaps. CLD learners from historically marginalized communities such as Black/African American, Latinx, and Indigenous youth are increasingly segregated in schools; disciplined at higher rates, with harsher consequences; disproportionately placed into the lowest academic tracks; and overrepresented in special education (Ford, 2012; Orfield, Kucsera, & Siegel-Hawley, 2012; Welton & Martinez, 2014). These youth have been systematically denied educational opportunities due to their race, native language, class, citizenship status, and learning differences, among other intersecting identities. As a result, CLD learners from historically marginalized communities experience an education system that is, at best, fragmented and irrelevant, and at worst, a systematic effort to marginalize, mis-educate, and disenfranchise generations of Americans (Salazar, 2013).

While some of our nation's children face persistent opportunity gaps along color lines, all of our nation's children are falling behind according to global comparisons. The Organisation for Economic Cooperation and Development (OECD) Programme for International Student Assessment (OECD, 2018) indicates that the achievement of U.S. students lags in comparison to their international peers. The PISA measures student performance in mathematics, reading, and science for 15 year olds in 72 countries. In 2015, the U.S. failed to make the top 20 nations in any category. Moreover, average mathematics scores dropped 11 points from the previous assessment, and reading and science scores remained flat (OECD, 2018).

An Intense Focus on Effective Teachers and Teacher Evaluation

Educational scholars and policy makers assert that the nation's children are in dire need of effective teachers (Darling-Hammond, 2013; Stronge, 2007). This assertion is bolstered by research demonstrating that no factor under a school's control affects student outcomes more than the quality of the teacher in the classroom (Darling-Hammond, 2009; Goe, 2007; Tucker & Stronge, 2005). Research based on value-added models indicates that effective teachers make a significant difference in student learning (Aaronson, Barrow, & Sander, 2007; Nye, Konstantopoulos, & Hedges, 2004; Rivkin, Hanushek, & Kain, 2005).

According to Darling-Hammond (2013), "teaching has become a major focus of policy attention, teacher evaluation is currently the primary tool being promoted to improve it" (p. 2). Ladson-Billings (1998) posits that the intense focus on teacher evaluation began in the 1980s with three key reports on teacher quality: "Teachers for Tomorrow's Schools" (U.S. Holmes Group, 1986), "A Nation Prepared: Teachers for the 21st Century" (Carnegie Task Force on Teaching as a Profession, 1986), and "A Nation at Risk" (U.S. Commission on Excellence in Education, 1983). Ladson-Billings explains that these reports revealed a need for improved assessment measures for pre-service and in-service teachers.

This focus intensified at the turn of the century with three key policy documents on teacher evaluation. The National Comprehensive Center for Teacher Quality released a report titled, "Approaches to Evaluating Teacher Effectiveness: A Research Synthesis." This report synthesizes methods of measuring teacher effectiveness, reveals a lack of consensus over what constitutes effective teaching, and asserts that there is no common method for evaluating teacher effectiveness (Goe, Bell, and Little, 2008).

The OECD (Isoré, 2009) released a report titled, "Teacher Evaluation: A Conceptual Framework and Examples of Country Practices." This report documents teacher evaluation practices from around the globe including: defining competencies, preparing evaluators, and using results. Consequently, it fostered a global sense of urgency related to teacher evaluation.

TNTP released a report published by TNTP titled, "The Widget Effect: Our National Failure to Acknowledge and Act on Differences in Teacher Effectiveness" (Weisberg et al., 2009). The report concludes that teaching effectiveness is the most important factor in improving student achievement. It recommends that districts adopt a comprehensive performance evaluation system for teachers based on classroom observations and student growth data. The report was widely read and had a major influence on policy (Di Carlo, 2014).

Spurred by these key policy reports, teacher evaluation reform has become a dominant focus in educational reform. It is important to note, however, that other factors, besides teachers, influence student achievement, including: school conditions; home and community supports or challenges; individual student factors; and validity issues with testing (Darling-Hammond, Amrein-Beardsley, Haertel, & Rothstein, 2012).

Although teachers are not solely responsible for students' educational success, teacher evaluation focuses on the quality of the teacher in the classroom. Thus, teacher evaluation models rely heavily on classroom-based observation tools: the most widely used measure of teacher effectiveness (Little, Goe, & Bell, 2009). The 2011–2012 Schools and Staffing survey showed that 99% of untenured teachers and 95% of tenured teachers are evaluated annually based on formal classroom observations (Cohen & Goldhaber, 2016). By 2013, all states required classroom observations as a component of their state teacher evaluation system (Hull, 2013).

Researchers indicate that classroom-based observation tools help improve teacher effectiveness and student achievement (Darling-Hammond, 2013; Rockoff & Speroni, 2010). Several teacher evaluation models based on classroom observation tools have emerged nationally, including: Danielson's Framework for Teaching (Danielson, 2013), the Marzano Teacher Evaluation Model (Marzano Center, 2017), and the Classroom Assessment Scoring System [CLASS] (Pianta, La Paro, & Hamre, 2006). All include widely used classroom observation tools (Brandt, Mathers, Oliva, Brown-Sims, & Hess, 2007).

The aforementioned teacher evaluation policy documents, and the national frameworks that define and measure effective teaching, have shaped the focus on teacher evaluation reform to date. However, as systematic teacher evaluation has become more widespread, scholars increasingly question whether current teacher evaluation models adequately address the needs of CLD learners (Cooper, 2013; Hawley & Irvine, 2011; Samson & Collins, 2012).

Culture, Pedagogy, Assessment, and Evaluation

The inquiry by scholars related to teacher evaluation models and CLD learners led us to explore the intersection between culture, pedagogy, assessment, and evaluation.

While there has been vast work to define culture, we offer a brief description. Nieto (1992) defines culture as "the ever-changing values, traditions, social and political relationships, and worldview created and shared by a group of people bound together by a combination of factors… and how these are transformed by those who share them" (p. 208). Culture is a creation of the human imagination, yet it is real and impacts every element of our lives.

How does culture intersect with pedagogy, assessment, and evaluation? This question is vital to our understanding of teacher evaluation. Goe et al. (2008) state, "What is measured is a reflection of what is valued, and as a corollary, what is measured is valued" (p. 4). Is culture valued in teacher evaluation? Hawley and Irvine (2011) address this question; they explain:

> Most of the protocols for measuring performance give inadequate attention to teaching practices that are particularly effective with students from diverse racial, ethnic, cultural, and linguistic backgrounds. By ignoring these research-based practices, generally called "culturally responsive pedagogy," or CRP, any high-stakes teaching evaluation is likely—unintentionally and ironically—to fail the very students most in need of highly effective teaching.
>
> *(p. 1)*

We are in agreement and assert that a comprehensive focus on CLD learners is conspicuously absent from teacher evaluation models. What is measured is a reflection of what is valued; this implies that meeting the needs of CLD learners is not valued. This assertion is supported in this book. Because we value CLD learners, we propose a new framework for teacher evaluation that merges culture, pedagogy, assessment, and evaluation. In the sections that follow we describe how *culturally responsive pedagogy* (CRP), *culturally responsive assessment* (CRA), and *culturally responsive evaluation* (CRE) intersect with teacher evaluation, to birth a new approach to teacher evaluation: *culturally responsive teacher evaluation* (CRTE).

Culturally Responsive Pedagogy (CRP)

What is CRP?

Irvine and Armento (2001) stress that culturally responsive pedagogy (CRP) is not a new concept; it has been widely implemented in schooling for White students. Consequently, the dominant culture has benefited from CRP for centuries. Scholars call on educators to enact CRP for historically marginalized CLD learners (Gay, 2000; Ladson-Billings, 2008; Salazar, 2013). Research supports the assertion that CRP has a positive impact on student learning as measured by academic, sociocultural, and social outcomes (Cammarota & Romero, 2009; Lee, 2001; Lipka, Webster, & Yanez, 2005; Nieto, 2017).

The term "culturally responsive" is often used synonymously with the terms culturally relevant, culturally congruent, culturally appropriate, and culturally compatible teaching. We use the term *culturally responsive pedagogy* (CRP) to align with literature on culturally responsive assessment and evaluation.

Ladson-Billings spurred the notion of CRP, "a pedagogy that empowers students intellectually, socially, emotionally, and politically by using cultural referents to impart knowledge, skills, and attitudes" (Ladson-Billings, 2009, p. 20). According to Ladson-Billings (1995), CRP rests on three criteria, teachers must: (a) develop students academically; (b) nurture and support cultural competence; and (c) develop sociopolitical or critical consciousness. Ladson-Billings (2014) encourages the "remix" of CRP to adapt to the needs of each generation of students. Recent remixed versions include *culturally sustaining pedagogy* (Paris, 2012) and *culturally sustaining/revitalizing pedagogy* (McCarty and Lee, 2014). Paris (2012) states that culturally sustaining pedagogy advances the notion that educators should "perpetuate and foster—to sustain—linguistic, literate, and cultural pluralism as part of the democratic project of schooling" (p. 93). McCarty and Lee (2014) build on Paris' work with the concept of culturally sustaining/revitalizing pedagogy, "an approach designed to address the sociohistorical and contemporary contexts of Native American schooling" (p. 103).

We conceptualize CRP as an approach that fosters CLD learners' growth and development (e.g., academic, intellectual, cultural, ethnic, linguistic, socioemotional, transformational, etc.) by providing access to the cultural knowledge and skills that are prized by the dominant society (e.g., culture of power), developing/sustaining/revitalizing cultural, linguistic, and familial resources, among others (e.g., power of culture), and engaging in critical thought and action to create change (e.g., power of change).

CLD learners need to navigate the *culture of power* (Delpit, 1988), the beliefs, skills, and attitudes prized by the dominant culture that advantage some and disadvantage others. This includes ideologies and behaviors that are privileged in U.S. society, such as: independence, individuality, competition, objectivity, linear modes of expression, Standard English, and positivism, to name a few (Darder, 1991). It is important to note that a singular focus on inculcating CLD learners with that which is prized by the dominant society can result in assimilation and cultural annihilation (Smith-Maddox, 1998). To foster an additive versus subtractive approach, as CLD learners learn to navigate the culture of power, they must develop/sustain/revitalize the power of their culture.

CLD learners need to draw from the *power of culture* (Pang & Barba, 1995), the linguistic, cultural, and familial resources, to name a few, that diverse learners draw on to survive and thrive. This construct is inclusive of Yosso's (2005) notion of community cultural wealth, or "an array of knowledge, skills, abilities, and contacts possessed and utilized by Communities of Color to survive and resist macro and micro forms of oppression" (p. 77). Community cultural wealth includes: aspirational, navigational, social, linguistic, familial, and resistant capital. Maintaining the power of one's culture can be an empowering source for student learning, engagement, and resiliency.

CLD learners need to engage in the *power of change*. This power is developed through *critical consciousness* (Freire, 1970), the process of "learning to perceive social, political, and economic contradictions, and to take action against the oppressive elements of reality" (p. 17). By developing critical consciousness, students learn to think critically about their own contributions and the contributions of society to the perpetuation of inequity, injustice, and oppression, and take transformative action (Salazar, 2013). Critical consciousness is vital for CLD learners because it is based on learning that is situated in their world(s). This approach allows CLD learners to grapple with questions, such as: Why do I need to learn this? How will this make a difference for me and my loved ones? How can this help me to make a difference for my family, my community, and my world? A focus on critical consciousness promotes equity and social justice in teaching and learning (Nieto, 2000). Yet, it is important to note that this focus is often lacking in the enactment of CRP. Ladson-Billings (2014) states, "Many practitioners, and those who claim to translate research to practice, seem stuck in very limited and superficial notions of culture… few have taken up the sociopolitical dimensions of the work" (p. 77). There is work to be done on the operationalization of CRP.

What Does CRP Look Like in the Classroom?

CRP is inclusive of the culture of power, the power of culture, and the power of change. The learning environment, planning, instruction, and professional leadership are grounded in culturally responsive approaches. Teachers who enact CRP:

- collaborate with students, families, and communities to set high expectations, and provide and solicit support;
- communicate a relentless belief in the power and potential of students, families, and communities;
- infuse *cariño* (caring), *confianza* (trust), *respeto* (respect), *buen ejemplos* (exemplary models), and *consejos* (verbal teachings);
- facilitate equitable classroom facilitation strategies that communicate care, support, respect, affirmation, and shared responsibility for the classroom community;
- include posters, anchor charts, word walls, resources, manipulatives, realia, books, and artifacts that are multicultural, multilingual, and promote critical consciousness;
- design classroom configurations that communicate a sense of safety, warmth, and home;
- supplement state standards and district curriculum with content and material resources that reflect students' diversity, challenge stereotypes, and advance social justice pursuits;
- create rigorous and relevant lessons that prepare students for college and career readiness, and local and global citizenship;
- build on students' cultural ways of knowing through instructional practices;
- design assessment practices that affirm and sustain students' cultural, linguistic, and familial resources, to name a few;
- advocate for students, their families, and their communities at school, district, local, and national levels; and
- reflect on own privileges and biases, and monitor and adjust the curriculum based on anti-oppression approaches.

Above all, the culturally responsive teacher is a force for equity and excellence in education. As a result of CRP, students are engaged, motivated, challenged, and empowered, because their learning is contextualized, relevant, and inclusive of their ways of knowing.

Culturally Responsive Assessment (CRA)

What Is CRA?

The growing body of literature on CRP spurred an interest in examining assessment practices in the classroom as they relate to culture and pedagogy. Thus, culturally responsive assessment (CRA) came to prominence in the 1990s. At this time, Gordon (1995) called on the assessment community to "be responsive to the complex realities, problems, and challenges of population diversity and contextual, cultural, and linguistic pluralism" (p. 361). Simultaneously, Ladson-Billings (1995) indicated that assessment measures that value and reward CRP had not yet been developed. She indicated that developing culturally responsive teacher assessment measures necessitates the following: (a) a focus on student academic achievement through the analysis of baseline data aligned to benchmarks; (b) inclusion of cultural competence though support for home and community culture, proficiency in cultures of schooling, and building student capacities to cope with prejudice and discrimination; and (c) the development of sociopolitical consciousness, or activism and social awareness.

In 1998, the *Journal of Negro Education* released a volume that generated seminal literature on CRA. The scholars highlighted in this volume asserted that culture plays a significant role in teaching and learning, and thus, culture plays a significant role in the assessment of teaching and learning (Smith-Maddox, 1998). The scholars emphasized the importance of grounding assessment in the cultural strengths and cultural context of Communities of Color (Hood, 1998).

Seminal and current scholarship indicates that CRA: acknowledges difference; is student- and community centered; sustains and builds on knowledge and skills that emerge from students' daily lives; incorporates diverse approaches to questioning, completing tasks, and processing feedback; includes varied methods that are authentic, performance-based, flexible, and contextualized; disaggregates data to identify disparities and inequities; eliminates bias; and improves student learning (Hood, 1998; Montenegro & Jankowski, 2017; Spinelli, 2008)

Students are at the center of CRA; they are involved "throughout the entire assessment process including the development of learning outcomes, assessment tool selection/development, data collection and interpretation, and use of results" (Montenegro & Jankowski, 2017, p. 10). In contrast, generic approaches to assessment signal to students that they must demonstrate their knowledge in a "standard way… or their learning 'doesn't count'" (Montenegro & Jankowski, 2017, p. 8). The standard way to demonstrate learning typically privileges: the English language; written form; linear, objective, and analytic modes of expression;

and positivist and quantitative outcomes. This is often in stark contrast to the ways of knowing of CLD learners.

While the interest in CRA continues, assessment practices have narrowed due to national initiatives that mandate standardized approaches to assessing student learning. Scholars make the argument that the current assessment landscape does not meet the needs of CLD learners. Montenegro and Jankowski (2017) state that the field of assessment clings to the notion that while students learn in multiple ways, they must demonstrate their learning in particular ways. They add, "There is no need to employ the same measure when what is desired is equity of results, not process" (p. 6). Montenegro and Jankowski explain that there is a distinction between assessing all students the same way versus making sure students demonstrate their learning through just and equitable means.

What Does CRA Look Like in the Classroom?

CRA emerges from understanding how CLD students learn. CLD learners often take holistic approaches to learning that are grounded in their cultural, linguistic, and familial resources, to name a few. Thus, assessment must be inclusive of students' ways of knowing in order to authentically capture their learning. Teachers who enact CRA:

- develop authentic assessments that include: real-world application; problem-solving; collaboration; choice; technology; community engagement; multicultural and global perspectives; use of cultural referents; and social justice pursuits;
- build assessments that promote a curriculum that validates CLD learners' strengths, needs, and resources;
- use frequent and formative assessment, provide continuous and explicit feedback, and continuously monitor CLD learners' understanding to make adjustments to instruction;
- include learning and test-taking strategies that support access to ways of knowing that are prized by the dominant society;
- minimize or eliminate bias in testing, and break down vocabulary that may impact student performance on assessments;
- develop test items that are reflective of CLD learners' experiential knowledge, ways of knowing, native language, and allow for multiple ways to demonstrate knowledge; and
- collect and analyze quantitative and qualitative data and disaggregate the data to identify disparities or inequities.

Above all, teachers who enact CRA do not see assessment as an end unto itself, but rather, it is a means for students to access the culture of power, sustain the power of their culture, and evoke the power of change, in order to promote their growth and development. As a result, students are engaged in demonstrating their learning in a way that is authentic, real, and meaningful in their world(s).

Culturally Responsive Evaluation (CRE)

What Is CRE?

While the field of education has grappled with the intersection between culture, pedagogy, and assessment for some time, the field of program evaluation has only recently begun to consider the link between culture and evaluation. Culturally responsive evaluation (CRE) is an approach that has emerged in the past 10 years in the field of program evaluation. CRE is based on the notion that culture and context influence the work of evaluation (Thomas & Parsons, 2017). Hood, Hopson, and Kirkhart (2015) state that CRE "recognizes that culturally defined values and beliefs lie at the heart of any evaluative effort" (p. 283). CRE is also known as culturally responsive, culturally competent, multicultural, and cross-cultural evaluation (Samuels & Ryan, 2011). Hood et al. (2015) indicate that "the historical foundations of CRE marry the theories of culturally responsive assessment and pedagogy with responsive evaluation" (p. 283).

CRE scholars indicate that the theory and practice of evaluation is laden with hidden factors that promote or hinder the inclusion of historically underrepresented people in evaluations; these include: social norms, political structures, stereotypes, and attitudes (Hood et al., 2015; Thomas & Parsons, 2017). Thomas and Parsons (2017) stress that a lack of responsiveness to cultural realities and complexities can render evaluation findings "inaccurate, incomplete, or seriously flawed, with potentially devastating consequences" (p. 3).

Key concepts embedded in a CRE approach include: (a) cultural competence (SenGupta, Hopson, & Thompson-Robinson, 2004); (b) authentic understanding of culture, identity, bias, privilege, and power (Kirkhart, 1995); and (c) responsiveness to stakeholders through the co-construction of knowledge (Thomas, 2004).

Askew, Green Beverly, and Jay (2012) summarize nine CRE guidelines for explicitly incorporating culture at the center of evaluation:

1. **Assemble the evaluation team.** Attend to the sociocultural context of the program or system by assembling a team of evaluators who are knowledgeable of and sensitive to the context.
2. **Engage stakeholders.** From beginning to end, seek out and involve members from all stakeholder groups, attending to distributions of power. Identify evaluation purpose and intent.
3. **Examine the context.** Consider the social and political climate of the program and the community in which it operates, paying particular attention to equitable distribution of resources and benefits.

4. **Frame the right questions.** Using a democratic process, assess whether the evaluation questions reflect the concerns and values of all significant stakeholders including the end users. The evaluators engage a diverse group of stakeholders from the development of the questions to the dissemination of the findings.

5. **Design comprehensive and appropriate evaluations.** Take advantage of qualitative and quantitative methods to examine and measure important cultural and demographic variables.

6. **Select and adapt instruments.** Instruments should be identified, developed, adapted and validated for the target population, using culturally sensitive language.

7. **Collect the data.** Select data collection methods that are appropriate and respectful of the cultural context of the program and the target population.

8. **Analyze the data.** Involve representatives from various stakeholder groups, as cultural interpreters, to review data and validate evaluators' inferences and interpretations.

9. **Disseminate and utilize results.** Distribute findings broadly using multiple modalities, in ways that are consistent with the original purpose of the evaluation and can be understood by a wide variety of audiences.

What Does CRE Look Like?

CRE often includes a team that:

- takes time to understand the context of the evaluation, including socio-political, sociocultural, and social justice elements;
- includes evaluators that are representative of the community that is being served by the evaluation;
- pays particular attention to power, privilege, equity, and social justice, and actively engages those who are traditionally silenced and marginalized;
- engages a diverse group of stakeholders in the entire process, from the development of the questions to the dissemination of the findings;
- selects, adapts, or develops evaluation instruments that are inclusive, sensitive, and appropriate to the community that is being served by the evaluation;
- uses data collection methods that are responsive, respectful, and appropriate given the context of the evaluation and the community that is being served;
- analyzes data using critical theoretical frameworks, and engages members of the community to interpret the data through culturally appropriate lenses; and
- disseminates the findings using multiple modalities that are responsive of community ways of knowing in order to make the findings accessible and encourage community action.

As a result of CRE, communities are deeply involved in the content and process of evaluation; thus the results have the potential for greater impact.

Culturally Responsive Teacher Evaluation (CRTE)

While research supports the assertion that CRP has a positive impact on educational practice, the teacher evaluation reform movement has yet to recognize that culture influences the work of teaching and evaluation. As a result, the field lacks a comprehensive framework that can assess a teacher's overall effectiveness in culturally responsive teaching (Powell, Cantrell, & Malo-Juvera, 2016).

Incorporating culture into teacher evaluation requires attention to be paid to both the content of the evaluation (CRP), and the process by which the evaluation is developed (CRE). We merge components from teacher evaluation reform efforts, culturally responsive pedagogy (CRP), and culturally responsive evaluation (CRE) to propose five tenets for culturally responsive teacher evaluation (CRTE). We envision CRA as a component of CRP.

We define CRTE as an approach that moves historically marginalized communities from the margins to the center of teacher evaluation through the following:

- develop equitable and excellent teachers;
- facilitate collaboration of diverse communities in co-construction of evaluation tools;
- incorporate targeted teacher competencies that promote student growth and development, particularly CLD learners;
- establish and monitor reliability and validity within a cultural context; and
- advance equity and social justice in student outcomes.

Table 1.1 presents a theoretical frame that illustrates the tenets of teacher evaluation reform, CRE, and CRP; these intersect to form the tenets of CRTE.

An example of CRTE in practice is provided in Chapter 4. In the sections that follow, we draw from literature on teacher evaluation reform efforts, CRE, and CRP, to further elaborate on the five tenets of CRTE.

Tenet 1: CRTE develops equitable and excellent teachers

Teacher evaluation reform emerged from a desire to ensure all students have effective teachers. However, efforts to meet the needs of *all* students have evolved into generic approaches that fail to consider the cultural context of teaching and learning. In contrast, CRE acknowledges inequity that is reproduced through evaluation approaches, and it takes a context-specific approach to evaluation by assessing how programs are meeting the needs of culturally diverse communities. CRP is also focused on the importance of culture, and asserts that culture and critical approaches are intertwined with teaching and learning.

CRTE promotes equitable teaching. McGee and Banks (1995) define equitable teaching as "teaching strategies and classroom environments that help students

TABLE 1.1 Theoretical frame for culturally responsive teacher evaluation (CRTE)

	Tenets of teacher evaluation reform	*Tenets of culturally responsive evaluation (CRE)*	*Tenets of culturally responsive pedagogy (CRP)*	*Tenets of culturally responsive teacher evaluation (CRTE)*
Purpose	Ensure all students have effective teachers	Evaluate how programs are meeting the needs of diverse communities	Promote culturally responsive teaching	Develop equitable and excellent teachers
Community engagement	Vary with regard to educator and policy maker consultation with communities	Sustain collaboration with diverse stakeholders/ communities from inception to dissemination	Encourage collaboration between educators and diverse communities in enactment of CRP	Facilitate collaboration of diverse communities in co-construction of evaluation tools
Content	Include generalized teacher competencies linked to student achievement	Varies based on needs of diverse communities	Focus on academic excellence, cultural competence, and critical consciousness	Incorporate targeted teacher competencies that promote student growth and development, particularly for CLD learners
Technical properties	Demonstrate reliability and validity	Determine reliability, validity, and multicultural validity	Varied and context specific	Establish and monitor reliability and validity within a cultural context
Outcome	Improve academic outcomes for students as measured by standardized tests	Further equity and social justice by improving the ability of programs to serve diverse communities; measurement varies and is context specific	Promote equity and social justice in student outcomes as measured by assessments of academic success, cultural competence, and critical consciousness	Advance equity and social justice in student outcomes as measured by assessments of students' full potential

Note. The tenets of CRTE are developed by Salazar and Lerner. These are derived from research on teacher evaluation reform (Darling-Hammond, 2012; Goe et al., 2008), CRE (Askew et al., 2012; Thomas & Parsons, 2017), and CRP (Ladson-Billings 1995, 2009; Nieto, 2017; Salazar, 2013).

from diverse racial, ethnic, and cultural groups attain the knowledge, skills, and attitudes needed to function effectively within, and help create and perpetuate, a just, humane, and democratic society" (p. 152).

CRTE also promotes excellent teaching, the result of equitable teaching. We make a conscious choice to use the term "excellent teaching" as opposed to "effective teaching." While we acknowledge the generalized knowledge, skills, and dispositions that are said to promote effective teaching, we push beyond these notions. Our conceptualization of excellence in teaching aligns with Delpit's (2013) notion:

> Part of truly honing the genius of our children would be consciously to organize institutions and instruction inside and outside of school buildings that expose the children to their intellectual legacy; clarify their position in a racialized society; ritually express expectations for hard work and academic, social, physical, and moral excellence; and create alternative reasons for success other than "getting a good job" – for your community, for your ancestors, for your descendants.
>
> *(p. 43)*

Delpit's description of what is possible helps us to imagine that excellent teaching has a soul; it is nourished by what was, what is, what can be, and what is just.

Tenet 2: CRTE facilitates collaboration of diverse communities in co-construction of evaluation tools

Teacher evaluation reform efforts vary widely. Reform efforts are often initiated by educators and policy makers, and they vary with regard to consultation with diverse communities. Teacher evaluation frameworks often emerge based on national, state, and local contexts. For example, many states have looked to the National Board for Professional Teaching Standards [NBPTS] (n.d.) and/or the Interstate Teacher Assessment and Support Consortium [InTASC] (2011) for guidance in developing teacher evaluation models. Both the NBPTS and InTASC were developed by a diverse group of stakeholders including: teachers, teacher educators, researchers, representatives from educational testing companies, and state policy leaders. It is unclear if these stakeholders are representative of the ethnic diversity of our nation's students.

From a CRE perspective, it is vital to collaborate with diverse stakeholders to evaluate programs from the inception to the dissemination of findings. We provide an example of collaboration with diverse stakeholders to develop culturally responsive evaluation tools. The Denver Public Schools (DPS) developed a model for educator support and evaluation, called Leading Effective Academic Practice (LEAP). The LEAP is the basis for the district's classroom-based evaluations. The LEAP is recognized nationally as a model for stakeholder collaboration because district leaders solicited feedback from diverse teachers, the local teacher's union, parents, students, and community members (Jerald, 2013). This input from stakeholders ensured that the evaluation of effective teaching was meaningful in their local context. While the LEAP includes a strong emphasis on language and culture, it is not inclusive of critical consciousness.

CRTE is co-constructed through collaboration between diverse communities. CRTE follows the guidelines set by Askew et al. (2012), previously described in this chapter, to ensure that the development process, from start to end, is responsive to the needs of diverse communities. As a part of this process, CRTE requires co-construction with diverse communities, such as: students, families, higher education faculty, teachers, administrators, and policy makers. It is important to include the voices and perspectives of diverse community members. The participants should mirror the demographics of the communities that will be served through CRTE.

Tenet 3: CRTE incorporates targeted teacher competencies that promote student growth and development, particularly CLD learners

The teacher evaluation reform movement was built on the notion that generalized teaching competencies can increase student achievement. However, in targeting generalized practices, teacher evaluation models have given "inadequate attention to teaching practices that are particularly effective for students from diverse racial, ethnic, cultural, and linguistic backgrounds" (Hawley & Irvine, 2011, p. 1). CRE is founded on the belief that the practice of evaluation is dependent on the needs of diverse groups. Thus, CRE promotes understanding the intersection between evaluation, culture, identity, bias, privilege, and power (Frierson et al., 2002; Thomas & Parsons, 2017). CRP aligns with CRE in that the needs of diverse communities are deemed to be essential for teaching and learning (Ladson-Billings, 1995).

CRTE incorporates targeted teaching competencies that promote student growth and development, particularly that of CLD learners. To promote student growth and development, CRTE targets competencies that promote knowledge of learning theory, CRP and ELL strategies, support for special needs students, native language support, and critical perspectives, to name a few. These are further explained in Chapter 4.

Tenet 4: CRTE establishes and monitors reliability and validity within a cultural context

The teacher evaluation reform movement advocates using teaching evaluations, along with other measures, for high-stakes decisions such as compensation, promotion, and dismissal. Thus, evaluators should be trained to rate teachers reliably.

Reliability refers to the degree to which the assessment produces stable and consistent results. Validity is also essential in teacher evaluation, and refers to the extent to which a construct measures what it was intended to measure.

CRE focuses on traditional measures of reliability and validity. However, it stresses the importance of establishing multicultural validity in evaluation approaches. Hopson and Kirkhart (2012) define multicultural validity as "the correctness or authenticity of understandings across multiple, intersecting cultural contexts" (p. 13). CRE also takes the characteristics of the raters into consideration. Thomas and Parsons (2017) assert that CRE "requires evaluators to have a 'shared lived experience' with the population under consideration and/or a keen awareness of the cultural context and an understanding of how this context might influence the behavior of individuals in programs" (p. 4). CRE stresses the importance of cultural competence among those conducting the evaluation. The Colorado Trust (2007) has identified the characteristics of culturally competent evaluators, including: consciousness of differences in cultures; willingness to engage in dialogue about culture, social identity, privilege, and power; and ability to design processes that consider the differences, similarities, and needs of stakeholders.

This perspective is closely aligned with Ladson-Billing's (1998) view of culturally responsive approaches to teacher evaluation. According to Ladson-Billings, "Few test constructors have ever considered the importance of cultural competence for students, nor would they even recognize it when it is being demonstrated by teachers" (p. 262). She contends that if teacher evaluation systems aim to capture culturally responsive teaching practice, assessors must be culturally responsive and capable of "cultural translations of pedagogical expertise" (p. 263). She adds that if assessors are not knowledgeable about culturally responsive teaching, they may not recognize those practices, or worse yet, they may misinterpret them as ineffective (Ladson-Billings, 1998).

CRTE is concerned with validity and reliability in a cultural context. Validity should be continuously monitored using quantitative and qualitative methods. The use of qualitative methods allows for integration of the experiential knowledge of diverse communities. Multicultural validity is particularly vital for CRTE. In the context of teacher evaluation, multicultural validity includes: a focus on relationship-building; alignment with culturally responsive and critical theories; inclusion of life experiences of those who are served by teacher evaluation; culturally appropriate methodologies; and action toward equity and social justice. Reliability is also essential. Evaluators should participate in ongoing rater training sessions. Those training sessions should include professional development on CRP, explicit and implicit biases, and the purpose of CRTE. The training should help evaluators understand that they have the "privilege and power to shed light on a social phenomenon by bringing attention to terms, concepts, and contextual conditions that might perpetuate or eliminate structural inequities..." (Colorado Trust, 2007, p. 13). It is also important that evaluators be representative of the demographics of the population that is being served by the evaluation.

Tenet 5: CRTE advances equity and social justice in student outcomes

Teacher evaluation reform efforts were founded on the expectation that teacher evaluation can improve academic outcomes for students (Papay, 2012). In this case, student outcomes are generally measured through standardized tests. CRE focuses on the broader goal of furthering equity and social justice by improving the ability of programs to serve diverse communities (Greene, 2006). CRE outcomes are measured through varied means that are context specific. CRP promotes equity and social justice in student outcomes.

CRTE is also focused on academic outcomes; however, this is not the sole focus. A singular focus on academic outcomes does not close the gap; it creates a chasm. The chasm results from the impetus to assimilate CLD learners; this practice denies students' full potential, including their academic, intellectual, cultural, ethnic, linguistic, sociocultural, and transformative capacities, to name a few. These can be defined and expanded on in a myriad of ways depending on local contexts.

Summary and Implications

In this chapter, we briefly describe the need for teacher evaluation reform. We assert that teacher evaluation reform has not met the needs of CLD learners. Thus, we propose a theoretical frame that merges culture, pedagogy, assessment, and evaluation – culturally responsive teacher evaluation (CRTE). The tenets of CRTE provoke the examination of teacher evaluation through the lens of culture, equity, and social justice. We encourage you to question and challenge the status quo of teacher evaluation. Does teacher evaluation meet the needs of CLD learners? How is culture included or excluded in teacher evaluation? How can teacher evaluation spur equity and social justice?

Critical Questions

The following critical questions are intended to extend your comprehension and help you relate the concepts to your own practice.

1. What is your perception of teacher evaluation reform? Is it positive, negative, or neutral?
2. Why does CRTE matter?
3. What are the strengths and weaknesses of CRTE?

4. What are your thoughts on the definitions of equity and excellence in teaching presented in this chapter? What are the strengths? What is missing? How do you define equity and excellence in teaching?
5. How do your state or district teacher evaluation tools align with and/or differ from the tenets of CRTE?

Resources for Further Reflection and Study

The following supplemental resources are intended to spur your personal and professional reflection, application of the concepts in your own context, and community outreach efforts.

Print

Greene, J. C. (2006). Evaluation, democracy, and social change. In I. F. Shaw, J. C. Greene, & M. M. Mark (Eds.), *The SAGE handbook of evaluation* (pp. 118–140). Thousand Oaks, CA: Sage.

Hood, S., Hopson, R., & Frierson, H. (2005). *The role of culture and cultural context: A mandate for inclusion, the discovery of truth, and understanding in evaluative theory and practice*. Greenwich, CT: Information Age Publishing.

Khalifa, M. A., Gooden, M. A., & Davis, J. E. (2016). Culturally responsive school leadership: A synthesis of the literature. *Review of Educational Research, 86*(4), 1272–1311.

McBride, D. F. (2011). Sociocultural theory: Providing more structure to culturally responsive evaluation. *New Directions for Evaluation, 2011*(131), 7–13.

SenGupta, S., Hopson, R., & Thompson-Robinson, M. (2004). Cultural competence in evaluation: An overview. *New Directions for Evaluation, 2004*(102), 5–19.

Sleeter, C. E. (2012). Confronting the marginalization of culturally responsive pedagogy. *Urban Education, 47*(3), 562–584.

Web

*   Eastern Evaluation Research Society
    Culturally responsive evaluation
    www.wcasa.org/file_open.php?id=869
*   Equity Alliance
    Culturally responsive teaching matters
    www.equityallianceatasu.org
*   National Education Association (NEA)
    Resources for culturally responsive teachers
    www.nea.org/archive/16723.htm
*   The Colorado Trust
    The importance of culture in evaluation: A practical guide for evaluators
    www.communityscience.com/pdfs/CrossCulturalGuide.r3.pdf

- The Education Alliance
  Culturally responsive teaching
  www.brown.edu/academics/education-alliance/teaching-diverse-learners/
  strategies-0/culturally-responsive-teaching-0

Media

- MyM&E
  Cultural responsiveness in equity-focused evaluations
  www.youtube.com/watch?v=XJpACQjfluI
- Public Consulting Group
  Best practices for teaching African American males
  www.youtube.com/watch?v=DeUFhei81wg
- Roses in Concrete
  Roses in Concrete trailer
  www.youtube.com/watch?v=bejCoWi88J8
- Teaching Tolerance
  Introduction to culturally responsive teaching
  www.youtube.com/watch?v=nGTVjJuRaZ8

Learning Opportunities

1. Use playdough, or a different medium, to create a visual representation of CRE, CRP, and/or CRTE.
2. Describe examples of culturally responsive teaching in your practice or practice you have observed. What did it look like, sound like, and feel like? How did students respond?
3. Reflect on your own K–12 education. How could your educational experience have been different if your teachers had been evaluated and supported using CRTE?
4. Compose a tweet (140 words or less) to summarize and advocate for CRTE.

Community Engagement Opportunities

1. Compose an email to your district/state school board members advocating for CRTE. Include the following:
   - Purpose
   - Benefits
   - Tenets
   - Potential impact on teaching and learning

2. Hold a town hall meeting with your school community, including school leaders, teachers, support staff, parents, and students. Explain the purpose of

teacher evaluation tools. Detail the strengths and weaknesses of such tools. Solicit feedback on your district/state evaluation tool. Use this feedback to advocate for CRTE.

3. Convene a group of diverse students. Ask them to complete the following sentence stems:
    *   Teachers/school leaders show they care by _____.
    *   Teachers help me learn by _____.
    *   Teachers make it hard for me to learn when they _____.
    *   My culture and other cultures are visible in my classroom and the school _____.
    *   A good teacher/school leader is _____.
    *   The advice I would give to a new teacher or school leader is _____.

References

Aaronson, D., Barrow, L., & Sander, W. (2007). Teachers and student achievement in the Chicago public high schools. *Journal of Labor Economics, 25*(1), 95–135.

Askew, K., Green Beverly, M., & Jay, M. L. (2012). Aligning collaborative and culturally responsive evaluation approaches. *Evaluation and Program Planning, 35*(4), 552–557.

Brandt, C., Mathers, C., Oliva, M., Brown-Sims, M., & Hess, J. (2007). *Examining district guidance to schools on teacher evaluation policies in the Midwest region. Issues & Answers.* REL 2007-No. 030. Regional Educational Laboratory Midwest. Retrieved from https://files.eric.ed.gov/fulltext/ED499235.pdf

Cammarota, J., & Romero, A. F. (2009). A social justice epistemology and pedagogy for Latina/o students: Transforming public education with participatory action research. *New Directions for Student Leadership, 123,* 53–65.

Carnegie Task Force on Teaching as a Profession (1986). *A nation prepared: Teachers for the 21st century: The report of the task force on teaching as a profession.* New York, NY: Carnegie Forum on Education.

Cohen, J., & Goldhaber, D. (2016). Observations on evaluating teacher performance: Assessing the strengths and weaknesses of classroom observations and value-added measures. In J. A. Grissom & P. Youngs (Eds.), *Improving teacher evaluation systems: Making the most of multiple measures* (pp. 8–21). New York, NY: Teachers College Press.

Colorado Trust (2007). *The importance of culture in evaluation: A practical guide for evaluators.* Retrieved from www.communityscience.com/pdfs/CrossCulturalGuide.r3.pdf

Cooper, P. M. (2013). Preparing multicultural educators in an age of teacher evaluation systems: Necessary stories from field supervision. *Teacher Education Quarterly, 40*(2), 7–27.

Danielson, C. (2013). *The Framework for Teaching: Evaluation instrument.* Princeton, NJ: The Danielson Group.

Darder, A. (1991). *Culture and power in the classroom: A critical foundation for bicultural education.* Westport, CT: Bergin and Garvey.

Darling-Hammond, L. (2009). Recognizing and enhancing teacher effectiveness. *The International Journal of Educational and Psychological Assessment, 3,* 1–24.

Darling-Hammond, L. (2012). *Creating a comprehensive system for evaluating and supporting effective teaching.* Stanford Center for Opportunity Policy in Education. Retrieved from https://edpolicy.stanford.edu/sites/default/files/publications/creating-comprehensive-system-evaluating-and-supporting-effective-teaching.pdf

Darling-Hammond, L. (2013). *Getting teacher evaluation right: What really matters for effectiveness and improvement.* New York, NY: Teachers College Press.

Darling-Hammond, L., Amrein-Beardsley, A., Haertel, E., & Rothstein, J. (2012). Evaluating teacher evaluation. *Phi Delta Kappan, 93*(6), 8–15.

Delpit, L. (1988). The silenced dialogue: Power and pedagogy in educating other people's children. *Harvard Educational Review, 58*(3), 280–299.

Delpit, L. (2013). *"Multiplication is for white people": Raising expectations for other people's children.* New York, NY: The New Press.

Di Carlo, M. (2014). *Revisiting the widget effect.* Albert Shanker Institute. Retrieved from www.shankerinstitute.org/blog/revisiting-widget-effect

Ford, D. (2012). Culturally different students in special education: Looking backward to move forward. *Exceptional Children, 78*(4), 391–405.

Freire, P. (1970). *Cultural action for freedom.* Boston, MA: Harvard Educational Review.

Frierson, H. T., Hood, S., & Hughes, G. B. (2002). Strategies that address culturally responsive evaluation. In J. Frechtling (Ed.), *The 2002 user-friendly handbook for project evaluation* (pp. 63–73). Arlington, VA: The National Science Foundation.

Gay, G. (2000). *Culturally responsive teaching: Theory, research, and practice.* New York, NY: Teachers College Press.

Goe, L (2007). *The link between teacher quality and student outcomes: A research synthesis.* National Comprehensive Center for Teacher Quality. Retrieved from https://files.eric.ed.gov/fulltext/ED521219.pdf

Goe, L., Bell, C., & Little, O. (2008). *Approaches to evaluating teacher effectiveness: A research synthesis.* National Comprehensive Center for Teacher Quality. Retrieved from https://files.eric.ed.gov/fulltext/ED521228.pdf

Gordon, B. M. (1995). Knowledge construction, competing critical theories, and education. In J. A. Banks & C. A. McGee Banks (Eds.), *Handbook of research on multicultural education* (pp. 184–202). New York, NY: Macmillan.

Greene, J. C. (2006). Evaluation, democracy, and social change. In I. Shaw, J. Greene, & M. Mark (Eds.), *The SAGE handbook of evaluation* (pp. 118–140). London, England: Sage.

Hawley, W. D., & Irvine, J. J. (2011). The teaching evaluation gap: Why students' cultural identities hold the key [Electronic version]. *Education Week, 31*, 30–31.

Hood, S. (1998). Culturally responsive performance-based assessment: Conceptual and psychometric considerations. *Journal of Negro Education, 67*(3), 187–196.

Hood, S., Hopson, R., & Kirkhart, K. (2015). Culturally responsive evaluation: Theory, practice, and future implications. In K. Newcomer, H. Hatry, & J. Wholey (Eds.), *Handbook of practical program evaluation* (pp. 281–317). San Francisco, CA: John Wiley & Sons, Inc.

Hopson, R., & Kirkhart, K. (2012). *Strengthening evaluation through cultural relevance and cultural competence.* Retrieved from www.wcasa.org/file_open.php?id=869

Hull, J. (2013). *Trends in teacher evaluation.* Alexandra, VA: National School Boards Association.

Interstate Teacher Assessment and Support Consortium [InTASC] (2011). *InTASC Model Core Teaching Standards and Learning Progressions.* Retrieved from https://ccsso.org/sites/default/files/2017-12/2013_INTASC_Learning_Progressions_for_Teachers.pdf

Irvine, J. J., & Armento, B. J. (2001). *Culturally responsive teaching: Lesson planning for elementary and middle grades.* New York, NY: McGraw-Hill.

Isoré, M. (2009). *Teacher evaluation: Current practices in OECD countries and a literature review.* OECD Education Working Papers, No. 23. Paris, France: OECD Publishing.

Jerald, C. R. (2013). *Defining a 21st century education.* Center for Public Education. Retrieved from www.mikemcmahon.info/21stCenturyEducationDefined.pdf

Kirkhart, K. E. (1995). 1994 conference theme: Evaluation and social justice seeking multicultural validity: A postcard from the road. *Evaluation Practice, 16*(1), 1–12.

Ladson-Billings, G. (1995). Toward a theory of culturally relevant pedagogy. *American Educational Research Journal, 32*(3), 465–491.

Ladson-Billings, G. (1998) Preparing teachers for diverse student populations: A critical race theory perspective, *Review of Research in Education, 24*, 211–247.

Ladson-Billings, G. (2008). Yes, but how do we do it? Practicing culturally relevant pedagogy. In W. Ayers, G. Ladson-Billings, G. Michie, & P. A. Noguera (Eds.), *City kids, city schools: More reports from the front row* (pp. 162–177). New York, NY: The New Press.

Ladson-Billings, G. (2009). *The dreamkeepers: Successful teachers of African American children* (2nd ed.). San Francisco, CA: Jossey-Bass.

Ladson-Billings, G. (2014). Culturally relevant pedagogy 2.0: Aka the remix. *Harvard Educational Review, 84*(1), 74–84.

Lee, C. C. (2001). Culturally responsive school counselors and programs: Addressing the needs of all students. *Professional School Counseling, 4*(4), 257–261.

Lipka, J., Webster, J. P., & Yanez, E. (2005). Introduction. *Journal of American Indian Education, 44*(3), 1–8.

Little, O., Goe, L., & Bell, C. (2009). *A practical guide to evaluating teacher effectiveness.* National Comprehensive Center for Teacher Quality. Retrieved from https://files.eric.ed.gov/fulltext/ED543776.pdf

Marzano Center (2017). *Marzano Teacher Evaluation Model.* Retrieved from www.marzanoevaluation.com

McCarty, T., & Lee, T. (2014). Critical culturally sustaining/revitalizing pedagogy and Indigenous education sovereignty. *Harvard Educational Review, 84*(1), 101–124.

McGee Banks, C. A., & Banks, J. (1995). Equity pedagogy: An essential component of multicultural education. *Theory into Practice, 34*(3), 152–158.

Montenegro, E., & Jankowski, N. A. (2017). *Equity and assessment: Moving towards culturally responsive assessment.* Retrieved from http://learningoutcomesassessment.org/documents/OccasionalPaper29.pdf

National Board for Professional Teaching Standards (NBPTS) (n.d.). *Five Core Propositions.* Retrieved from www.nbpts.org/standards-five-core-propositions/

Nieto, S. (1992). *Affirming diversity: The sociopolitical context of multicultural education.* White Plains, NY: Longman.

Nieto, S. (2000). Placing equity front and center: Some thoughts on transforming teacher education for a new century. *Journal of Teacher Education, 51*(3), 180–187.

Nieto, S. (2017). *Language, culture, and teaching: Critical perspectives* (3rd ed.). New York, NY: Routledge.

Nye, B., Konstantopoulos, S., & Hedges, L. V. (2004). How large are teacher effects? *Educational Evaluation and Policy Analysis, 26*(3), 237–257.

OECD (2018). *PISA results in focus.* OECD. Retrieved from www.oecd.org/pisa/pisa-2015-results-in-focus.pdf

Orfield, G., Kucsera, J., & Siegel-Hawley, G. (2012). E pluribus… separation: Deepening double segregation for more students. *Journal of Urban Education, 50*(5), 535–571.

Pang, V. O., & Barba, R. H. (1995). The power of culture: Building culturally affirming instruction. In C. A. Grant (Ed.), *Educating for diversity: An anthology of multicultural voices* (pp. 341–358). Boston, MA: Allyn & Bacon.

Papay, J. (2012). Refocusing the debate: Assessing the purposes and tools of teacher evaluation. *Harvard Educational Review, 82*(1), 123–141.

Paris, D. (2012). Culturally sustaining pedagogy: A needed change in stance, terminology, and practice. *Educational Researcher, 41*(3), 93–97.

Pianta, R. C., La Paro, K. M., & Hamre, B. K. (2006). *Classroom Assessment Scoring System: Manual K-3 version.* Charlottesville, VA: Center for Advanced Study of Teaching and Learning.

Powell, R., Cantrell, S. C., Malo-Juvera, V., & Correll, P. (2016). Operationalizing culturally responsive instruction: Preliminary findings of CRIOP research. *Teachers College Record, 118*(1), 1–46.

Rivkin, S. G., Hanushek, E. A., & Kain, J. F. (2005). Teachers, schools, and academic achievement. *Econometrica, 73*(2), 417–458.

Rockoff, J. E., & Speroni, C. (2010). Subjective and objective evaluations of teacher effectiveness. *The American Economic Review, 100*(2), 261–266.

Salazar, M. (2013). A humanizing pedagogy: Reinventing the principles and practice of education as a journey toward liberation. *Review of Research in Education, 37*(1), 121–148.

Samson, J. F., & Collins, B. A. (2012). *Preparing all teachers to meet the needs of English language learners: Applying research to policy and practice for teacher effectiveness.* Retrieved from https://files.eric.ed.gov/fulltext/ED535608.pdf

Samuels, M., & Ryan, K. (2011). Grounding evaluations in culture. *American Journal of Evaluation, 32*(2), 183–198.

SenGupta, S., Hopson, R., & Thompson-Robinson, M. (2004). Cultural competence in evaluation: An overview. *New Directions for Evaluation, 102,* 5–19.

Smith-Maddox, R. (1998). Defining culture as a dimension of academic achievement: Implications for culturally responsive curriculum, instruction, and assessment. *Journal of Negro Education, 67*(3), 302–317.

Spinelli, C. (2008). Addressing the issue of cultural and linguistic diversity and assessment: Informal evaluation measures for English Language Learners. *Reading and Writing Quarterly, 24*(1), 101–118.

Stronge, J. H. (2007). *Qualities of effective teachers.* Alexandria, VA: ASCD.

Thomas, V. G. (2004). Building a contextually responsive evaluation framework: Lessons from working with urban school interventions. *New Directions for Evaluation, 101,* 3–23.

Thomas, V. G., & Parsons, B. A. (2017). Culturally responsive evaluation meets systems-oriented evaluation. *American Journal of Evaluation, 38*(1), 1–22.

Tucker, P. D., & Stronge, J. H. (2005). *Linking teacher evaluation and student achievement.* Alexandria, VA: ASCD.

U.S. Commission on Excellence in Education (1983). *A nation at risk: The imperative for educational reform.* Washington DC: United States Department of Education.

U.S. Department of Education Office of Planning, Evaluation, and Policy Development (2016). *The state of racial diversity in the educator workforce.* Retrieved from www2.ed.gov/rschstat/eval/highered/racial-diversity/state-racial-diversity workforce.pdf

U.S. Holmes Group (1986). *Tomorrow's teachers: A report of the Holmes Group.* Lynnwood, WA: Holmes Group.

Weisberg, D., Sexton, S., Mulhern, J., Keeling, D., Schunck, J., Palcisco, A., & Morgan, K. (2009). *The widget effect: Our national failure to acknowledge and act on differences in teacher effectiveness.* The New Teacher Project. Retrieved from https://files.eric.ed.gov/fulltext/ED515656.pdf

Welton, A. D., & Martinez, M. A. (2014). Coloring the college pathway: A more culturally responsive approach to college readiness and access for students of color in secondary schools. *The Urban Review, 46*(2), 197–223.

Yosso, T. J. (2005). Whose culture has capital? A critical race theory discussion of community cultural wealth. *Race Ethnicity and Education, 8*(1), 69–91.

2

EXAMINING TEACHER EVALUATION FROM THE CULTURAL LENSES OF THE DEVELOPERS

> **Chapter Overview:** This chapter makes the case that developers of teacher evaluation models advance notions of teaching that emerge from their own lived experiences and interpretive frames. The authors of this book, a Latina and a White scholar, each share their lived experiences and interpretive frames, from the margins and the center. These experiences influence the lenses used to conceptualize teaching and teacher evaluation.

In the previous chapter, we described the context of teacher evaluation and proposed a theoretical frame for culturally responsive teacher evaluation (CRTE). In this chapter, we propose that teacher evaluation models are not neutral and objective. We share how our own cultural experiences and interpretive frames impact the way we conceptualize CRTE.

Culture and Teacher Evaluation

The culturally responsive evaluation (CRE) literature emphasizes that the evaluation process is influenced by the cultures of the participants, including the evaluators. While CRE scholars underscore the importance of culture in evaluation, the constructs of culture and teacher evaluation rarely intersect. The primary focus of the literature on teacher evaluation is on technical and organizational aspects (Murphy, Hallinger, & Heck, 2013). The technical aspects include definitions of effective teaching; methods, instrumentation, and procedures; evaluator training; and implementation (Danielson & McGreal, 2000). The organizational aspects include school and/or district goals; resources; and collective bargaining and legal requirements (Millman & Darling-Hammond, 1990, p. 19).

While much of the focus on teacher evaluation is on the technical and organizational aspects, Millman and Darling-Hammond (1990) consider environmental aspects in teacher evaluation; these include "individuals and institutions outside of the immediate school organization" (p. 38). This focus is also described in the CRE literature. Guzman (2003) makes reference to the environmental context of evaluation; this includes individual, familial, community, and societal influences on evaluation. In the CRE literature, the cultural lenses of evaluators matter. Thomas and Parsons (2017) indicate that it is important to include evaluators who have a shared lived experience with the population the evaluation is intended to serve.

We contend that the environmental aspects that impact teacher evaluation include the social identities of those who are served by the evaluation, those who define the construct that is to be evaluated, the evaluators, and the developers of evaluation models. Social identities that impact evaluation include race, language, gender identity, socioeconomic status, sexual orientation, citizenship status, religion, and abilities, to name a few. Important questions about the environmental aspects that impact teacher evaluation include:

- Who is served by the teacher evaluation model?
- How are diverse communities included in the development of teacher evaluation models?
- Who defines effective teaching?
- Who is creating the professional teaching standards that teacher evaluation models are based on?
- Who are the developers of teacher evaluation models?

One important environmental consideration is the cultural lenses used by developers of teacher evaluation models. In effect, developers of teacher evaluation models advance notions of teaching that emerge from their own lived experiences and interpretive frames; these include assumptions of quality and worth (Flynn, 2015). According to the U.S. Department of Education Schools and Staffing Survey (SASS), approximately 82% of teachers and 80% of school leaders identify as White (U.S. Department of Education, 2016). Because educators are overwhelmingly White and middle class, teacher evaluation models are laden with the values, beliefs, and ways of knowing and becoming that are prized by the dominant culture. This is important because evaluation is "inherently directed at making a judgment of worth about something" (Millman & Darling-Hammond, 1990, pp. 19–20).

CRE requires that "the evaluator spend time reflecting upon his or her own values and how these might influence their work" (Mertens, 2008, p. 96). In this chapter, we, a Latina and a White scholar, each share stories of our lived experiences, from the margins and the center. We describe how these experiences and our interpretive frames influence the cultural lenses we use to conceptualize teaching and teacher evaluation. The stories that we share follow guidelines adapted from the work of Albert and Couture (2014): personal narrative, interpretation, and theorizing.

The Cultural Lens of a Latina Scholar

Maya Angelou (2014) proclaims, "There is no greater agony than bearing an untold story inside of you" (p. 47). In the section that follows, I, María del Carmen Salazar, share four *testimonios* (testimonies) of my lived experiences. These are followed by the interpretive frames, bolstered by research literature, I use to make meaning of my experience and the collective experience of the *other*. I conclude by theorizing about how my cultural lenses shape the way I envisage teaching and teacher evaluation.

A Rosebud in the Concrete

A legendary American poet, philosopher, composer, Rock and Roll Hall of Fame artist, and rap music extraordinaire – Tupac Shakur – captures the essence of growing up in urban environments. Shakur (2009) describes his experience in the inner city using an analogy of a rose growing from a crack in the concrete. He writes:

> Did you hear about the rose that grew from concrete? Proving nature's law is wrong, it learned to walk without having feet. Funny it seems, but by keeping its dreams, it learned to breathe fresh air. Long live the rose that grew from concrete when no one else cared.
>
> *(p. 89)*

Shakur's (2009) poetry pays homage to the roses that grew from concrete. I am a rose that grew from concrete. A Mexican immigrant, I was torn from the nurturing embrace of my motherland as an infant. I was only two weeks old when my parents crossed the border into the United States to settle in Denver, Colorado. I may be considered an immigrant; but in reality, I am a nomad. I am a citizen of nowhere, *ni de aqui, ni de alla* (not from here, nor from there). I am perceived as an alien in the two countries whose borders I straddle. My sense of "twoness" is aptly described by Du Bois (1903): "two souls, two thoughts, two unreconciled strivings; two warring ideals in one dark body, whose strength alone keeps it from being torn asunder" (p. 46).

A confluence of individual, familial, community, and school factors set me on a trajectory to be left behind. My father and mother are both Mexican immigrants. My father has a third-grade education and my mother has a sixth-grade education. My father was taken out of school to help with the family farm. My mother was taken out of school because her father believed that she did not need an education to fulfill her future duties as a wife and mother. My parents speak limited English and have limited literacy skills in English and Spanish. When I was growing up, my father worked in a factory and my mother worked in maintenance. We received government assistance at various points throughout my childhood. They were not "involved" in my education according to traditional measures (e.g., attending parent teacher conferences, monitoring grades, participating in school events, attending field trips, participating on the PTA, etc.).

In my childhood, there was debilitating trauma in my family. One of my earliest memories as a six-year-old child was seeing my mother hold the lifeless body of my five-year-old brother, Ricardo. I can still hear her shattering wails as she cradled his pale and limp body in her arms. It was as if she were in a trance, she rocked back and forth, clenching her dead child in her arms. It was as though she willed him back to life with each desperate motion. The events that preceded my brother's death are unforgettable. We had been playing hide-and-go-seek on a farm in Mexico. We think my little brother hid in a water well. We searched for him for hours until my father emerged from the well with my brother's flaccid body. I couldn't tell if my father was crying because he was soaking wet, but the devastated look on his ashen face was unmistakable. He tenderly placed the shell that was my brother in my mother's violently trembling arms. It was then that my mother started to sob and scream uncontrollably, like *La Llorona*, the crying woman. Her cries are impossible to describe; they did not sound human. Her cries are seared into my soul.

When we returned to the United States, I remember hearing my mother call someone at my school. She told them my little brother would not be starting kindergarten because he was dead. The torment inside my parents' hearts exploded; my home became a battlefield. My parents and my older brother, he was 11 at the time of my brother's death, did not know how to deal with my brother's loss. So they hurt themselves and those around them. While my parents managed to deal with their grief at some point and stop punishing one another, my older brother continued to punish himself. He embarked on a destructive life-long journey to obviate his grief through alcohol. Close to 40 years after the death of my little brother, I cared for my older brother while he was in a drunken stupor. I witnessed his eyes fill with terror and desperation as he called out, "Where is my brother? I can't find my brother!" His unquenchable pain and inexorable alcohol addiction took his life at the age of 50. My family recently traveled to Mexico to bury my older brother, Javier, next to my little brother, Ricardo. My family walked through the town of my birth, trailing behind my brother's casket that was transported in a hearse. In my mind, I went back in time; I was six years old again, walking through the town trailing the body of my brother. I watched my father's shoulders slump in the same way, heavy with the weight of his grief. His eyes drooped in the same way, loaded with pain and regret. We reached the cemetery… again. I said goodbye to my brother… again. As I watched Javier's casket being lowered into the ground next to the resting place of my little brother Ricardo, my tears erupted like a dormant volcano that was awakened. I pressed my forehead against my brother Ricardo's resting place and sobbed uncontrollably. My grief gushed out as I thought, "*Al fin* (at last). Javier found our little brother."

My familial challenges were virtually insurmountable. I also faced challenges related to community and school factors. When I was growing up in North Denver, a community I believed to be 100% Mexican, I experienced many struggles. My neighborhood was replete with liquor stores; we had few grocery stores and restaurants; we had no recreation centers. Most of the homes in my neighborhood were modestly maintained, and some were dilapidated and run down. It was not uncommon to hear gunshots at night and listen to tales about gang violence the next day. My siblings and I stayed close to home and were supervised by our parents who feared for our safety.

Upon my entry into school, I was shackled with the following labels: minority, Limited English Proficient (LEP), Free and Reduced Lunch (FRL), low SES, at risk, and underprivileged. The vast majority of the students in the Denver Public Schools I attended were of Mexican or Mexican American origin. We were segregated, mis-educated, and forgotten. Our teachers suffered from the "*pobrecito syndrome*" (Garcia, 1992). The word pobrecito means "poor little ones" and is indicative of having low expectations. Our teachers pitied us; they lowered the bar so we could step over it with little effort or exertion. We knew without a doubt that they did not believe we were capable. I was one of few who graduated from my high school, a "dropout factory" (Orfield, 2009).

To survive so many challenges, I found the escape routes that were hidden in the pages of books. I loved to read and anxiously awaited the bookmobile that would come into our neighborhood. It was a bus filled with books, my treasures. I experienced other worlds through the characters that came to life in my imagination. I found solace and peace, my mind quieted when I read. I was able to leave my troubles behind. Reading helped me find my wings; I soared far away from home when I read and traveled to different worlds. My love of reading helped me to imagine my future possibilities.

An outsider might only see the harshness of the concrete that was my early life. Yet, as an insider, I can see beauty in the jagged edges and harshness of the concrete. My parents loved me and did their best to protect my siblings and me from the harshness of our surroundings. While I experienced trauma that I wish I could change, it has made me who I am. I am resilient, strong, and brave. Today, I know I can survive and thrive, no matter the circumstances that surround me. Moreover, today, my parents and siblings are my greatest support. They have always been by my side, throughout every accolade and tribulation I have experienced. They believe in me and have proudly heralded my accomplishments. They helped me reach every milestone in my life, and they have helped me to raise my three children, whom they love beyond anything imaginable.

Amidst all of the challenges, my parents, siblings, extended family, fictive kin, and community swathed me in a cocoon of culture, belonging, and love. I was enveloped in a *sarape* (shawl) that was replete with the familial and community treasures that emerged from our Mexican culture. These included: *solidaridad* (solidarity), *humildad* (humility), *fe* (faith), *perserverancia* (perseverance), *coraje* (courage), *ganas* (effort), and *comunidad* (community). These treasures made it possible for me to embrace the concrete with resilience and hope. To this day, the concrete resides inside of me. I do not ever want to leave it behind; I draw my strength from its beauty and its harshness.

My First-grade Teacher Stole My Humanity

After the death of my brother, with turmoil in my heart and in my home, I entered the first grade. I lamented having to leave Mr. Lopez, my kindergarten teacher, and my bilingual classroom. Mr. Lopez encouraged me to bring all of my treasures to kindergarten, including my *lenguaje* (language), *cultura* (culture), and *familia* (family). Mr. Lopez taught me English and Spanish. He told me I was so smart that I could learn in two languages, not just one. I felt so proud and capable.

I left my treasures behind when I moved to the first grade. I was mainstreamed into an English-only classroom. It was sink or swim; I felt that I would sink if I held onto my treasures. When I recall the first grade, the words that come to mind are: harsh, cold, frightening, and lonely. I remember vividly how Mrs. Kowalski would test me relentlessly in the English language. She wielded her pen like a sharp blade, slashing at the paper, leaving vivid crimson marks. I did not know the traitorous English words. The paper bled profusely. It was in one of those moments that I came to realize there was something wrong with me. I came to understand that my native language did not have value. My teacher did not care about what I knew in Spanish. I deduced that if my native language did not have value, my culture did not have value, my parents did not have value; thus, I did not have value. It was then that I began to reject all that was native to me. I refused to speak Spanish. I felt ashamed of my culture and my parents. I hated when my father would show up to my school in his Mexican *guaraches* (sandals); they became a symbol of the ways I wanted to repel so desperately. My brownness became a source of shame and pain.

My first-grade teacher gave me a new set of treasures that included U.S. cultural ways of knowing and the English language. Her learning environment, curriculum, instruction, and assessment made it blatantly clear that English and whiteness were prized. As a result, I wanted desperately to be White and worthy. My first-grade teacher stole my humanity. Most of my teachers who came after her were complicit in this thievery. To this day, I continue the struggle to reclaim my humanity.

Reclaiming My Treasures

My schooling was agonizing. Having a border drawn at my classroom door meant that I became a perpetual border crosser. I left myself at the boundary of my classroom door and changed into my other self. The constant movement between two worlds at odds with one another was overwhelming, exhausting, and confusing. The values prized by my teachers, such as independence and competition, were sources of conflict in my home because my parents stressed dependence on the family and collaboration. I struggled to navigate my two worlds. I thought that "becoming White" would be the answer to my woes. I share this story in an article I wrote on humanizing pedagogy (Salazar, 2013):

> I am filled with endless stories of advertent and inadvertent messages of inferiority that compelled me to crave whiteness as a young child. In the third grade, I desperately wanted to be White. My teachers privileged whiteness through the English language and U.S. culture, and they excluded all that was native to me; hence, I ascertained that White children were smarter, more attractive, and affluent. As a result, I became a connoisseur of whiteness when I was eight years old. I observed my White classmates closely and dissected their behaviors until I discovered a common pattern; every White student in my class was in the highest reading group. Thus, I hypothesized that if I propelled myself into the top reading group, the Red Robins, the color of my skin would change and I would become White and worthy. I achieved my goal and my name was called to join the Red Robins. I ran home that day and examined my complexion in the mirror, to no avail; my skin remained the color of burnt toast. I waited anxiously for days, yet the transformation never ensued, and I became distressed that I would have to live in my dark skin forever as *la morena*, the dark-skinned girl.
>
> *(p. 122)*

Despite these struggles, with the help of a handful of good teachers, I managed to graduate from high school with honors. When I told my father I was going to college he said, "*¿Que estas loca hija?*" "Are you crazy daughter?" He did not understand why I would put off working to continue with school. He grew up in extreme poverty and was only allowed to go to school until the third grade. He had focused on survival his entire life, not esoteric dreams. He was never given the opportunity to dream. He also wanted to keep me safe; he was afraid of the unknown. I am the only sibling out of seven in my family to attain a higher education. I did not know one person in my extended family or community who had graduated from college. I navigated the college admissions process on my own. It was daunting and overwhelming. I felt incompetent, intimidated, and lost.

Because I graduated with honors from high school, this made it possible for me to get into a reputable four-year college. While it appeared that my teachers closed the gap, in reality, they created a chasm. Not only had they taken my treasures and stripped me of my humanity, the *pobrecito* approach left me unprepared for college-level work. I struggled with the basics when I started college, including: listening, note-taking, reading comprehension, writing, and math. Moreover, I experienced intense culture shock in the predominantly White institution (PWI) that I attended, even though it was only two miles from the community where I grew up. Fortunately, I obtained a job working with the Hispanic Student Services on campus. This group was housed with the Native American, Asian, and African American Student Services. I found a cocoon. I flourished with the *others*, and for the first time, I saw the beauty in our collective *otherness*. It was then that I began the fight to reclaim the treasures that I left behind. Like Coates (2015), I needed to see the beauty of my brown world, acknowledge its violent creation, and hail our survival. Coates captures my angst at this time in my life:

> I needed this vantage point before I could journey out. I needed to know that I was from somewhere, that my home was as beautiful as any other… though it was forged in the shadow of the murdered, the raped, the disembodied, we made it all the same.
>
> *(pp. 120–121)*

I waited patiently for my university professors to give me access to knowledge of myself and my heritage that was denied to me in my K-12 education. To no avail, my professors wielded the Western canon like a weapon that would secure America's greatness and protect them from the others. In response, I took the initiative to learn about my family, history, and heritage; the contributions of my people to the Americas; the oppression of my people and their resistance; and our place in making America, and the world, great. I discovered my *mestizo* heritage, a mixture of Indigenous and European. We are descendants of Mayans, Aztecs, and Europeans. We are mathematicians, scientists, astronomers, engineers, healers, philosophers, and so much more. I came to the epiphany that we are the oppressed and the oppressor, and thus we have the ultimate duty to uphold social justice. To this day, I strive to sustain my own, my children's, and all children's humanity through my work for equity and excellence in education.

Teaching with Color

When I graduated from college, I stumbled upon my calling. I worked as a paraprofessional in a high school and saw firsthand the impact of teaching CLD youth. I became a high school social studies teacher because I wanted youth to know about the history and contributions of historically marginalized communities. I started teaching at the high school I graduated from, the dropout factory. Nothing had changed. It was heartbreaking. I saw firsthand the systemic racism inherent in an educational system that treats CLD youth as though they are incapable and uneducable. My students were segregated, mis-educated, and forgotten. They moved about the hallways as ghost-like figures, mere wisps; they had been stripped of their humanity and their treasures. The teachers at the school were infected with the *pobrecito* syndrome; they lowered the bar so the youth, who were predominantly of Mexican descent, could step over it with little exertion.

I could not bear to be in such a dehumanizing environment. I moved to another high school that had a population of 30% Students of Color. However, I faced different challenges. I was the only Teacher of Color in the school. Teaching with color was powerful and traumatic. The Latinx and Black/African American students gravitated to me. I was a brown beacon of hope in a sea of whiteness. My students and I started a multicultural student organization called Pride; the membership included Latinx, Black/African American, and biracial students. My colleagues and school administrators reacted negatively when I allowed the students to use the symbol of a raised fist on printed material. The raised fist is attributed to the Black Power movement of the 1960s; it is a symbol of resistance, solidarity, pride, and social justice (Goodnow, 2006). My colleagues perceived this to be a symbol of violence. They wanted the group to adhere to picturesque images of "kumbaya" diversity that included fun, food, fiestas, and friendship. My high school students and I continued to use the image of the fist. The students felt empowered by the symbol, and I vowed that I would never take that power from them.

At the same time, some of my White high school students waged an attack on me. This happened in response to a unit I taught called "Discovery or Genocide." This unit was on the colonization of the Americas, the rise to power of Europeans, and the decimation of Indigenous and African peoples. I taught the unit using multiple perspectives from primary and secondary sources. On one memorable occasion, a White female raised her hand and said, "This can't be true. I've never learned these things about Christopher Columbus. Our teachers would have taught us this if it were true." Subsequently, a group of White students contacted the principal and stated that I favored the Students of Color, I was telling lies about U.S. history, and I was making the White students feel bad.

My experience as a Teacher of Color was marked by my humanistic commitment to equity and social justice. I did not want to perpetuate the lies my teachers told me or steal any child's humanity. I wanted my students to bring their treasures into my classroom; however, some of my White students felt that I was taking away their treasures, namely the masternarratives of their White superiority. Teaching with color was empowering in that I made a difference in students' lives, particularly for the Students of Color. It was also marked by a constant struggle to develop students' critical consciousness of race and racism, and other issues of diversity, whether they wanted this knowledge or not. Eventually, the isolation of being the only Teacher of Color pushed me out of the high school classroom. I decided to become a teacher educator so that I could impact students though the preparation of their teachers. Thus, I completed a Ph.D. in bilingual and multicultural education and entered the Ivory Tower. In this predominantly White space, I experience the isolation of being one of the few tenured Women of Color at a university founded in 1864. I am the first Woman of Color to receive tenure in a college of education that was founded in 1890. To this day, I struggle to profess with color.

Interpretive Frame: A Collective Experience

My *testimonios* represent but a fragment of the collective experience of the CLD learners from historically marginalized communities in U.S. schools. CLD learners are:

- isolated from the social, cultural, historical, and political contexts of our lives (Nieto, 2017);
- perceived through *deficit perspectives* (Valencia, 2012) that fuel *subtractive schooling* intended to "divest youth of important social and cultural resources, leaving them progressively vulnerable to academic failure" (Valenzuela, 2010, p. 3);
- stripped of the cultural, linguistic, and familial resources we need to survive and thrive, including our *funds of knowledge* (Moll, Amanti, Neff, & Gonzalez, 1992) and *community cultural wealth* (Yosso, 2005);
- robbed of our culture, language, history, values, and our sense of self (Salazar, 2013);
- engulfed in the *whitestream*, or "the cultural capital of whites in every facet of U.S. society" (Urrieta, 2010, p. 181);
- shackled by a mis-education that reproduces opportunity gaps and persistent disparities in access to quality education (Milner, 2012; Welner & Carter, 2013); and
- *dehumanized* (Freire, 1970) by approaches that silence and denigrate us, and instill a sense of internalized failure and self-contempt (Quiroz, 2001).

Yet, we resist. We find power in the margins. hooks (1990) states, "I am located in the margin… a site of resistance… a location of radical openness and possibility" (p. 53). We reside in the margins and resist through our humanistic commitments to equity and social justice (Achinstein, Ogawa, Sexton, & Freitas, 2010). We persist because of, not in spite of, our community, familial, cultural, and linguistic treasures. Shakur (2000) eloquently captures our reality:

> You see, you wouldn't ask why the rose that grew from the concrete had damaged petals. On the contrary, we would all celebrate its tenacity. We would all love its will to reach the sun. Well, we are the roses, this is the concrete, and these are my damaged petals.
>
> *(track 12)*

We, the roses, embrace the harshness and beauty of the concrete from which we have emerged. The concrete makes us who we are. We proudly display our damaged and exquisite petals. We have the tenacity and the will to reach the sun. Even as we reach the sun, we choose to remain in the concrete, to grow more roses.

Perspective on Teaching and Teacher Evaluation

My positionality at the margins impacts the way I see teaching and teacher evaluation.

I believe that teachers need to be prepared to nourish the roses that grow in concrete. In an article titled, "Hope Required When Growing Roses in Concrete," Duncan-Andrade (2009) connects the prose of Shakur to teaching and states:

> The quality of our teaching, along with the resources and networks we connect our students to, are those cracks. They do not create an ideal environment for growth, but they afford some leaking in of sunlight, water, and other resources…
>
> *(p. 5)*

The roses that grow in concrete need teachers that hold a relentless belief in their potential; set high expectations; provide support; sustain their community cultural wealth and funds of knowledge; give them the opportunity to learn the knowledge and skills prized by the dominant society; and teach them to challenge the status quo and agitate for social justice. They need teachers who can help them see the beauty of their worlds, and can see and draw from their full potential. They need teachers who communicate to the roses: "You exist. You matter. You have value… You have every right to be you. And no one should deter you from being you. You have to be you. And you can never be afraid to be you" (Coates, 2015, p. 113). In turn, the roses that grow in concrete can develop a sense of empowerment that fosters their own and their community resiliency, persistence, and success, as defined by them.

I believe it is vital to prepare equitable and excellent teachers that sustain the humanity of students, and their families, by providing access to the culture of power, sustaining the power of their culture, and evoking their power to create change. To do anything less is to steal the humanity of our children. I envision CRTE as a powerful tool for equity and excellence in education because it positions CLD learners at the center, not at the periphery.

The Cultural Lens of a White Scholar

My parents were both raised in working-class families. My dad left home at 17 to join the Navy. My mom went to college, but decided to leave after one semester. Her father passed away suddenly. My dad traveled the world in the Navy – working as a mechanic on a ship. He would later leverage those skills to start his own small appliance repair company. When my parents met as young adults in the 1970s, they were both ready to leave their small hometown. Together, they set off for the open spaces of the Rocky Mountains. They settled in a tiny mountain town where my brother and I spent our early childhood. My mom started a career as a real estate agent and worked long hours. We played with the neighborhood kids, riding our bikes until dark. One neighbor let me come over every day after the school bus dropped us off at the top of the dirt road. Her house was always warm and she let me help her cook homemade tortillas. Aside from one Latina/o family, the town was working class and White.

When I was six, my parents divorced. We stayed with my mom in the mountains during the week and with my dad, closer to the city, every other weekend. My mom struggled to support us by herself. She couldn't afford the heat bill, so she made a fire in the wood-burning stove every night. She came home from work in the evening to a cold house and pulled wood in from the snow to get the fire started. Eventually, we moved to the city where my aunt and cousins lived. Our extended family offered us a soft landing, but school looked much different in the city.

Making Meaning Out of Forced Integration

I started fourth grade in the city. We rented a house in a working-class White neighborhood and attended the neighborhood school. The district was forced to integrate after the Supreme Court ruled in the 1970s that the district had intentionally segregated schools. Every day the bus dropped off African American and Latina/o kids from other neighborhoods. I did not understand the larger political context. In my mountain town, I took the bus to the closest school, so I assumed those kids just lived outside of walking distance. My class was about one-third White, one-third Black, and one-third Latina/o.

My parents felt strongly allied with the civil rights movement in the 1960s and they taught me that racism was wrong. But, I was shocked by how different I felt from the Students of Color. I remember staring at the African American girls' braids and listening closely to the way they talked. We were all there together, but we were separated by race. No one discussed the purpose of integration or acknowledged race in any way. We were left to construct meaning from those experiences on our own.

I loved my third-grade teacher when I lived in the mountains. She was young and enthusiastic and she told me I was a gifted writer. I cried and hugged her on the last day of school. My fourth-grade teacher in the city was mean. She sat at her desk all day and we completed worksheets in silence. She left me alone because I was quiet. But I could tell that she hated some of the kids in our class. We all could. She especially hated Reggie. Reggie was an African American boy with a round face. He was friendly, funny, and goofy. Every day she battled with Reggie – often sending him to the office for talking in class. I do not know how she felt about integration, but it was clear how she felt about Reggie. In retrospect, the experience was much more jarring for the Students of Color than it was for me. While kids in my neighborhood were also bused to other schools at that time, I went to school in a White neighborhood where Students of Color were brought in from across town. While I wasn't raised in a wealthy family, my teachers never doubted my ability based on the color of my skin. In fact, my whiteness likely shielded me from the cruelty that Reggie experienced.

Separate and Unequal

Though forced busing would eventually come to an end, it was still in place during my middle and high school years. Just like in elementary school, African American, Latina/o, and White students were together, but we were separate. In middle and high school, we were systematically segregated through tracking. The advanced track was mostly White students; the Students of Color were mostly in the lower tracks. The teacher of the seventh-grade advanced science class was very strict and maintained high academic standards. We had to work hard and show her respect. But the classroom right next door was a low-track science class and we could see them through a window in the separating door. The low-track classroom next door had several teachers over the course of the year. Each one seemed less competent than the one before. Without any academic or behavior expectations, the classroom devolved into chaos. We would see spit balls fly through the air. Our teacher frequently stepped into the other room to intervene so we would not be distracted by the noise. We were in the same building, but in two different worlds.

In high school, we were separated again – this time by advanced and non-advanced courses. The advanced courses had mostly White students. The only advanced history course offered was European history. Peer groups were primarily delineated by race. As far as I could tell, there was no effort made by the school to promote equity and inclusivity. Difference was ignored; we were encouraged to be color blind. Some students challenged the status quo and formed a Black Student Alliance. These students advocated for themselves without a teacher sponsor. They were, at best, tolerated by the school. At the same time, some White students asked, "Why can't there be a White student alliance?"

Teaching as a Transformative Experience

I knew my parents would not be able to pay for college, but I was determined to go. I took every advanced class I could and finished second in my high school class. I went to the local state university with the help of grants and loans. I graduated with a degree in biology and then began working as a substitute teacher while I thought about what to do next. I worked as a substitute teacher at an elementary school labeled "high poverty." They offered me a job as a science teacher and

I started right away through an emergency licensure program. As a teacher, I was strict, but fun. I fell in love with teaching and the students. I remember thinking that my students had a twinkle in their eyes; a light shining inside of them. The teaching staff was mostly young and White, though there were a couple of African American and Latina teachers. Many of us had no formal training prior to our first day on the job. The school was labeled as "hard to staff" and some teaching positions went unfilled late into the school year – a series of substitutes filling in for a few days at a time. By this time, mandated segregation had ended. Students walked to school. Though the school I taught in was in a historically Black neighborhood, the demographics were changing as more Latina/o families moved in. It was about half Black and half Latina/o and nearly every family qualified for free or reduced lunch.

Most of the teachers worked hard and cared about their students, but the academic standards were very low. The first year the state standardized test was administered, the local paper published grades for every school based on the percentage of students who scored proficient. Our school received an F. Discouraged, the teachers traded stories about the students' home lives and gossiped about their parents. We speculated about why a student's dad went to jail and whether his mom was on drugs. We said we loved the students, but we saw their home lives as an obstacle to their success at school. If a student fell asleep in class, we let them sleep, assuming their living conditions must be rough. Just like my own school experience, as teachers we did not talk about race, culture, or poverty. We shook our heads when so few parents showed up to teacher conferences. We assumed they did not care.

As I got to know my students, I started to know their families too. One little girl named Nakia was living with her grandparents. The word in the teachers' lounge was that her mom was in jail for drugs or prostitution. "It's so sad," we said, "What a terrible mom." One day I was teaching a lesson when someone knocked on the classroom door. It was Nakia and her mom. Her mom looked at me with tears in her eyes and said, "I'm sorry to bother you. I just wanted to thank you for everything you have done for Nakia. She tells me all about the work she does in class and I am grateful for what you have taught her." She looked down at Nakia, who was hugging her arm, and smiling up at her mom proudly. Nakia's mom was referring to the fact that I held high academic expectations for my students. I realized what they can do; I pushed them and they improved.

That moment with Nakia and her mother changed me. I realized then what seems so obvious now: every parent wants what is best for their child. I felt so ashamed about the judgement I made about her as a mom. Maybe it was easier to believe that low-income parents of color did not care. Parents, especially poor parents, are an easy scapegoat. Looking back, I wish I could have drawn on the parents' resources and included them as a true partner in their child's education. I wish I would have seen Nakia's mother's resilience and dedication instead of her limitations. I wish I would have praised my students' bilingualism instead of focusing so intently on their limited English.

As a liberal White woman, I never would have thought of myself as racist. I knew what racism was – it was confederate flags and hate speech, and of course I was opposed to all of that. But now I think about pervasive low academic expectations, deficit assumptions about families, and discounting students' cultural and linguistic resources. That was racism too – subtle yet systematized, and real. My own kids are now in middle school. They attend a racially diverse, "low-income" school, but they are White and economically privileged. We chose this school because we want our kids to be a part of a community that discusses issues related to race and inequity instead of being "color blind." We want them to experience diverse perspectives as they form their perceptions of the world. When I read about culturally responsive teaching, it is often positioned as a set of teaching strategies for CLD students. I agree that confronting educational inequity is the ultimate goal. But, I think White students, like my own kids, can be a part of that mission. They can learn to recognize inequity when they see it and be a part of the struggle for social justice.

Perspective on Teaching and Teacher Evaluation

Eventually I moved out of the classroom to be an instructional coach. As I moved from classroom to classroom, the difference in quality from one teacher to the next was shocking. Some teachers pushed their students academically; some did not expect much. Some teachers invited parents into their classrooms every day; some explicitly excluded them. Some teachers wanted to learn and improve their instructional practice; others had no interest in changing. A student could end up with a terrific teacher or a terrible one. It was painful to watch. Some kids ended up with ineffective teachers several years in a row. They headed off to middle school without the skills they needed. The realization that so much of a student's future depends on the quality of his or her teacher made me an advocate for teacher evaluation reform.

My positionality at the center impacts the way I see teaching and teacher evaluation. I believe that integrated schools are good for students, but shifting the demographics within a school is not enough. I believe we need more Teachers of Color. But, changing teacher demographics is not enough either. We must teach about race and culture in schools. We must acknowledge our own biases and systematic injustices so that CLD learners feel empowered and so White students can be allies. I believe that CRP and CRTE are a moral imperative – and not just for those of us who work primarily with CLD learners. A White teacher in a school made up of predominantly White students can learn to be culturally responsive. S/he can learn to talk about power and privilege and see the strengths of diverse cultures. S/he can learn to recognize inequity and join in the struggle for social justice.

Summary and Implications

In this chapter, we asserted that the cultural lenses used to develop teacher evaluation models matter. We presented our own lived experience and interpretive frames, and theorized about how these impact our perspectives on teaching and teacher evaluation. The content of this chapter leads us to an intriguing question: Is it necessary for developers of teacher evaluation models to be representative of diverse cultural backgrounds? This may not be the case if you believe good teaching is just good teaching. However, if you believe that culture impacts teaching and learning, then the answer to the question is, unequivocally, yes! We believe that it is imperative that historically marginalized Communities of Color are included in the development of teacher evaluation models because they can envision teaching and learning from a perspective that is rooted in their experiences in the margins. It is also essential that those from the dominant culture who are developing teacher evaluation models be reflective of their position at the center, including their power, privilege, and biases. Ultimately, when developing teacher evaluation models, it is essential to include a diverse group of participants that are representative of the community the model is intended to serve.

Critical Questions

The following critical questions are intended to extend your comprehension and help you relate the concepts to your own practice.

1. What inspires you to teach and/or lead?
2. How does culture impact the way you teach and/or lead?
3. What are the consequences of excluding students' cultures from teaching, learning, and leading?
4. What aspects of our lived experiences made an impact on you? How are your lived experiences similar or different from ours?
5. How have your lived experiences impacted your perspectives on teaching, school leadership, and teacher evaluation?

Resources for Further Reflection and Study

The following supplemental resources are intended to spur your personal and professional reflection, application of the concepts in your own context, and community outreach efforts.

Print

Akinbode, A. (2013). Teaching as lived experience: The value of exploring the hidden and emotional side of teaching through reflective narratives. *Studying Teacher Education, 9*(1), 62–63.

Carter, M. (2003). Telling tales out of school: "What's the fate of a Black story in a White world full of White stories?" In G. R. Lopez & L. Parker (Eds.), *Interrogating racism in qualitative research methodology* (pp. 29–48). New York, NY: Peter Lang.

Howard, T. C. (2010). Culturally relevant pedagogy: Ingredients for critical teacher reflection. *Theory Into Practice, 42*(3), 195–202.

Kose, B. W. (2009). The principal's role in professional development for social justice: An empirically-based transformative framework. *Urban Education, 44*(6), 628–663.

Popham, W. J. (2001). *The truth about testing: An educator's call to action.* Alexandria, VA: Association for Supervision and Curriculum Development.

Web

- Edutopia
  Teacher using the lived experiences of students
  www.edutopia.org/blog/teach-using-lived-experiences-your-students-rebecca-alber
- National Association for Elementary School Principals
  How Effective Principals Encourage their Teachers
  www.naesp.org/sites/default/files/resources/2/Principal/2007/J-Fp48.pdf
- National Association for Multicultural Education
  How do I know if my biases affect my teaching?
  www.nameorg.org/learn/how_do_i_know_if_my_biases_aff.php
- National Institute for Urban School Improvement
  Cultural Identity and Teaching
  www.niusileadscape.org/docs/FINAL_PRODUCTS/NIUSI/toolkit_cd/4%20%20Implementing%20Change/OnPoints/OP_cultural_identity.pdf

Media

- Jeff Duncan-Andrade, TED Talk
  Growing roses in the concrete
  www.youtube.com/watch?v=2CwS60ykM8s
- María Salazar
  The InTASC teaching standards: Reprofessionalizing teaching
  www.youtube.com/watch?v=8joyeG5oE88
- Melissa Crum, TED Talk
  A tale of two teachers
  www.youtube.com/watch?v=sgtinODaW78
- Pearl Arredondo
  My story, from gangland daughter to star teacher
  www.ted.com/talks/pearl_arredondo_my_story_from_gangland_daughter_to_star_teacher

- National Education Association
  English language learners: Culture, equity, and language
  www.youtube.com/watch?v=5HU80AxmP-U
- Tupac Shakur
  The rose that grew from concrete
  https://genius.com/2pac-the-rose-that-grew-from-concrete-lyrics

Learning Opportunities

1. Write a critical self-reflection of your lived experiences in five short stories that include: early life, community experiences, P-12 educational experiences, higher education educational experiences, teaching experiences. Describe how these impact your interpretive frame (or the lens you use to see the world) and perspectives on teaching/leading and teaching evaluation.
2. Write an "I Am Poem." Include a minimum of nine stanzas that describe your personal/social identities. Example:

I am.
I am from two cultures.
at peace
at war
the oppressor
the oppressed
I am filled with treasures.
familia
cultura
lenguaje
coraje
I am powerful.
bold
brilliant
beautiful

I am.

3. Create a personal treasure box. Add five to eight artifacts that illustrate your most valued treasures (i.e., social identities: race, language, ethnicity, culture, citizenship, gender, sexual orientation, socioeconomic class, special needs, religion, social justice pursuits, family, hobbies, academic pursuits, etc.). How do these treasures impact your teaching and/or leadership?
4. Create a community treasure box. Add five to eight artifacts that illustrate the treasures of the community you serve as an educator (i.e., social identities: race, language, ethnicity, culture, heritage, history, citizenship, gender,

sexual orientation, socioeconomic class, special needs, religion, social justice pursuits, resiliency, etc.). How can these treasures be integrated into teaching and/or leadership?

5. Compare and contrast your personal treasure box and the community treasure box. What are the differences and similarities? How might these differences impact the way effective teaching is defined and assessed?

Community Engagement Opportunities

1. Conduct a mini ethnography of the community where you serve as an educator. Explore the community. Draw a map of the area. Note what types of commercial businesses are located in the community. Note the material culture of the community such as: posters, art, graffiti, signs, names of businesses, street names, language(s), etc. Describe what it looks, feels, tastes, smells, and sounds like. Describe the people and their verbal and non-verbal interactions. Reflect on the following questions: What surprised you? What stood out to you? What are their challenges? What are their treasures? What are the implications for teaching, learning, school leadership, and equity?

2. Create a bulletin board in your classroom or school that displays the community's cultural treasures. Invite members of the community to create it with you.

3. Have a conversation, or conduct a semi-structured interview, with youth from historically marginalized Communities of Color. Ask them the following:

    *   Describe the best teachers/school leaders you've had in school.
    *   How have your teachers impacted you in positive and negative ways?
    *   How have your school administrators helped or hindered your success?
    *   How have your race, culture, or other social identities impacted your experience in school?

4. Write a blog about how your lived experiences impact the way you teach and learn. Be brave. Ask critical questions. Share your hopes and fears. Describe how your lived experiences can positively or negatively impact your students.

References

Achinstein, B., Ogawa, R. T., Sexton, D., & Freitas, C. (2010). Retaining teachers of color: A pressing problem and a potential strategy for "hard-to-staff" schools. *Review of Educational Research, 80*(1), 71–107.

Albert, M. N., & Couture, M. M. (2014). To explore new avenues: Experiential testimonio research. *Management Decision, 52*(4), 794–812.

Angelou, M. (2014). *Rainbow in the cloud: The wisdom and spirit of Maya Angelou.* New York, NY: Random House Incorporated.

Coates, T. (2015). *Between the world and me.* New York, NY: Spiegel & Grau.

Danielson, C., & McGreal, T. L. (2000). *Teacher evaluation to enhance professional practice.* Alexandria, VA: ASCD.

Darling-Hammond, L. (1990). Teaching and knowledge: Policy issues posed by alternate certification for teachers. *Peabody Journal of Education, 67*(3), 123–154.

Du Bois, W. E. B. (1903). *The talented tenth* (pp. 102–104). New York, NY: James Pott and Company.

Duncan-Andrade, J. (2009). Note to educators: Hope required when growing roses in concrete. *Harvard Educational Review, 79*(2), 181–194.

Flynn, J. E. (2015). Racing the unconsidered: Considering whiteness, rubrics, and the function of oppression. In M. Tenam-Zemach & J. E. Flynn (Eds.), *Rubric nation: Critical inquiries on the impact of rubrics in education* (pp. 201–221). Charlotte, NC: Information Age Publishing Inc.

Freire, P. (1970). *Cultural action for freedom*. Boston, MA: Harvard Educational Review.

Garcia, E. (1992). *Teachers for language minority students: Evaluating professional standards.* Retrieved from https://files.eric.ed.gov/fulltext/ED349821.pdf

Goodnow, T. (2006). On Black Panthers, blue ribbons, & peace signs: The function of symbols in social campaigns. *Visual Communication Quarterly, 13*(3), 166–179.

Guzman, B. L. (2003). Examining the role of cultural competency in program evaluation: Visions for new millennium evaluators. In S. I. Donaldson & M. Scriven (Eds.), *Evaluating social programs and problems: Visions for the new millennium* (pp. 167–181). Mahwah, NJ: Lawrence Erlbaum.

hooks, b. (1990). Marginality as a site of resistance. In R. Ferguson, M. Gever, M. T. Trinh, & C. West (Eds.), *Out there: Marginalization and contemporary cultures* (pp. 341–343). Cambridge, MA: MIT.

Mertens, D. M. (2008). *Transformative research and evaluation*. New York, NY: Guilford Press.

Millman, J., & Darling-Hammond, L. (Eds.). (1990). *The new handbook of teacher evaluation: Assessing elementary and secondary school teachers*. Thousand Oaks, CA: Corwin Press.

Milner, H. R. (2012). Beyond a test score: Explaining opportunity gaps in educational practice. *Journal of Black Studies, 43*(6), 693–718.

Moll, L., Amanti, C., Neff, D., & Gonzalez, N. (1992). Funds of knowledge for teaching: Using a qualitative approach to connect homes and classrooms. *Theory into Practice, 32*(2) 132–141.

Murphy, J., Hallinger, P., & Heck, R. H. (2013). Leading via teacher evaluation: The case of the missing clothes. *Educational Researcher, 42*(6), 349–354.

Nieto, S. (2017). *Language, culture, and teaching: Critical perspectives* (3rd ed.). New York, NY: Routledge.

Orfield, G. (2009). *Reviving the goal of an integrated society: A 21st century challenge*. Los Angeles, CA: The Civil Rights Project/Proyecto Derechos Civiles at UCLA. Retrieved from https://cloudfront.escholarship.org/dist/prd/content/qt2bw2s608/qt2bw2s608.pdf

Quiroz, P. A. (2001). The silencing of Latino student "voice": Puerto Rican and Mexican narratives in eighth grade and high school. *Anthropology & Education Quarterly, 32*(3), 326–349.

Salazar, M. (2013). A humanizing pedagogy: Reinventing the principles and practice of education as a journey toward liberation. *Review of Research in Education, 37*(1), 121–148.

Shakur, T. (2000). The rose that grew from concrete [Recorded by Nicci Giovanni]. On *The rose that grew from concrete vol. 1* [CD]. Marin City, CA: Amaru Entertainment Inc.

Thomas, V. G., & Parsons, B. A. (2017). Culturally responsive evaluation meets systems-oriented evaluation. *American Journal of Evaluation, 38*(1), 1–22.

Urrieta, L. (2010). Whitestreaming: Why some Latinas/os fear bilingual education. *Counterpoints, 371*, 47–55.

U.S. Department of Education (2016). *The state of racial diversity in the educator workforce.* Office of Planning, Evaluation, and Policy Development. Retrieved from www2. ed.gov/rschstat/eval/highered/racial-diversity/state-racial-diversity-workforce.pdf

Valencia, R. R. (Ed.). (2012). *The evolution of deficit thinking: Educational thought and practice.* New York, NY: Routledge.

Valenzuela, A. (2010). *Subtractive schooling: US-Mexican youth and the politics of caring.* New York, NY: SUNY Press.

Welner, K. G., & Carter, P. L. (2013). Achievement gaps arise from opportunity gaps. In P. L. Carter & K. G. Welner (Eds.), *Closing the opportunity gap: What America must do to give every child an even chance* (pp. 1–10). Oxford, UK: Oxford University Press.

Yosso, T. J. (2005). Whose culture has capital? A critical race theory discussion of community cultural wealth. *Race Ethnicity and Education, 8*(1), 69–91.

3

UNVEILING TEACHER EVALUATION FROM THE CENTER AND INTERROGATING NATIONAL MODELS

> **Chapter Overview:** This chapter interrogates teacher evaluation through the lens of critical race theory (CRT). CRT is applied to the analysis of nationally recognized teacher evaluation models to unveil a masternarrative of objectivity and neutrality that positions the dominant culture at the center of teacher evaluation, and CLD learners at the margins. This chapter considers the impact of teacher evaluation from the center.

In the previous chapter, we made the case that the cultural lenses used to develop teacher evaluation models matter. In this chapter, we expand on this notion with the help of critical race theory (CRT). We examine the tenets of CRT to reveal that the lenses used to develop teacher evaluation models center the dominant culture and marginalize CLD learners. We provide examples of this from nationally recognized teacher evaluation models, and conclude the chapter by addressing the impact of teacher evaluation from the center.

Critical Race Theory and Education

Anzaldúa (1990) wrote, "If we have been gagged and disempowered by theories, we can also be loosened and empowered by theories" (p. xxvi). CRT is a body of oppositional scholarship that challenges discourses, ideologies, and structures that reproduce racism and inequity (Solorzano & Yosso, 2000). The historical roots of CRT can be traced to the turn of the 20th century with the work of race scholars such as W. E. B. DuBois (Yosso, Smith, Ceja, & Solórzano, 2009). Contemporary CRT emerged out of critical legal studies in the 1980s as a response to the persistence of racism in the U.S. legal system and society (Delgado, 1995).

While CRT emerged from legal studies, its principles have been applied to countless disciplines, including education. CRT in education is defined as: "a framework or set of basic perspectives, methods, and pedagogy that seeks to identify, analyze, and transform those structural, cultural, and interpersonal aspects of education that maintain the marginal position and subordination of Students of Color" (Solorzano & Yosso, 2000, p. 42). Ladson–Billings and Tate (1995) generated seminal work on CRT in education in the mid-1990s through the identification of five tenets of CRT that are embedded in the ideologies, policies, and practices of schooling: (a) centrality of race and racism; (b) challenge to the dominant ideology; (c) commitment to social justice; (d) importance of the experiential knowledge of Communities of Color; and (e) the use of interdisciplinary perspectives. The sections that follow delineate the intersection of the tenets of CRT with education, teaching, and learning.

The Centrality of Race and Racism

Why do race and racism matter? CRT foregrounds race as the most essential construct for analyzing inequity, challenging oppressive systems, and identifying solutions for a more just society (Zamudio, Russell, Rios, & Bridgeman, 2011). Race is socially constructed; thus, "the meanings, messages, results, and consequences of race are developed and constructed by human beings" (Milner & Laughter, 2015, p. 351). Being part of a race is akin to being bound to people who share the struggles, beauty, and power of belongingness. While race is central to CRT, it intersects with multiple constructs, including, but not limited to: class, gender, sexuality, abilities, citizenship, language, culture, and nation (Espinoza & Harris, 1998; Urrieta & Villenas, 2013).

Racism is a systemic and structural phenomenon that fortifies oppression and privilege along color lines. Worse yet, racism "is the need to ascribe bone-deep features to people and then humiliate, reduce, and destroy them" (Coates, 2015, p. 7). Racism is a chameleon; it can morph, change, and camouflage its presence. As an example, Bonilla-Silva (2017) describes "new racism" as a racial order that: (a) maintains White privilege without fanfare; (b) safeguards White racial interests; (c) acknowledges Whites' resentment against minorities; (d) sanctions claims about reverse racism; and (e) allows Whites to claim they are not racists. Bonilla-Silva refers to this phenomenon as "racism without racists" (p. 4). Thus, new racism is normalized, sanctioned, and systematized.

Racism is deeply rooted into educational structures in U.S. society; thus, it is often unrecognizable (Taylor, 2006). CRT in education reveals the intersection of race and racism with school policies and practices. Consequently, CRT exposes structural racism in educational systems that maintains opportunity gaps and reifies inequality (Lynn & Parker, 2006). Despite decades of efforts by critical race scholars, race and racism continue to be under-researched and under-theorized in education, and particularly in teacher education (Howard & Navarro, 2016; Milner, 2008).

Challenge to Dominant Ideology

How does race privilege some and marginalize others? One of the most important functions of CRT is to deconstruct and counteract masternarratives. Masternarratives are defined as a "mindset of positions, perceived wisdoms, and shared cultural understandings brought to the discussion of race" (Fránquiz, Salazar, & DeNicolo, 2011, p. 282). Masternarratives are also known as majoritarian tales and masterscripts (Solorzano & Yosso, 2000).

Masternarratives are generated to position the dominant culture as the standard or the norm. These are generated through countless tales that become normative and universal, fuel the pathologization of Communities of Color, camouflage White privilege and racial oppression, and fortify White racial domination (Leonardo, 2004). An example is the tale that whiteness is not a race or culture. Nieto (2008) states that "Whites frequently do not experience their culture *as a culture* because… it 'just is'…" (p. 135). Nieto adds that at the same time, the dominant ideology of Whites is positioned as the most valued. Messages of value and superiority are deeply engrained in U.S. systems and institutions; thus, whiteness is the sanctioned norm. Consequently, whiteness is "omnipresent yet invisible because it is everywhere and nowhere all at once" (West, 2005, p. 386).

Another masternarrative is that of color-blindness: "I don't see color, just people" (Bonilla-Silva, 2017, p. 1). Ladson-Billings (2009) maintains that color-blind, or race-neutral, perspectives, portray "a homogenized 'we'" (p. 29), thus universalizing the dominant group's interests, namely fortifying the dominant culture and assimilating Communities of Color. Dyer (1997) vows:

> As long as race is something only applied to non-white peoples, as long as white people are not racially seen and named, they/we function as a human norm. Other people are raced, we are just people. There is no more powerful position than that of being 'just' human.
>
> *(p. 10)*

While some Whites see themselves as cultureless or color-blind, others proudly proclaim their whiteness and advocate for nativism and culture wars. They claim they are not racist, they are proud of their White culture and want to protect their ways (Weller, 2017). They fail to acknowledge that they have protected their ways for thousands of years across the globe, to the detriment of the *others*.

While critics of CRT decry the demonization of whiteness (Trainor, 2002), CRT scholars explain that they analyze whiteness as a system. West (2005) states that the objective of the study of race is not to demonize whiteness, but instead, to catalogue how the construction of whiteness reinforces privilege, power, exclusion, and othering. CRT does not seek to demonize whiteness, but to deconstruct it, and challenge the inequities and injustice that result from systems that ascribe opportunity along color lines.

In his book titled *Between the World and Me*, Coates (2015) writes to his son, "The entire narrative of this country argues against the truth of who you are"

(p. 99). The depth of this statement is hard to fathom, yet it plays out every day in schools. The culture, ideals, and beliefs of the dominant White culture are privileged in education (Lynn, 2006). Students of Color are denied the truth of who they are. Moreover, schooling perpetuates masternarratives that propagate color-blind approaches, while at the same time spewing deficit-based ideologies of Communities of Color. Deficit notions of Students of Color are deeply embedded in educational practice. Valencia (2010) defines deficit thinking as "the idea that minority students labor under intellectual handicaps because of their family structure, linguistic background, and culture" (p. ix). The implication is that Students of Color are damaged, and the goal of schooling should be assimilation and cultural replacement or eradication.

Experiential Knowledge of Communities of Color

What is the value of race? CRT acknowledges that while race is a social construct, the experiential knowledge that emerges from Communities of Color is real and has value. The experiential knowledge of Communities of Color is "an asset, a form of community memory, a source of empowerment and strength, and not a deficit" (Villalpando, 2003, p. 46). Experiential knowledge emerges from many elements, but particularly from one's culture. To best serve the needs of Students of Color, schools should implement affirming approaches that sustain the multiplicity of students' resources (Paris & Alim, 2014). Such resources are inclusive of Yosso's (2005) conceptualization of "community cultural wealth," or the aspirational, linguistic, familial, social, navigational, and resistance capital that marginalized communities draw from as resources for learning.

The experiential knowledge of Communities of Color is often invisible, dismissed, or rejected, and thus relegated to the margins. Students of Color are often denied access to the power of their culture due to deficit-based instructional approaches and assimilationist policies that minimize, exclude, prohibit, or eradicate their cultural resources (Salazar, 2013). As a result, they may experience a loss in motivation and engagement and may ultimately resist subtractive schooling (Valenzuela, 2010).

Social Justice

Why must we challenge racism? Critical race scholars champion social justice by challenging practices that reproduce injustice (Salazar & Rios, 2016). CRT is hostile toward color-blind approaches, deficit ideologies, and racism. Instead, CRT embraces the assets of marginalized communities, and engages in action that benefits marginalized communities (Salazar & Rios, 2016).

Yamamoto (1997) advocates for concrete approaches that translate CRT to frontline action. Stovall (2006) concurs that social justice in education should be conceived as "an individual contribution to the collective efforts to articulate the day-to-day process and actions… for the purpose of changing our conditions" (p. 14). It is essential for educators to transform elements of education that maintain subordination and domination by engaging in action that improves the lives of historically marginalized communities.

Interdisciplinary Perspectives

How can we examine race and racism from multiple viewpoints? CRT scholars advocate for the use of interdisciplinary epistemologies, perspectives, and methodological tools to examine race and challenge racism in educational theory and practice (Howard & Navarro, 2016). Interdisciplinary approaches promote an understanding of the intersectionality of race with other socially constructed identities, such as: class, language, gender, abilities, citizenship, and sexual orientation. Howard and Navarro (2016) indicate that "intersectionality is a way to conceptualize how oppressions are socially constructed and affect individuals differently across multiple group categories" (p. 263). The examination of race through intersectionality captures the multiplicity of identities that diverse students embody as learners. These are integral to students' lived experiences and influence their growth and development.

Critical Race Theory and Teacher Evaluation

The tenets of CRT can help educators reconceptualize the construct of teacher evaluation. We focus on one particular aspect of teacher evaluation, frameworks for teaching. Frameworks for teaching are commonly used performance-based teacher evaluation models that define, assess, and develop effective teaching through performance-based competencies, rubrics of performance, and field-based observation instruments (New Teacher Project, 2011). In the sections that follow, we uncover the masternarrative of objectivity and neutrality that is rampant in frameworks for teaching. In doing so we reveal that frameworks for teaching center whiteness and marginalize CLD learners.

Challenging the Masternarrative of Objectivity and Neutrality

Frameworks for teaching are often based on a general consensus of what teachers should know and be able to do. Darling-Hammond (2012, pp. 2–3) summarizes the knowledge and skills that foster effective teaching, including:

- understanding content concepts;
- connecting content to prior knowledge and experiences;
- scaffolding learning;
- facilitating standards- and outcome-based instruction;
- providing students with opportunities to apply knowledge and master content;

- assessing student learning, making instructional adjustments, and supporting students in monitoring their own learning;
- giving explicit feedback; and
- managing student behavior and classroom routines.

This general knowledge and skills can be perceived as objective and neutral, and thus be seen as promoting effective teaching for *all* students. Mirra, Garcia, and Morrell (2015) challenge notions of objectivity. They state, "What is seen as objective, in fact, represents the experience of those who possess more societal power, while the experiences of marginalized others are downplayed or outright ignored" (p. 17). Flynn (2015) challenges notions of neutrality as false promises, myth-making, and bamboozling. He adds, "The very creation of a tool happens in a context with a certain set of assumptions, intentions, and repercussions (both intended and unintended)" (p. 212).

We reiterate our point from the previous chapter – the lenses used by the developers of teacher evaluation models matter. We contend that objective, neutral, or generalized approaches place whiteness at the normative center by fortifying the "whitestream" (Grande, 2000). Urrieta (2010) describes the notion of "whitestreaming" as: "a coercive force that imposes white history, mores, morals, language, customs, individualism, cultural capital, and other forces as the norm or standard U.S. in society" (p. 47). It is important to note that the whitestream is "not exclusively the work of Whites. Any person, including People of Color, actively promoting or upholding white models as the goal or standard is also involved in whitestreaming" (Urrieta, 2010, p. 181).

How is whiteness at the center of frameworks for teaching? The ideologies, norms, ways of knowing, and discourses of the dominant culture are often at the core of generic teaching competencies. We use the terms dominant culture, whiteness, and Eurocentric interchangeably. The use of the term Eurocentric implies Whites also have culture. We assert that generic teaching camouflages the following:

- Standards and assessments privilege the Western Canon and Eurocentric knowledge (e.g., contributions of Europeans/European Americans; English and the written word).
- Instruction emphasizes Eurocentric ways of knowing (e.g., individualism; competition; linear modes of expression; positivist ways of knowing; minimization of emotions).
- Application of content knowledge and skills aligns to interests of the dominant culture (e.g., real-world connections to dominant culture; excludes social justice pursuits).
- Assessment of student learning reinforces Eurocentric ways of knowing (e.g., detached; quantitative; standardized; culturally biased).
- Management of student behavior targets the perceived deficits of diverse learners (e.g., mechanistic; detached; punitive; assimilationist); and

- Standards of professional behavior reinforce neutrality and objectivity (e.g., color-blindness; devoid of critical consciousness; exclude a focus on advocacy).

In addition, frameworks for teaching often omit culturally responsive competencies that sustain and revitalize CLD learners, and promote their growth and development. We contend that frameworks for teaching must explicitly address the needs of CLD learners by incorporating culturally responsive teaching competencies. These are described in detail in Chapter 4 of this book. Table 3.1 contrasts examples of generic teaching competencies with culturally responsive teaching competencies.

Culturally responsive teaching competencies can emerge from, and extend, research-based effective teaching competencies. They explicitly include the *culture of power*, the *power of culture*, and *power of change*. We strongly advocate for the inclusion of culturally responsive teaching competencies in teacher evaluation models.

Teacher Evaluation from the Center

We assert that the generic teaching knowledge and skills promoted in teacher evaluation models situate the dominant culture at the center of definitions of effective teaching and omit culturally responsive teaching competencies, thus resulting in the systematic marginalization of CLD learners. Consider Salazar's *testimonio* (testimony) about the consequences of centering whiteness and marginalizing the "other":

> I entered kindergarten with my maleta (suitcase). It was filled with all of my treasures. Mr. Lopez encouraged me to bring my maleta into his bilingual classroom. He made me feel that I was so smart and capable because I could sustain two languages and cultures. I entered his classroom every morning with my head held high; I imagined that my treasures sparkled brilliantly like the star of Bethlehem. This came to an abrupt halt when I entered first grade, a mainstream classroom. Mrs. Kowalski directed me to leave my maleta at the classroom door. She gave me a new maleta, one that she believed would serve me better. It was filled with the U.S. culture, U.S. ways of knowing, and the English language. I felt afraid, confused, and lost without my maleta. Over time, I adjusted to my new maleta. I did so by rejecting my treasures; they had lost their luster. I did not want that old maleta anymore.

In centering whiteness and excluding my (Salazar) cultural, linguistic, and familial resources, my first-grade teacher, and the vast majority of my teachers, stripped me of the most essential parts of my humanity. My testimony reveals the potential negative impact of teacher evaluation models that center the dominant culture.

In the sections that follow, we interrogate the most frequently used teacher evaluation models in the United States: Danielson's Framework for Teaching, the Marzano Teacher Evaluation Model, and the Classroom Assessment Scoring

TABLE 3.1 Generic teaching competencies versus culturally responsive teaching competencies

	Generic teaching competencies	Culturally responsive teaching competencies
Learning environment	Build positive relationships	Develop respectful relationships with students, families, and communities in ways that affirm their diversity
	Set norms for appropriate behavior and enforce consequences for misbehavior	Co-construct asset-based classroom norms with students and families and develop a culturally responsive system of rewards and consequences
	Set high expectations	Set high expectations and communicate belief in students and a commitment to their growth and development
	Engage students	Ensure active engagement for every learner that is inclusive of their diverse ways of knowing
Content knowledge	Connect content to prior knowledge and experiences	Connect content concepts to students' lives and diversity
	Enact approved curriculum	Ensure curriculum includes content that represents the contributions and perspectives of diverse communities
	Engage students in applying knowledge	Engage students in applying knowledge in real world contexts that promote social justice
Planning and instruction	Use standards to plan instruction	Use culturally relevant curriculum planning
	Identify learning objectives	Identify content and language objectives
	Enact research-based instructional strategies	Enact research-based instructional strategies for diverse students
	Provide opportunities for high-level learning	Engage students in high-level learning that is relevant to their lives, and promotes critical consciousness and social justice
Assessment	Assess student learning using established criteria	Develop and implement authentic assessments based on students' interests and diversity
	Use standardized assessments	Minimize or eliminate bias in testing
	Have students monitoring their own learning	Engage students in continuously assessing their progress and setting individual and group learning goals
	Provide explicit feedback	Provide students with frequent, timely, specific, individualized, and group feedback

TABLE 3.1 (Cont.)

	Generic teaching competencies	*Culturally responsive teaching competencies*
Differentiation	Group students based on abilities	Group students based on assessment data and diverse learning needs
	Consider individual student needs	Use data to assess and meet individual and subgroup needs (e.g., ELL, special needs, gifted, gender, etc.)
	Include multiple learning styles	Incorporate multiple modalities that are inclusive of diverse ways of knowing

Note. This table is derived from the research base described in the previous chapters. The research base for culturally responsive competencies will be further described in Chapter 4.

System (CLASS). These teacher evaluation models are currently in widespread use in the United States and/or have been included in national-level research on teacher effectiveness. We briefly describe each model and conduct a systematic analysis to assess the equity focus of each model. We compare these to Salazar and Lerner's Framework for Equitable and Excellent Teaching (FEET), a culturally responsive teacher evaluation model, presented in detail in Chapter 4 of this book (see Appendix B: FEET Dimensions, Competencies, and Indicators).

We assess the use of equity-based words in the four aforementioned teacher evaluation models (i.e., Danielson, Marzano, CLASS, FEET) using the following procedure. First, we compile a list of equity-based words included in the FEET; these align with the concept of equity described in Chapter 1 (see Appendix A: FEET Equity-based Words). We do not claim that this list is inclusive of all possible equity-based words; however, we assert that the words in this list provide evidence of an equity focus. Second, we examine the first three levels of descriptors (e.g., domain, competency, indicator) in each model and conduct a frequency count of equity-based words. We assign a score for each descriptor: 0 for the absence of equity-based words and 1 for presence of equity-based words. Third, we determine a quantitative tally, in percentage form, of equity-based words for the first three levels of descriptors. Last, we describe qualitative examples of the focus on equity in each tool. The result of our analysis of the equity focus in the four previously mentioned tools follows.

Danielson's Framework for Teaching

Charlotte Danielson's Framework for Teaching is the most widely used approach in the United States to define and evaluate effective teaching (Malmberg, Hagger, Burn, Mutton, & Colis, 2010; Pianta & Hamre, 2009). This framework is used in teacher preparation, mentoring and induction, professional development, and teacher evaluation (Danielson, 2013). Danielson's Framework for Teaching was first published in 1996. The most recent edition, released in 2013, was adapted in response to the instructional implications resulting from the adoption of the Common Core State Standards. Danielson's Framework received national attention for its inclusion in the Bill & Melinda Gates Foundation's Measure of Teacher Effectiveness (MET) study (Kane, McCaffrey, Miller, & Staiger, 2013). It "has been adopted as the single model, or one of several approved models, in over 20 states" (Danielson, 2013).

Danielson's Framework includes 4 domains, 22 components, and 76 elements of effective teaching. It promotes generic teaching skills such as: demonstrating knowledge of content and pedagogy; demonstrating knowledge of students; setting instructional outcomes; demonstrating knowledge of resources; designing coherent instruction; designing student assessments; creating an environment of respect and rapport; establishing a culture for learning; managing classroom procedures; managing student behavior; organizing physical space; communicating with students; using questioning and discussion techniques; engaging students in learning; using assessment in instruction; demonstrating flexibility and responsiveness; and communicating with families.

Educators have found a useable framework for teacher evaluation in Danielson's Framework. However, in settling for convenience, educators have turned a blind eye to the fact that the Framework fails to serve CLD learners. Danielson's description of her Framework illustrates this point. She states:

> It is a description of good teaching, in any context. One of the common themes – and there are seven – focuses on differentiating instruction to appropriately teach all students, including those with special needs. The framework doesn't give specific guidance on how to address diverse needs, – it's generic and applies to all teaching situations, subjects, and grade levels – and I don't think there is any frame work published that does offer that type of guidance.
>
> *(DeWitt, 2011)*

Danielson stresses that the framework for teaching is a generic representation of good teaching that applies to *all* teaching situations; yet, she states that it does not offer guidance on how to address the diverse needs of learners. Danielson's own words affirm that generic teacher competencies are "good" teaching for all students, despite the fact that they are not inclusive of the needs of diverse learners.

Table 3.2 illustrates the frequency, in percentage form, of equity-based words in Danielson's Framework at the first three levels of performance: domains, components, and elements. As noted in the table, no equity-based language was evident at the "domain" and "component" levels, and only 1% of the words at the "element" level were equity-based.

Further examination of Danielson's Framework suggests that it promotes generic teaching competencies that center the dominant culture and exclude CLD learners.

TABLE 3.2 Percentage of equity-based words in Danielson's Framework for Teaching

	Domains	*Components*	*Elements*
Percentage of equity-based words	0%	0%	1%

First, Danielson includes two elements that relate to CLD learners; however, these lack detail. These elements include the following: "knowledge of students' interests and cultural heritage," and "suitability for diverse students." While Danielson's Framework states that "knowledge of students' interests and cultural heritage" is important, little detail is provided related to how teachers show evidence of this other than accompanying indicators that suggest teachers "participate in community cultural events" and provide "opportunities for families to share their heritages." The lack of detail promotes the following issues:

- Knowledge of students' cultural heritage does not automatically equate to teachers valuing, building on, and sustaining/revitalizing CLD learners' resources.
- While the accompanying scoring rubric states that teachers should incorporate knowledge of students' cultural heritages into planning, detail is missing related to planning relevant lessons that leverage students' cultural, linguistic, familial, and community resources.
- The lack of detail related to "cultural heritage" and "cultural events" can reinforce a "fun, food, and fiesta approach" (Salazar, 2010, p. 120). In fact, the examples provided in the accompanying rubrics for Danielson's Framework suggest surface-level approaches, including: reading a Hanukkah book in December; discussing students' ancestry in a unit on South America; and attending a local Mexican heritage day and meeting students' family members.

In terms of "suitability for diverse learners," this element is described as "setting outcomes that are appropriate for all students in the class." Again, the focus is on *all* students without regard to student diversity. No further description is provided that relates to CLD learners.

Second, there are glaring omissions across the framework related to meeting the needs of CLD learners. For example, in the component "demonstrating knowledge of resources" there is no mention of materials that emphasize equity or reflect CLD learners. Instead of encouraging the incorporation of CLD resources in the curriculum, a teacher can score "distinguished" on the accompanying rubric if s/he "maintains a log of resources for student reference" or "facilitates student contact with resources outside the classroom."

Third, we contend that Danielson's Framework describes generic teacher performances that can reify whitestream ways of knowing. As a case in point, the Danielson Framework includes aspects related to the classroom environment such as structure, respect, active listening, turn-taking, physical proximity, politeness, time, and fairness. These are cultural constructs that vary according to the norms of diverse cultures (Gay, 2000). As an example, turn-taking in some cultures includes overlapping speech and/or call-and-response interactions. A teacher that approaches teaching through the whitestream may interpret cultural differences in communication as misbehavior, disengagement, disrespect, and/or resistance. Rather than making a generalized statement about aspects related to the classroom environment, the Framework should explicitly acknowledge that students navigate different cultural systems, and thus it is essential to build a classroom community in collaboration with students and families.

In sum, Danielson's Framework for Teaching has virtually no focus on equity, promotes a "tourist approach to diversity" (Jones & Derman-Sparks, 1992), and fails to explicitly identify culturally responsive practices. Ultimately, the Framework's omissions effectively render CLD learners invisible. Danielson (2007) acknowledges that educators have criticized her framework for excluding important elements such as cultural awareness. In response, Danielson makes the claim that "implicit in the entire framework is a commitment to equity" (p. 32) because *all* students are included. In reality, Danielson's Framework for Teaching centers the whitestream and relegates CLD learners to the margins of teaching and learning.

Marzano's Teacher Evaluation Model

Marzano's Teacher Evaluation Model is a teacher evaluation framework that has been implemented in school across the nation (Marzano Center, 2017). Marzano's original teacher evaluation framework, released in 2010, was based largely on a meta-analysis of instructional strategies correlated with student achievement gains. Updated versions of the model, released in 2014 and 2017, were intended to provide greater clarity and focus on key pedagogical principles. The Marzano Center (2017) indicates that the goal of the evaluation model is "to ensure that teachers understand exactly how to improve their teaching to affect measureable gains in student achievement" (p. 6).

A major update of the Marzano Teacher Evaluation Model took place in 2017 resulting in the Marzano Focused Teacher Evaluation Model (Carbaugh, Marzano, & Toth, 2017). This teacher evaluation model is intended to simplify evaluation. It consists of four domains, or areas of expertise: standards-based planning, standards-based instruction, conditions for learning, and professional responsibilities. These domains are further developed into 23 elements that support a teacher's developing expertise within the four areas of expertise. Evidence is provided for reaching the specified element. The model promotes generic teaching skills, including: establish and communicate learning goals, track student progress, and celebrate success; help students effectively interact with new knowledge; help students practice and deepen their understanding of new knowledge; help students generate and test hypotheses about new knowledge; engage students; establish and maintain

TABLE 3.3 Percentage of equity-based words in Marzano's Focused Teacher
Evaluation Model

	Domains	Elements	Evidence
Percentage of equity-based words	0%	0%	10%

TABLE 3.4 Percentage of equity-based words at the evidence-level by domain in
Marzano's Focused Teacher Evaluation Model

	Standards-based Planning	Standards-based Instruction	Conditions for Learning	Professional Responsibilities
Percentage of equity-based words at the "evidence" level	4%	1%	3%	2%

classroom rules and procedures; recognize and acknowledge adherence and lack
of adherence to classroom rules and procedures; establish and maintain effective
relationships with students; communicate high expectations for all students; and
develop effective lessons organized into a cohesive unit.

Table 3.3 illustrates the frequency, in percentage form, of equity-based words
in the 2017 Marzano Focused Teacher Evaluation Model. As reflected in the table,
no equity-based words are found at the first two levels: "domains" and "elements."
Ten percent of the words at the third level, "evidence," are equity based.

First, a closer look at Marzano's Model reveals that, of the 23 elements, only
two elements appear to address the needs of CLD learners: "planning to close
the achievement gap using data," and "communicating high expectations for
each student to close the achievement gap." Both competencies use the deficit language of "achievement gaps." Gutiérrez (2008) makes the case that the
achievement gap focus offers "little more than a static picture of inequities,
supporting deficit thinking and negative narratives about Students of Color and
working-class students, perpetuating the myth that the problem (and therefore
solution) is a technical one, and promoting a narrow definition of learning and
equity" (p. 357).

Second, we conducted an analysis of the language in at the third level, to
further examine how the evidence by domain level includes an equity focus.
Table 3.4 illustrates the frequency, in percentage form, of equity-based words at
the "evidence" level for each of the four domains of the Marzano Focused Teacher
Evaluation Model.

Our analysis indicates that the majority of the equity-based words are found
in the standards-based planning domain (4%). The fewest equity-based words are
in the standards-based instruction domain (1%). This is significant because an

evaluation tool is typically geared toward assessing instruction in the classroom. Thus, in Marzano's Model, 1% of instruction promotes equity.

Third, the Marzano model does not explicitly include culturally responsive teaching competencies at the domain and element levels. While the third level, evidence, does include some culturally responsive competencies, approximately 24/236, this makes up 1% of the evidence that evaluators can draw from to assess effective teaching.

In sum, Marzano touts that the revised 2017 model has a more focused approach. However, from our perspective, the updated version is more focused on maintaining the whitestream and marginalizing CLD learners.

Classroom Assessment Scoring System (CLASS)

The Classroom Assessment Scoring System (CLASS) is a teaching observation instrument developed to assess classroom quality in kindergarten through twelfth-grade classrooms (Teachstone, 2008). The developers indicate that the CLASS is based on developmental theory and research that suggests student learning results from interactions between students and adults (Pianta, La Paro, & Hamre, 2008). While the CLASS K-3 Manual (Pianta et al., 2008) was published in 2008 for kindergarten through third-grade classrooms, the upper elementary and secondary classroom manuals (Pianta, Hamre, & Mintz, 2012a, 2012b) were published in 2012. The CLASS is organized into domains, dimensions, indicators, and behavioral markers. At the broadest level are the three *domains*: Emotional Support, Classroom Organization, and Instructional Support. The K-3 *dimensions* include the following: positive climate, negative climate, teacher sensitivity, regard for student perspective, behavior management, productivity, instructional learning formats, concept development, quality of feedback, and language modeling. The upper elementary and secondary dimensions include the aforementioned dimensions and add instructional dialogue and student engagement. The *indicators* are short descriptors of effective interactions between teachers and students; these are accompanied by *behavioral markers* that provide examples of how teacher–student interactions can be assessed.

The CLASS has been implemented in 23 states (Teachstone, 2008) and has received national attention for its inclusion in the Bill & Melinda Gates Foundation's Measure of Teacher Effectiveness (MET) study (Kane et al., 2013).

Table 3.5 illustrates the frequency, in percentage form, of the inclusion of equity-based words in the CLASS. Based on our analysis, the CLASS has no equity-based language in four levels of descriptors. We examined four levels in the CLASS because we found no focus on equity in the first three levels.

In addition to the evidence above, further examination reveals no equity focus. This reality is best captured in the statement: "The CLASS resembles a 'well-oiled machine' where everybody knows what is expected and how to go about doing it" (Pianta et al., 2012b, p. 49). This well-oiled machine systematizes the marginalization of CLD learners.

TABLE 3.5 Percentage of equity-based words in the CLASS

	Domains	Dimensions	Indicators/behavioral markers
Percentage of equity-based words	0%	0%	0%

First, the CLASS does not delineate culturally responsive practices in its observation tools. Instead, it takes a generic focus that reifies the whitestream. As an example, the description of behavior management in the CLASS (Pianta et al., 2012b) emphasizes teacher control such as: telling students what to do, monitoring and redirecting student behavior, curbing student aggression or defiance, and ensuring student compliance. Rather than emphasizing the co-construction of classroom norms with students and families, the CLASS emphasizes a teacher-centered approach based on teacher control of student behavior. What does student aggression and defiance look like? Can the ways of knowing of CLD learners be interpreted as aggressive or defiant? Must CLD learners comply with norms of "good behavior" that are determined by White ways of being? These are all important questions to consider.

Moreover, the CLASS takes a deficit-based approach using terminology such as "at risk for school failure" (Pianta et al., 2008, p. 3). The CLASS perpetuates deficit views through the use of the following terms: at risk, failure, low-risk, high-risk, and behind. The emphasis on what students *can't do* reinforces ideologies that that the "poor little ones" are at a disadvantage. This is in contrast to views that all students bring strengths and they *can do* when given the opportunity to learn.

In sum, the CLASS blatantly renders CLD learners to the margins through a total lack of disregard for equity and culturally responsive practices, the use of deficit language, and generic approaches that reinforce whitestream ways of being.

Framework for Equitable and Excellent Teaching (FEET)

The FEET consists of three levels of descriptors of equitable and excellent teaching: domains, competencies, and indicators. This framework will be described in detail in Chapter 4. At the first level, 100% of the domains include equity-based words. At the second and third levels, competencies and indicators, 50% or above include equity-based words. Table 3.6 reflects the percentage use of equity-based words in each of the three levels of descriptors in the FEET.

Overall, the FEET reflects a significantly higher percentage of equity-based words at the three levels of descriptors of teaching. In addition to the inclusion of equity-based words, the FEET includes culturally responsive practices; these are delineated in Chapter 4. The FEET takes a significantly stronger focus on equity in comparison to the three teacher evaluation models described in this chapter.

TABLE 3.6 Percentage of equity-based words in the Framework for Equitable and Excellent Teaching

	Domains	Competencies	Indicators
Percentage of equity-based words	100%	53%	50%

Comparison of Teacher Evaluation Models

Table 3.7 provides a comparison of the total percentage of descriptors (e.g., domains, competencies, indicators), at the first three levels, that contain equity-based words for the four teacher evaluation models: Danielson's Framework for Teaching, the Marzano Teacher Evaluation Model, the Classroom Assessment Scoring System (CLASS), and Salazar and Lerner's Framework for Equitable and Excellent Teaching (FEET). This comparison shows a clear distinction in the focus on equity.

As evidenced in Table 3.7, the FEET far outpaces the Danielson Framework for Teaching, the Marzano Teacher Evaluation Model, and the Classroom Assessment Scoring System in its equity focus.

The Impact of Teacher Evaluation from the Center

We reject notions of objectivity and neutrality in teacher evaluation. Current teacher evaluation models position the dominant culture at the center, as the standard, the norm, and the default setting. Thus, they serve as a powerful mechanism for fortifying whiteness. Concomitantly, the positioning of CLD learners at the margins promotes assimilation, fuels deficit notions, and subtracts the resources of CLD learners.

Who will challenge the status quo of teacher evaluation? New iterations of teacher performance assessments continue to bolster the status quo. Gargani and Strong (2014) proclaim that they have developed an instrument that can identify a successful teacher "better, faster, and cheaper" (p. 390). The Rapid Assessment of Teacher Effectiveness (RATE) includes shorter segments of instruction, fewer observations, less training, and simpler scoring criteria. The authors claim to generate teacher evaluations that are more reliable, predictive, and inexpensive. The RATE includes six items based on teacher competencies related to lesson objectives, instructional delivery, questioning strategies, clarity of concepts, time on task, and student understanding. The authors do not claim that the items are good teaching. Instead, they assert that the items can identify a successful teacher by predicting student learning as reflected on standardized tests. We contend that this impetus for efficiency and standardization, and the persistent disregard for CLD learners, is simply a better, faster, and cheaper method to assimilate and thus dehumanize CLD learners.

TABLE 3.7 Comparison of descriptors with equity-based words in teacher evaluation models

	Total no. of descriptors with equity-based words	Total no. of descriptors	Total % of descriptors with equity-based words
Danielson	4	102	.04%
Marzano	24	263	.09%
CLASS	0	Varies by level	0%
FEET	42	79	53%

Note. The CLASS varies by levels: K-3, upper elementary, and secondary.

When confronted with the egregious news that teacher evaluation models marginalize CLD learners, some educators vociferously uphold the status quo through a litany of excuses: "We have to use our state's teacher evaluation model." "It would be too resource intensive to develop and implement a new model." "A tool focusing on equity would not be applicable to White students." Why do these educators not feel a sense of urgency? Why do they sit on the sidelines and watch our CLD children languish and struggle to find their power in the margins? Why can't they see there is no room for neutrality? Milner (2015) states that: "Educators are either fighting for equitable education for all students, or they are fighting against it. *There is no neutral space in this work*" (p. 11; emphasis in original). Do not proclaim to fight for equity while you sit on the sidelines and wait for change.

We assert that the struggle for equity in education is for all children. CRTE does not position educators for Students of Color and against White students. To the contrary, CRTE serves the needs of all students; White students have culture too. Ultimately, exposing all students to different ways of knowing and being in the world will prepare them to thrive in an increasingly globalized space. It is important to note that making the case that White students will not be left behind is necessary from a CRT perspective. This is because White communities may not advocate for the needs of CLD learners unless they perceive interest convergence, that is, their own interests align with those of Communities of Color (Milner, 2008).

We challenge current approaches to teacher evaluation. We challenge how "the center is always trying to contain the margin, to bring it under the power of definition and limitation" (Walker, 1999, p. 36). We proclaim that the most commonly used teacher evaluation models across our nation: center the dominant culture and reinforce the whitestream; seek to assimilate CLD learners; and render CLD learners invisible at the margins. The result – a systematic approach to leave America's most vulnerable children behind. We call you to action in the remaining chapters of this book. Be the change.

Summary and Implications

In this chapter, we unveiled the masternarrative of objectivity and neutrality in teacher evaluation. We revealed whiteness at the normative center of these evaluation systems. We have made the case that evaluation models privilege the dominant culture through "generic" teaching competencies, and marginalize the "others" by negating their cultural, linguistic, and familial resources. This chapter affirms the claim we made in the previous chapter: The cultural lenses used to develop teacher evaluation models matter. We ask you to be a critical consumer of these models. Who is included? Who is excluded? Do they meet the needs of CLD learners? What has been omitted? Why are generic teacher evaluation models being implemented on a state-wide and national scale? What can we do to advocate for the inclusion of CLD learners' resources and needs in teacher evaluation models? Why does this matter?

Critical Questions

The following critical questions are intended to extend your comprehension and help you relate the concepts to your own practice.

1. One of the central assertions in this chapter is that teacher evaluation models reinforce the dominant culture and exclude CLD learners. Do you agree or disagree with this assertion? Explain your reasoning.
2. Consider the following statement: Generic teacher evaluation tools advance teacher knowledge and skills that assimilate Students of Color and steal their humanity. Do you agree or disagree with this statement? Explain your reasoning.
3. What values are evident in your state or district teacher evaluation model?
4. How does your state or district teacher evaluation tool meet the needs of CLD students?
5. What changes must be made to teacher evaluation models to advance equity?

Resources for Further Reflection and Study

The following supplemental resources are intended to spur your personal and professional reflection, application of the concepts in your own context, and community outreach efforts.

Print

Fine, M., Weis, L., Powell Pruitt, L., & Burns, A. (2004). *Off White: Readings on power, privilege, and resistance* (2nd ed.). New York, NY: Routledge.

Jupp, J. C., Berry, T. R., & Lensmire, T. J. (2016). Second-wave White teacher identity studies: A review of White teacher identity literatures from 2004 through 2014. *Review of Educational Research, 86*(4), 1151–1191.

Kivel, P. (2002). *Uprooting racism: How white people can work for racial justice* (Rev. ed.). Gabriola Island, BC, Canada: New Society Publishers.

Rothenberg, P. S. (Ed.). (2005). *White privilege: Essential readings on the other side of racism* (2nd ed.). New York, NY: Worth Publishers.

Shireav, E. B., & Levy, D. A. (2016). *Cross-cultural psychology: Critical thinking and contemporary applications* (5th ed.). New York, NY: Routledge.

Web

- Chryssikos, K., Marshall, T., Melitski, J., & Palushi, M.
  The culture of power
  https://prezi.com/mb3bfkqiqrdw/the-culture-of-power/
- LA RED Week
  Practical application of critical race theory in Latina/o responsive evaluation
  http://aea365.org/blog/la-red-week-practical-application-of-critical-race-theory-in-latinao-responsive-evaluation/
- Racial Equity Tools
  Whiteness and White privilege
  www.racialequitytools.org/fundamentals/core-concepts/whiteness-and-white-privilege

Media

- Charlotte Danielson
  Making teacher evaluations meaningful
  www.youtube.com/watch?v=KzDcYuSsU2E
- Lisa Hollenbach
  Are you prepared to talk about race?
  www.teachingchannel.org/blog/2017/08/18/talk-about-race/
- National Public Radio – Educate Podcast
  Talking about race in schools
  www.npr.org/podcasts/381443931/american-radioworks
- The Education Gadfly
  DC teachers speak out about teacher evaluations
  www.youtube.com/watch?v=LoaidrMJ6wk

Learning Opportunities

1. Create a time capsule of artifacts that illustrate the tenets of CRT in your current educational context. Include a brief description explaining how each artifact illustrates the tenets of CRT.
2. Identify two to three examples in your own context to support or challenge the following statement: Frameworks for teaching center whiteness and marginalize Communities of Color.

3. Examine your school/district teacher evaluation tool. Make a list or draw a visual representation of the values that are transmitted based on what is, and is not, present in the evaluation tool. What are the most common values that emerged? What are the implications for teaching, learning, school leadership, and equity?
4. Engage with the following scenario: You are a school administrator who is responsible for teacher evaluation. Upon reviewing your district teacher evaluation tool you come to the conclusion that it excludes CLD learners. You ask your district area superintendent to meet with you to discuss your concerns. Your district administrator encourages you to document your concerns. Create a one-page document in which you: (a) summarize your three main concerns about the teacher evaluation tool used in your district; (b) suggest an alternative approach; and (c) explain your reasoning for suggesting the alternative approach.

Community Engagement Opportunities

1. Create a professional learning community (PLC) that examines race. Search "Race in America" on YouTube. View four or five videos of your choosing. Summarize the main points of the videos in half a page. Describe how the videos impacted your views about race. Discuss the implications for teaching and learning.
2. Attend a cultural event in the community you serve or a culturally diverse community. What does it look, sound, taste, smell, and feel like? What values are represented in the diverse cultures? How can you draw on their resources to improve teaching, learning, and leading?
3. Explore the community you serve as an educator. Speak to community members. Ask them questions such as: How long have you lived in this community? How has your community changed? What do you love about your community? What are your best community resources? What would you change? How have the local schools helped or hurt your community? How can I help you and your community to thrive? Share their lived experiences with your school community.

References

Anzaldúa, G. (1990). *Making faces, making soul = haciendo caras: Creative and critical perspectives of feminists of color.* San Francisco, CA: Aunt Lute Press.
Bonilla-Silva, E. (2017). *Racism without racists: Color-blind racism and the persistence of racial inequality in America.* Boulder, CO: Rowman & Littlefield.
Carbaugh, B., Marzano, R., & Toth, M. (2017). *The Marzano focused teacher evaluation model: A focused, scientific behavior evaluation model for standards-based classrooms.* West Palm Beach, FL: Learning Sciences International.
Coates, T. (2015). *Between the world and me.* New York, NY: Speigel & Grau.

Danielson, C. (2007). *Enhancing professional practice: A framework for teaching*. Alexandria, VA: ASCD.

Danielson, C. (2013). *The Framework for Teaching: Evaluation instrument*. Princeton, NJ: The Danielson Group.

Darling-Hammond, L. (2012). *Creating a comprehensive system for evaluating and supporting effective teaching*. Stanford Center for Opportunity Policy in Education. Retrieved from https://edpolicy.stanford.edu/sites/default/files/publications/creating-comprehensive-system-evaluating-and-supporting-effective-teaching.pdf

Delgado, R. (1995). *Critical race theory: The cutting edge*. Philadelphia, PA: Temple University Press.

DeWitt, P. (2011). *A framework for good teaching: A conversation with Charlotte Danielson*. Retrieved from http://blogs.edweek.org/edweek/finding_common_ground/2011/10/a_framework_for_good_teaching_a_conversation_with_charlotte_danielson.html

Dyer, R. (1997). The matter of whiteness. White privilege: Essential readings on the other side of racism. In P. Rothenberg (Ed.), *White privilege: Essential readings on the other side of racism* (pp. 9–14). New York, NY: Worth Publishers.

Espinoza, L., & Harris, A. (1998). Embracing the tar-baby: LatCrit theory and the sticky mess of race. *La Raza Law Journal, 10*(1), 499–559.

Flynn, J. E. (2015). Racing the unconsidered: Considering whiteness, rubrics, and the function of oppression. In M. Tenam-Zemach & J. E. Flynn (Eds.), *Rubric nation: Critical inquiries on the impact of rubrics in education* (pp. 201–221). Charlotte, NC: Information Age Publishing, Inc.

Fránquiz, M. E., Salazar, M. D. C., & DeNicolo, C. P. (2011). Challenging majoritarian tales: Portraits of bilingual teachers deconstructing deficit views of bilingual learners. *Bilingual Research Journal, 34*(3), 279–300.

Gargani, J., & Strong, M. (2014). Can we identify a successful teacher better, faster, and cheaper? Evidence for innovating teacher observation systems. *Journal of Teacher Education, 65*(5), 389–401.

Gay, G. (2000). *Culturally responsive teaching: Theory, research, and practice*. New York, NY: Teachers College Press.

Grande, S. (2000). American Indian identity and intellectualism: The quest for a new red pedagogy. *International Journal of Qualitative Studies in Education, 13*(4), 343–359.

Gutiérrez, R. (2008). A "gap-gazing" fetish in mathematics education? Problematizing research on the achievement gap. *Journal for Research in Mathematics Education, 39*(4), 357–364.

Howard, T. C., & Navarro, O. (2016). Critical race theory 20 years later: Where do we go from here? *Urban Education, 51*(3), 253–273.

Jones, E., & Derman-Sparks, L. (1992). Meeting the challenge of diversity. *Young Children, 47*(2), 12–18.

Kane, T. J., McCaffrey, D. F., Miller, T., & Staiger, D. O. (2013). *Have we identified effective teachers? Validating measures of effective teaching using random assignment*. Retrieved from http://k12education.gatesfoundation.org/download/?Num=2676&filename=MET_Validating_Using_Random_Assignment_Research_Paper.pdf

Ladson-Billings, G. (2009). *The dreamkeepers: Successful teachers of African American Children* (2nd ed.). San Francisco, CA: Jossey-Bass.

Ladson-Billings, G., & Tate, W. (1995). Toward a critical race theory of education. *Teachers College Record, 97*, 47–68.

Leonardo, Z. (2004). The color of supremacy: Beyond the discourse of 'white privilege'. *Educational Philosophy and Theory, 36*(2), 137–152.

Lynn, M. (2006). Dancing between two worlds: A portrait of the life of a black male teacher in South Central LA. *International Journal of Qualitative Studies in Education, 19*(2), 221–242.

Lynn, M., & Parker, L. (2006). Critical race studies in education: Examining a decade of research on U.S. schools. *The Urban Review, 38*(4), 257–290.

Malmberg, L., Hagger, H., Burn, K., Mutton, T., & Colis, H. (2010). Observed classroom quality during teacher education and two years of professional practice. *Journal of Educational Psychology, 102*(4), 916–932.

Marzano Center (2017). *Marzano Focused Teacher Evaluation Model.* Retrieved from www. marzanoevaluation.com

Milner IV, H. R. (2008). Critical race theory and interest convergence as analytic tools in teacher education policies and practices. *Journal of Teacher Education, 59*(4), 332–346.

Milner IV, H. R. (2015). *Rac(e)ing to class: Confronting poverty and race in schools and classrooms.* Cambridge, MA: Harvard Education Press.

Milner IV, H. R., & Laughter, J. C. (2015). But good intentions are not enough: Preparing teachers to center race and poverty. *The Urban Review, 47*(2), 341–363.

Mirra, N., Garcia, A., & Morrell, E. (2015). *Doing youth participatory action research: Transforming inquiry with researchers, educators, and students.* New York, NY: Routledge.

New Teacher Project (2011). *Rating a teacher observation tool: Five ways to ensure classroom observations are focused and rigorous.* Retrieved from http://tntp.org/assets/documents/TNTP_RatingATeacherObservationTool_Feb2011.pdf?files/TNTP_RatingATeacherObservationTool_Feb2011.pdf

Nieto, S. (2008). Culture and education. *Yearbook of the National Society for the Study of Education, 107*(1), 127–142.

Paris, D., & Alim, H. S. (2014). What are we seeking to sustain through culturally sustaining pedagogy? A loving critique forward. *Harvard Educational Review, 84*(1), 85–100.

Pianta, R. C., & Hamre, B. K. (2009). Conceptualization, measurement and improvement of classroom processes: Standardized observation can leverage capacity. *Educational Researcher, 38*, 109–119.

Pianta, R. C., Hamre, B. K., & Mintz, S. (2012a). *Classroom Assessment and Scoring System: Upper elementary manual.* Charlottesville, VA: Teachstone.

Pianta, R. C., Hamre, B. K., & Mintz, S. (2012b). *Classroom Assessment and Scoring System: Secondary manual.* Charlottesville, VA: Teachstone.

Pianta, R. C., La Paro, K. M., & Hamre, B. K. (2008). *Classroom Assessment and Scoring System: K-3 manual.* Charlottesville, VA: Teachstone Training, LLC.

Salazar, M. (2010). Pedagogical stances of high school ESL teachers: Huelgas in high school ESL classrooms. *Bilingual Research Journal, 33*(1), 111–124.

Salazar, M. (2013). A humanizing pedagogy: Reinventing the principles and practice of education as a journey toward liberation. *Review of Research in Education, 37*(1), 121–148.

Salazar, M., & Rios, F. (2016). Just scholarship: Publishing academic research with a social justice focus. *Journal of Multicultural Perspectives, 18*(1), 3–11.

Solorzano, D., & Yosso, T. (2000). Toward a critical race theory of Chicana and Chicano education. In C. Tejeda, C. Martinez, and Z. Leonardo (Eds.), *Charting new terrains of Chicana(o)/Latina (o) education* (pp. 35–65). Cresskill, NJ: Hampton Press Inc.

Stovall, D. (2006). Forging community in race and class: Critical race theory and the quest for social justice in education. *Race Ethnicity and Education, 9*(3), 243–259.

Taylor, E. (2006). A critical race analysis of the achievement gap in the United States: Politics, reality, and hope. *Leadership and Policy in Schools, 5*(1), 71–87.

Teachstone (2008). *CLASS*. Retrieved from http://teachstone.com/

Trainor, J. S. (2002). Critical pedagogy's" other": Constructions of whiteness in education for social change. *College Composition and Communication, 53*(4), 631–650.

Urrieta, L. (2010). Whitestreaming: Why some Latinas/os fear bilingual education. *Counterpoints, 371*, 47–55.

Urrieta, L., & Villenas, S. A. (2013). The legacy of Derrick Bell and Latino/a education: A critical race testimonio. *Race Ethnicity and Education, 16*(4), 514–535.

Valencia, R. R. (2010). *Dismantling contemporary deficit thinking*. New York, NY: Routledge.

Valenzuela, A. (2010). *Subtractive schooling: US-Mexican youth and the politics of caring.* New York, NY: SUNY Press.

Villalpando, O. (2003). Self-segregation or self-preservation? A critical race theory and Latina/o critical theory analysis of findings from a longitudinal study of Chicana/o college students, *International Journal of Qualitative Studies in Education, 16*(5), 619–646.

Walker, J. (1999). When texts collide: The re-visionist power of the margin. *Colby Quarterly, 35*(1), 35–48.

Weller, R. C. (2017). 'Western' and 'White civilization': White nationalism and Eurocentrism at the crossroads. In R. C. Weller (Ed.), *21st-century narratives of world history* (pp. 35–80). London, UK: Palgrave Macmillan.

West, T. R. (2005). White power, white fear. *Rhetoric Review, 24*(4), 385–388.

Yamamoto, E. K. (1997). Critical race praxis: Race theory and political lawyering practice in post-civil rights America. *Michigan Law Review, 95*(4), 821–900.

Yosso, T. J. (2005). Whose culture has capital? A critical race theory discussion of community cultural wealth. *Race Ethnicity and Education, 8*(1), 69–91.

Yosso, T., Smith, W., Ceja, M., & Solórzano, D. (2009). Critical race theory, racial microaggressions, and campus racial climate for Latina/o undergraduates. *Harvard Educational Review, 79*(4), 659–691.

Zamudio, M., Russell, C., Rios, F., & Bridgeman, J. L. (2011). *Critical race theory matters: Education and ideology*. New York, NY: Routledge.

PART II

Culturally Responsive Teacher Evaluation

Part II describes practical examples based on culturally responsive approaches to teacher evaluation. Chapter 4 provides an exemplar of a culturally responsive teacher evaluation (CRTE) model known as the Salazar and Lerner Framework for Equitable and Excellent Teaching (FEET). Chapter 5 offers narratives of the instructional practice of five in-service teachers who were prepared with the FEET. Chapter 6 delineates scenarios to guide practicing and prospective teachers and school leaders to advance CRTE.

4

PROPOSING AN EXEMPLAR
OF CULTURALLY RESPONSIVE
TEACHER EVALUATION

Chapter Overview: This chapter proposes a counternarrative to the masternarrative of objectivity and neutrality in teacher evaluation. The authors reposition the margins to the center of teacher evaluation through a culturally responsive teacher evaluation (CRTE) model, the Salazar and Lerner Framework for Equitable and Excellent Teaching (FEET). The development and testing of the FEET is described based on the tenets of CRTE.

In the previous chapter we unveiled the masternarrative of objectivity and neutrality that positions the dominant culture at the center of teacher evaluation models. In this chapter we propose a counternarrative that demonstrates how to move the margins to the center of teacher evaluation. We describe the development of the Salazar and Lerner Framework for Equitable and Excellent Teaching (FEET) based on the tenets of culturally responsive teacher evaluation (CRTE). The FEET is a sound exemplar of a teacher evaluation model that is culturally responsive, empirically based, and psychometrically sound. It foregrounds the cultural, linguistic, familial, and community resources of historically marginalized CLD communities.

The FEET evaluation model measures teacher performances, or skills, based on 4 dimensions, 15 competencies, and 60 indicators of equitable and excellent teaching for K-12 learners (see Table 4.1). The performances (e.g., competencies and indicators) rated according to accompanying rubrics of performance on a four-level rating scale. Moreover, an 11-item field-based observation protocol provides both summative and formative assessment of teacher performance. Appendices related to the FEET can be found at the end of the book, including: FEET Dimensions, Competencies, and Indicators (B); FEET

TABLE 4.1 FEET dimensions, competencies, and indicators

Dimensions	Competencies	Indicators
Engage students in an inclusive and supportive learning community.	1.1 Develop affirming relationships with students and families.	E.1 Express value, respect, and asset perspectives of students' language(s), culture(s), and communities.
		E.2 Foster positive rapport (e.g., patience, caring) with students and facilitate positive interactions between students.
		E.3 Communicate belief in capacity of all learners to achieve at high levels (e.g., college and career readiness, high expectations, growth mindset).
		E.4 Collaborate with parents/guardians/families to identify student interests and needs and set shared goals for student learning and development.
	1.2 Maintain an equitable classroom environment.	E.5 Facilitate classroom norms and routines, in collaboration with students/families, that promote a positive learning community (e.g., clear expectations, positive reinforcement, individualized support).
		E.6 Guide student behaviors through teacher moves (e.g., tone, movement, positioning, cues, key phrases, direct speech) and a system of incentives that promotes student empowerment.
		E.7 Use predictable transition strategies to maintain students' focus on learning.
		E.8 Use a systematic process to ensure students have necessary materials for learning.
	1.3 Actively engage students in learning.	E.9 Use a variety of active engagement strategies to ensure each student participates through discussion and movement (e.g., interactive technology, assistive technology, total physical response, call-and-response, storytelling, props, simulations, scenarios, games, music/rhythm, arts integration, visual and performing arts).
		E.10 Incorporate modalities that facilitate content learning (e.g., auditory, visual, kinesthetic, tactile, and intra/interpersonal, musical, naturalistic, logical, verbal, technological).
		E.11 Provide opportunities for students to experience joyful learning that includes discovery, application, collaboration, and/or advocacy for social justice issues.

TABLE 4.1 (Cont.)

Dimensions	Competencies	Indicators
		E.12 Demonstrate student-centered approach by consistently incorporating student voice, choice, teaching, and leadership.
Plan rigorous, culturally responsive, standards- and outcome-based lesson and unit plans.	2.1 Use culturally responsive backward design curriculum planning to develop units.	P.1 Identify big ideas, essential questions, enduring understandings, and social justice themes that are relevant to students' interests and diversity.
		P.2 Create engaging units of study that are aligned to relevant content, language, and college and career readiness standards.
		P.3 Supplement or adapt district-approved curriculum to reflect student diversity, and promote cultural competence and critical consciousness.
		P.4 Include materials and resources that reflect students' cultures and include a variety of cultures.
		P.5 Design rigorous, relevant, and authentic unit performance tasks.
		P.6 Develop a sequence of lessons aligned to unit goals and social justice pursuits.
	2.2 Design measurable, challenging, and culturally responsive lessons.	P.7 Set clear, rigorous, measureable content and language objective (CLO) based on unit goals.
		P.8 Create a logical sequence with each lesson component aligning to objectives and assessments.
		P.9 Develop rationale that connects lesson objective with unit goals, students' lives, real-world application, and social justice pursuits.
		P.10 Incorporate topics that draw on student diversity (e.g., race, ethnicity, culture, gender, class, abilities, sexual orientation, religion) and include the contributions of diverse populations.
		P.11 Provide opportunities for students to identify oppression locally and globally, counteract stereotypes, develop critical consciousness, and see themselves as agents of change.

(*continued*)

TABLE 4.1 (Cont.)

Dimensions	Competencies	Indicators
	2.3 Integrate culturally responsive assessment into planning.	P.12 Analyze assessments for validity, reliability, and bias (e.g., culture, language, gender, class, religion, etc.).
		P.13 Include a variety of assessment tools (e.g., formative, summative, authentic, project-based) to gather data on student learning.
		P.14 Analyze standardized and classroom-based student assessment data to set SMART learning targets.
		P.15 Use assessment data to identify individual and subgroup (e.g., EB/ELL, special needs, gifted) learning goals and design differentiated learning experiences.
		P.16 Use technology to collect, track, analyze, and share assessment data with students and families, and analyze trends in student progress to make planning decisions.
	2.4 Demonstrate knowledge of content and student development.	P.17 Analyze current research related to content pedagogy, and identify implications for teaching, learning, and equity.
		P.18 Understand how students' typical and atypical development (e.g., cognitive, socioemotional, linguistic) impacts learning.
		P.19 Identify prerequisite content and language knowledge and skills, and typical student errors, misconceptions, and challenges.
		P.20 Use knowledge of content to plan rigorous and relevant units and lessons that develop literacy and numeracy.
Teach equitably by setting high expectations and providing support for student growth and development.	3.1 Set context for lesson.	T.1 Post, preview, and review concise, rigorous, and measurable content and language objective (CLO).
		T.2 Engage students in discussing lesson rationale that connects content to students' diversity, prior content knowledge and skills, and interests.
		T.3 Promote real-world application of content in local, national, and global contexts.
		T.4 Clearly define performance expectations orally and in writing using student-friendly language.

TABLE 4.1 (Cont.)

Dimensions	Competencies	Indicators
	3.2 Facilitate clear and rigorous learning experiences.	T.5 Provide clear, concise, and relevant explanations of content (e.g., mental models, culturally responsive examples, accessible language).
		T.6 Use gradual release lesson cadence (I do, we do, you do) to scaffold students' independent application of learning.
		T.7 Align learning experiences to objectives.
		T.8 Adequately pace learning experiences by attending to student learning cues and progress on learning tasks.
	3.3 Promote rigorous academic talk.	T.9 Promote higher-order thinking skills by providing opportunities for students to use academic language, make claims, and articulate reasoning.
		T.10 Facilitate academic conversations by posing high-level questions, and asking students to pose questions and explain their thinking (e.g., elaborate, clarify, provide examples, build on or challenge ideas, paraphrase, synthesize).
		T.11 Set discussion norms with students and facilitate student conversations that foster critical consciousness (e.g., analyze multiple perspectives, ask critical questions, advocate for systemic change).
	3.4 Make content and language comprehensible for all learners.	T.12 Incorporate students' home language (e.g., heritage language, vernaculars, code-switching, translanguaging) into instruction and include materials in students' home language.
		T.13 Preview vocabulary to support understanding of concepts and context, and development of academic language.
		T.14 Incorporate sensory, graphic, and interactive supports (e.g., technology, visuals, manipulative/realia, key vocabulary, graphic organizers, concept maps, sentence stems, total physical response, modeling, and cooperative learning).
	3.5 Use formal and informal assessment data to monitor student progress toward learning targets.	T.15 Collect data on individual student progress toward content and language objective and analyze data to adjust instruction for individuals and subgroups (e.g., EB/ELL, special needs, gifted).

(continued)

TABLE 4.1 (Cont.)

Dimensions	Competencies	Indicators
		T.16 Engage students in continually assessing their own progress toward unit/lesson objectives and personal/group goals.
		T.17 Provide students with frequent, timely, specific, and individual/group feedback.
		T.18 Frequently check for understanding and adjust instruction according to evidence of student learning.
	3.6 Differentiate instruction to challenge students and meet diverse student needs.	T.19 Use assessment data to differentiate instruction according to student needs (e.g., language levels, special needs, socioemotional needs, learning modalities,).
		T.20 Implement flexible grouping strategies to meet diverse student needs.
		T.21 Provide options for differentiated content, learning experiences, and/or assessments that allow for student choice and expression of cultural ways of knowing.
		T.22 Collaborate with support specialists to develop and apply specific accommodations for individual students based on language needs, IEPs, and other legal requirements.
Lead by exemplifying professionalism and community advocacy.	4.1 Meet professional standards of practice.	L.1 Adhere to ethical and legal responsibilities for students' learning, behavior, safety, confidentiality, and civil rights as specified in local, state, and federal statutes.
		L.2 Maintain professional demeanor and communication in accordance with school, district, and/or university policy.
		L.3 Collaborate with community and school partners to support students' needs (e.g., parents/guardians, community organizations, school psychologists, counselors, social workers, nurses).
	4.2 Demonstrate growth and commitment to students and communities.	L.4 Recognize own biases and how these affect teaching and learning, and take action to monitor and eliminate bias.
		L.5 Use feedback and data to set clear and measurable goals to improve instruction and promote student learning and development.

TABLE 4.1 (Cont.)

Dimensions	Competencies	Indicators
		L.6 Participate in school, district, and community initiatives and advocate for community needs (e.g., professional development opportunities, school events, community engagement).

Note 1. We include examples (e.g.,) with indicators in order to provide examples of culturally responsive practices. These can be removed if desired.
Note 2. The book's appendices provide additional resources related to the FEET. The rubrics can be accessed at: http://portfolio.du.edu/MSALAZAR.

Observation Instrument (C); FEET Supervisor Training Protocol (D); and FEET Standards Matrix (E). The FEET is used to evaluate teacher performance during teaching events in the field. While this model was designed and tested with pre-service teachers, it is a measure of equitable and excellent teaching and thus can be used for in-service teachers. We offer the FEET as an exemplar of CRTE. The sections that follow describe the development and testing of the FEET based on the five tenets of CRTE.

Development and Testing of the FEET

Tenet 1: The FEET develops equitable and excellent teachers

We present the FEET as a counternarrative to the masternarrative that promotes generic practices for meeting the needs of all students. A counternarrative is a tool for "making visible the structures, processes, and practices that contribute to continued racial inequality" (Zamudio, Russell, Rios, & Bridgeman, 2011, p. 5). Counternarratives can be used to challenge structural aspects of education by critically examining a phenomenon that maintains the marginalization and subordination of Communities of Color (Solórzano & Yosso, 2002). The FEET is a teacher evaluation model that develops equitable and excellent teachers who disrupt inequity and advocate for equity and social justice. To achieve this aim, the FEET enacts critical race theory (CRT) in that it:

- establishes the centrality of race/culture;
- decenters whiteness and repositions the resources of CLD learners from historically marginalized communities at the center;
- rejects color-blind approaches to teacher evaluation;
- foregrounds the experiential knowledge of historically marginalized Communities of Color;

- promotes equity and social justice; and
- incorporates interdisciplinary approaches through the tenets of CRTE.

The FEET was developed and tested through the use of CRT methodology. Delgado Bernal (1998) suggests that critical race scholars use their cultural intuition during the research process. Cultural intuition emerges from data sources such as: (1) existing literature on the topic; (2) professional experience; (3) personal experience; and (4) data gathered from the research process. The FEET was developed and tested through the process of cultural intuition. It is inclusive of existing literature, the professional and personal experiences of Salazar and Lerner, the professional expertise of mentor teachers, and qualitative and quantitative data gathered from the research process. Quantitative measures used in isolation may negate the experiences of diverse participants; including qualitative measures allows for a deeper understanding of the cultural context (Thomas & Parsons, 2017). The FEET was developed over a 10-year time span through three phases of research: development, field testing, and psychometric testing. These are described in Table 4.2 and the sections that follow.

Tenet 2: The FEET facilitates collaboration of diverse communities in co-construction of evaluation tools

In the first phase, the FEET was developed through a three-year exploratory qualitative research project. In this phase, we developed a framework for teaching that is foregrounded in equity and excellence. We used the following procedures: (1) identify performance-based expectations; (2) determine the structure and organization of the framework; (3) develop rubrics of performance; and (4) design field-based observation instruments.

First, we conducted an exploratory qualitative research study to identify the performance-based expectations for equitable and excellent teachers. We conducted purposeful selection and analysis of standards, models, instruments, and literature related to effective, equitable, and excellent teaching. The data sources included: the InTASC Model Core Teaching Standards and Learning Progressions (2013); the National Board for Professional Teaching Standards (n.d.); two nationally recognized frameworks for teaching: Danielson Framework for Teaching and Teach for America Teaching as Leadership Framework; and targeted peer-reviewed journal articles, book chapters, and books. Salazar was a member of the InTASC Committee and was able to bring her learning from this work to the development of the FEET beginning in 2009.

The literature review included the following methods: search, screening, appraisal, data extraction, and analysis. We searched four electronic databases (i.e., ERIC, EBSCO, ProQuest, Google Scholar) to identify peer-reviewed journal articles, books, and book chapters based on the following keyword searches related to teaching: effective, excellent, quality, good, culturally responsive, linguistically responsive, equity, social justice, critical pedagogy, multicultural, and humanizing.

TABLE 4.2 Phases of FEET research

Phase	Objective	Research question	Research method	Outcome	Timeline
1 – Research and development	– Define and evaluate equitable and excellent teaching for pre-service teachers through a framework for teaching.	RQ1– What are the dimensions, competencies, and indicators of equitable and excellent teaching?	Exploratory qualitative research: Document analysis; literature review; coding schemes; wisdom of practice	– Framework for Equitable and Excellent Teaching – Rubrics of performance – Summative and formative observation tools	2007–2010
2 – Field testing	– Pilot and assess the FEET for ease of use, clarity, and accuracy. – Establish the clarity and accuracy of the FEET. – Revise the FEET based on empirical findings.	RQ2– How do supervisors and candidates describe the strengths and weaknesses of the FEET evaluation model?	Qualitative research: Surveys	– Revised FEET, rubrics, and observation tools	2011–2013
3 – Reliability and validity testing	– Estimate psychometric properties of the FEET. – Revise the FEET and supervisor training based on empirical findings.	RQ3– To what extent are the psychometric properties (scale use, fit, consistency, convergent validity) of the FEET adequate?	Quantitative research: Many-Facet Rasch Model, correlation with validation measures	– Revised FEET evaluation model and training of supervisors	2014–2017

Next, we used snowballing techniques to review the references of selected journals, books, and book chapters for relevant sources that aligned with the construct of equitable and excellent teaching. The targeted research was published between 1995 and the present. The initial year was selected based on Ladson-Billings' (1995) seminal work on culturally relevant pedagogy.

The screening phase included the completion of annotated bibliographies to ensure alignment with the keyword search. In the appraisal phase, the sources were narrowed to 165 peer-reviewed journal articles, book chapters, and books that met the keyword search criteria in the abstract. A significant proportion of the literature, approximately 70%, highlights pedagogical practices that address the needs of CLD learners. Moreover, approximately 55% of the literature originates from Scholars of Color.

We extracted and analyzed the data through a macro-level deductive content analysis to identify themes for performance expectations. Subsequently, we used qualitative research computer software, ATLAS.ti (ATLAS.ti, 2015), to conduct micro-level inductive content analysis and develop open, axial, and selective coding schemes used to generate subthemes. The emerging data transformation resulted in codes by tallying the number of times concepts occurred in the textual data. This approach revealed key themes and subthemes of equitable and excellent teaching that recurred across the data sources. We determined how the emerging themes and subthemes would be represented as domains, competencies, and indicators based on degree of specificity. We then conducted an extensive review of performance expectations for alignment, coherence, clarity, appropriate sequence, and practical usage. Next, we compared the data with literature on culturally responsive pedagogy from distinguished CRP scholars to strengthen the focus. We also drew from our own personal and professional experiences, from the margins and the center, to develop the performance expectations.

Once the performance-based expectations were defined, we determined the structure and organization of the FEET by considering the structures of two national frameworks for teaching, the Danielson Framework (Danielson, 2007, 2013) and the Teach for America Teaching as Leadership Framework (Farr, 2010). We selected these frameworks because they were the two leading national frameworks at the time. We gleaned the importance of moving from the simple to the complex. The FEET is structured in a way that moves from the simple themes related to equitable and excellent teaching (e.g., dimensions), to more detailed descriptions of performances (e.g., competencies), and evidence of behaviors indicating the performances are evident (e.g., indicators).

Next, we developed rubrics of performance and an observation measure. The FEET rubrics are based on a four-level rating scale (e.g., unsatisfactory, developing, proficient, advanced) employed with items that reflect the competencies and indicators of equitable and excellent teaching. The proficient rating is aligned with the first two levels of the InTASC Learning Progressions (InTASC, 2013). This allows for the inclusion of indicators of teaching readiness (level 1) along with additional challenge (level 2). The advanced rating is aligned with level 3 of the InTASC Learning Progressions. This allows for teachers to reach for the highest level of competency in teaching.

Subsequently, we developed observation instruments to facilitate the practical implementation of the FEET, thus allowing for summative ratings of performance, formative feedback, and reflection. The FEET observation instruments include a numerical rating scale. Summative data is used to guide formative assessment that includes targeted feedback. Feedback is diagnostic and facilitates reflection and discussion based on teacher self-assessment and goal-setting. The focus of the observation instrument is on developing equitable and excellent teaching practice that positively impacts student growth and development.

In the second phase of the research, the FEET evaluation model was field-tested with 120 pre-service teachers at the University of Denver Teacher Education Program. A 15-item quantitative and qualitative survey was distributed to 68 respondents, including field supervisors, pre-service teachers, and mentor teachers. The purpose of the survey was to collect feedback from respondents on the technical properties of the FEET performance expectations, rubrics, and observation instruments. Using a two-point scale (adequate/inadequate), the respondents were asked to rate the FEET's clarity, ease of use, and accuracy in identifying equitable and excellent teaching practices. The pilot and survey results were used to revise the FEET to improve its clarity, accuracy, and ease of use.

The FEET was developed through the contributions of diverse communities including: the authors of this book, literature by Scholars of Color, literature on teaching CLD learners, pre-service teachers, mentor teachers, and university supervisors. A weakness of the FEET is that it was not created with feedback from diverse students and parents. Our future goal is to establish the content validity of the FEET with diverse students and parents.

Tenet 3: The FEET incorporates targeted teacher competencies that promote student growth and development, particularly CLD learners

The first and second phases of the FEET resulted in the identification of targeted culturally responsive teaching competencies linked to student growth and development. The FEET is a framework for teaching that incorporates the knowledge and skills that are prized by the dominant culture (e.g., culture of power), the knowledge and skills that are treasured by diverse communities (e.g., power of culture), and reflection and action toward equity and social justice (e.g., power of change).

The FEET includes performances that fall into the broad categories of effective teaching defined by Darling-Hammond (2012). Thus, the FEET incorporates the culture of power in developing a teacher's ability to:

- integrate skills for college and career readiness (Darling-Hammond, Wilhoit, & Pittenger, 2014; Yamamura, Martinez, & Seanz, 2010);

- set high academic expectations (Delpit, 2013;Villegas & Irvine, 2010);
- communicate a belief in students' capacity to achieve at high academic levels (Ladson-Billings, 2014; McAllister & Irvine, 2002);
- develop students' academic language (Genesse, Lindholm-Leary, & Saunders, 2006;Walqui & Van Lier, 2010);
- facilitate the acquisition of content knowledge and skills through higher-order thinking skills (Darling-Hammond, 2012; Delpit, 2006); and
- design units and lessons based on state and national content standards (Childre, Sands, & Pope, 2009; Stronge 2007).

The FEET is infused with culturally responsive teaching competencies designed to draw students' diverse resources. Thus, the FEET incorporates the power of culture in developing a teacher's ability to:

- build positive relationships with diverse students and parents (Baquedano-López, Alexander, & Hernandez, 2013; Nieto, 2017);
- engage the resources of diverse communities (Moll, 2015;Yosso, 2005);
- incorporate multiple learning modalities (Banks & McGee Banks, 2010; Irvine, 2003);
- provide students with authentic and relevant opportunities for discovery, application, and collaborative learning (Gay & Howard, 2000; Morrell & Duncan-Andrade, 2002);
- use instructional strategies that support English language learners and students with special needs (Ford, 2011; Lucas & Villegas, 2013);
- integrate multicultural materials and resources (Nieto, 2017; Sleeter & Flores Carmona, 2016);
- use culturally responsive explanations and representations of content (Gay, 2010;Villegas & Lucas, 2002);
- develop relevant lessons that reflect the cultures of students (Grant & Sleeter, 2011; Hollins, 2011; Irvine & Armento, 2001);
- include the histories and contributions of diverse populations (Gay & Kirkland, 2003; Fránquiz & Salinas, 2011);
- connect content to students' diversity, background experiences, prior knowledge, skills, and/or interests (McCarty & Lee, 2014; Milner, & Lomotey, 2013; Salazar, 2013);
- promote real-world application that facilitates social justice pursuits (Gay, 2013; Oakes, Lipton, Anderson, & Stillman, 2015); and
- integrate students' native language into instruction (Lipka & Ilutsik, 2014; Lucas & Villegas, 2013; Salazar, 2010).

Marginalized youth must also be provided with opportunities to develop critical consciousness. Freire (2000) defines critical consciousness as the process of "learning to perceive social, political, and economic contractions, and to take action against the oppressive elements of reality" (p. 17). Critical consciousness empowers marginalized communities to advocate for equity and social justice. Cochran-Smith et al. (2018) declare that: "Teacher candidates need to have a strong equity perspective. This means that they need to have not only the knowledge and skills to teach well, but also critical consciousness about the structures and processes that produce and reproduce inequities…" (p. 175). The FEET nurtures critical consciousness in teachers and students by developing their ability to:

- incorporate topics that draw on diverse identity groups (e.g., race, ethnicity, gender, class, ability, sexual orientation, religion, culture) (Gay, 2010; Nieto, 2017);
- express their voice and have choice (Cammarota, 2014; Duncan-Andrade, 2004; Morrell, 2015);
- counteract stereotypes (Fine, Torre, Burns, & Payne, 2007; Grant & Sleeter, 2011);
- identify oppression locally and globally (Gorski, 2006; Matias, 2013);
- engage in social justice pursuits (Duncan-Andrade, 2007; Kumashiro, 2015; Sleeter, 2017); and
- interrogate multiple perspectives, ask probing questions, and take critical stances (Darder, Baltodano & Flores, 2003; McLaren, 2014).

In sum, the FEET is grounded in teacher knowledge and skills that help students to: (a) navigate the dominant culture; (b) sustain/revitalize their cultural, linguistic, familial, and community resources; and (c) develop critical consciousness. While the FEET is strategically focused on CLD learners from historically marginalized communities, these students experience intersecting social identities that include their religion, gender, sexual orientation, and legal status, to name a few. The FEET attempts to capture broader elements of diversity, while maintaining a targeted approach to CLD learners. The FEET is also inclusive of White students. The FEET immerses all students in the culture of power, the power of culture, and power of change. For those who believe the FEET is too focused on CLD learners, we are unapologetic in our approach to centering CLD learners in teacher evaluation. We believe this approach is necessary to advance equity and excellence in education.

Tenet 4: The FEET establishes and monitors reliability and validity within a cultural context

CRTE stresses the importance of reliability and validity in teacher evaluation; however, this is examined within a cultural context. In the third phase of the research, we, along with a team of research methods and statistics researchers, tested the measurement quality of the FEET though an estimation of its reliability and validity. The sections that follow detail the assessment of the FEET's reliability and validity.

Reliability

To estimate the reliability of the FEET, we conducted a reliability study with 60 pre-service teachers and 8 field supervisors in the University of Denver Teacher Education Program. Multiple factors need to be examined to assess the reliability of a measure. Therefore, we applied a Many-Facet Rasch Model (MFRM) to examine the reliability of the FEET. With the MFRM, interactions among facets can be modeled, allowing unusual interactions between raters and items, or raters and participants. In sum, MFRM generates information from different facets that affect the functioning of an instrument, and provides feedback for each facet that can be used to improve the utility of a measure. We examined four variables, or facets: item function (e.g., item difficulty); teacher candidate performance (e.g., supervisor FEET ratings), change of teacher candidate performance over time (e.g., supervisor FEET ratings over time), and rater stability (e.g., severity and leniency of supervisor ratings). We used FACETS (Version 3.71.2; Linacre, 2013) software to analyze the resulting data. Results indicated the:

- distribution of items from low to high difficulty captures different levels of teaching skill;
- candidates demonstrate different proficiency levels;
- gradual increase in the pre-service teachers' proficiency over time;
- supervisors used the full range of the rating scale and were able to distinguish the items; and
- supervisor ratings were within an accepted range, but there were statistically distinctive levels in rater severity.

Overall, the facet analysis indicates that the FEET has adequate measurement quality. The majority of candidates demonstrated that their teaching proficiency increased over time. The distribution of items was adequate, although the items appeared to be grouped into easy and difficult categories. The supervisors showed a good understanding and use of the FEET evaluation instrument. There was no randomness in the way supervisors assigned the ratings. The supervisors also showed evidence of distinguishing the candidates' abilities and rating them at different performance levels. While the supervisor ratings were fitting, there were also significant differences in the severity of the candidate ratings. To use the FEET most effectively, the program faculty revised items to ensure a range of difficulty (e.g., easy, intermediate, difficult), and conducted additional and ongoing training to ensure less variation in rater severity.

We conducted a second replication study. The purpose of this replication study was to reassess the quality of the FEET instrument after adjustments were made as a result of the initial study. The replication study focused on examining item difficulty and rater severity. In terms of the items, all items were distributed with different level of difficulty. In terms of the raters, they showed similarities in rating their teacher candidates. All supervisors were fitting within range of productive measurement (Linacre, 2013). A bias-interaction analysis of the raters revealed that the raters did not have specific biases for some of the items. However, the supervisors did show a significant difference in severity ratings. A closer examination indicated that the rater positions were not far apart with the exception of one rater. The results of the analysis indicated that ongoing supervisor training is needed. However, overall, the findings provide support for the FEET as yielding reliable ratings.

Convergent Validity

The research team also correlated candidate scores with a validation measure to estimate the convergent validity for the FEET. This allowed the researchers to test if the concepts developed in the FEET were highly correlated with other instruments designed to measure a theoretically similar construct.

The researchers used a pre-service teacher self-report of teaching competencies survey known as the *Core Competency Survey* (CCS) (Seidel, Green, & Briggs, 2011). This survey is administered to teacher program graduates as a self-report of teaching competencies. The basis for the Core Competencies (CC) was the Survey of Enacted Curriculum developed by researchers at the University of Wisconsin-Madison (Blank, Kim, & Smithson, 2000) and existing teacher observation protocols such as the Classroom Assessment Scoring System (Pianta, La Paro, & Hamre, 2008).

The CCS is an appropriate referent for establishing convergent validity because it is inclusive of culturally responsive practices such as developing a classroom culture that is responsive to diverse learners, using culturally responsive instructional strategies, and supporting English language learners (ELLs). While the CCS includes culturally responsive practices, it differs from the FEET in that it does not include a focus on critical consciousness. Moreover, it is used as a self-assessment of teaching practice, not as an observation instrument.

The instrument contains 46 items aligned with eight competencies of effective teaching: (1) demonstrating mastery of and pedagogical expertise in content taught; (2) managing the classroom environment to facilitate learning for students; (3) developing a safe, respectful environment for a diverse population of students; (4) planning and providing effective instruction; (5) designing and adapting assessments, curriculum & instruction; (6) engaging students in higher-order thinking and expectations; (7) supporting academic language development and English language acquisition; and (8) reflection and professional growth.

The items on the CCS were triple-banked, with responses regarding the extent to which the CC was emphasized in classroom work, in field experiences, and how well prepared the novice teacher is with respect to that CC. The response scale asks participants to report how well prepared they are by their teacher education program on a 1–4 response scale where 1=not well prepared and 4=very well prepared. The scores from the third response scale, how well prepared the respondent is, were used in this part of the project.

The study of the convergent validity of the FEET revealed reliabilities between the FEET measure and CCS multi-item subscales were .95 and .96. The subscales showed adequate correlation, suggesting evidence for convergent validity between the FEET measure and the CCS. Thus, evidence of convergence with external measures was found, supporting the convergent validity of the FEET.

Multicultural Validity

In addition to establishing the convergent validity of the FEET, we thought it was vital to conduct a self-assessment of the FEET's multicultural validity. We consider the justifications set forth by Hopson & Kirkhart (2012):

- Relational: quality of the relationships that surround the evaluation process.
- Theoretical: alignment of theoretical perspectives underlying the program, evaluation, and assumptions of validity.
- Experiential: congruence with the life experience of participants in the program and in the evaluation process.
- Methodological: cultural appropriateness of epistemology and method.
- Consequential: social consequences of understandings and the actions taken.

We assert that the FEET demonstrates multicultural validity in the following ways:

- Strong relationships with preservice and inservice teachers involved in the evaluation process.
- Stakeholder commitment to equity and excellence through teacher evaluation.
- Theoretical soundness, drawing from multiple bodies of research including teacher evaluation, culturally responsive evaluation, culturally responsive pedagogy and assessment, and critical race theory.
- Inclusivity of the experiential knowledge of Communities of Color through the main author's experiences, and also through educational research and literature.
- Cultural appropriateness in research methodology through a mixed methods approach.
- Focus on reflection and action for equity and social justice.

Tenet 5: The FEET Advances Equity and Social Justice in Student Outcomes

The FEET develops equitable and excellent teachers who foster students' full potential, including their academic, cultural, and transformative capacities, to name a few. It is important to note that, at present, we have not established a link between the FEET and student outcomes. Thus, we have not established the predictive validity of the FEET. We are conscious of the perspective of researchers who assert that a teacher evaluation tool is valid only if it is associated with student outcomes on standardized tests. While we are aware of the importance of assessing the degree to which CLD learners are making academic gains, we also caution that linking student achievement to standardized student test scores can be a measure of how well CLD learners have been assimilated. Standardized tests do not measure the full potential of CLD learners, but rather measure their ability to adopt the tools of the whitestream. Research suggests that teachers who promote academic achievement are not always competent in supporting students' social, emotional, or cultural well-being (Dever, Raines, & Barclay, 2012; Jennings & DiPrete, 2010). We are not opposed to exploring the potential of the FEET to predict gains in student academic outcomes. However, this is insufficient. In the future, we plan to conduct a research study that provides empirical evidence of the impact of the FEET on K-12 students' academic, cultural, and transformative capacities. To do this, we will have to go beyond the boundaries of student assessment to devise a measure, or set of measures, that does not currently exist.

Summary and Implications

In this chapter, we presented an example of a CRTE model. The development, field testing, and psychometric testing of the FEET aligns with the tenets of CRT and CRTE, thus resulting in a culturally responsive, empirically based, and psychometrically sound teacher evaluation model designed to move the margins to the center of teacher evaluation. The FEET demonstrates adequate measurement quality, thereby indicating the capability of the FEET observation instrument to assess and develop equitable and excellent teaching. Measurement quality is important in the whitestream, and so we make a case for the measurement quality of the FEET.

Critical Questions

The following critical questions are intended to extend your comprehension and help you relate the concepts to your own practice.

1. What has been your experience with performance evaluation in education or in another industry? Did you perceive the measures to be reliable, valid, and culturally inclusive?
2. What aspects of the FEET stand out to you and why? What are its strengths and weaknesses?
3. Compare and contrast the FEET with the teacher evaluation tool used in your current school district. What are the similarities? What are the differences?
4. A criticism of CRTE may be that it is exclusive to historically marginalized communities. How might you counter this criticism?
5. What have you learned about teacher evaluation in your preparation program? How does this align or differ with the contents of this chapter?

Resources for Further Reflection and Study

The following supplemental resources are intended to spur your personal and professional reflection, application of the concepts in your own context, and community outreach efforts.

Print

Applin, J. L. (2007). The development of the Culturally Responsive Teaching Assessment Instrument. *Kentucky Teacher Educator.* Retrieved from https://digitalcommons.wku.edu/kte/4/

LaFrance, J., & Nichols, R. (2008). *Indigenous Evaluation Framework: Telling our story in our place and time.* Alexandria, VA: American Indian Higher Education Consortium (AIHEC).

Thomas, V. G. (2004). Building a contextually responsive evaluation framework: Lessons from working with urban school interventions. In V. G. Thomas & F. I. Stevens (Eds.), *Co-constructing a contextually responsive evaluation framework: The Talent Development Model of School Reform.* New Directions for Evaluation (No. 101, pp. 3–23). San Francisco, CA: Jossey-Bass.

Thomas, V. G., & Parsons, B. A. (2017). Culturally responsive evaluation meets systems-oriented evaluation. *American Journal of Evaluation, 38*(1), 1–22.

Wagner, T. (2008). Closing the gap: Schools that work. *The global achievement gap: Why even our best schools don't teach the new survival skills our children need-and what we can do about it* (pp. 207–253). New York, NY: Perseus Books Group.

Web

- Colorado Department of Education
  Practical strategies for culturally competent evaluation
  www.cdc.gov/dhdsp/docs/cultural_competence_guide.pdf
- University of Illinois
  Center for Culturally Responsive Evaluation and Assessment
  https://crea.education.illinois.edu

Media

- Brian Lozenski, TED Talk
  Bringing cultural context and self-identity into education
  www.youtube.com/watch?v=bX9vgD7iTqw
- Institute of Educational Sciences
  Increasing educator effectiveness with culturally responsive teaching and learning
  www.youtube.com/watch?v=6nYEZ1N5zf4

- National Equity Project
  Calibrating ideas about culturally responsive teaching with Zaretta Hammond
  www.youtube.com/watch?v=9nMK1nepwvk

Learning Opportunities

1. Create a hashtag that captures the purpose of the FEET.
2. Identify five culturally responsive practices in the FEET that you can build into your own practice. Set a timeline to implement these into your practice.
3. Use the FEET as a self-evaluation tool. Evaluate your skill in enacting the FEET dimensions and competencies. Would you rate yourself advanced, proficient, developing, or unsatisfactory? Set two to three goals to improve your practice.
4. Have a colleague evaluate you using the FEET. How does this evaluation compare to your self-evaluation using the FEET? How does it compare to your district/school evaluation? What did you learn about your teaching from this activity?
5. Create a Venn diagram to compare and contrast the teacher evaluation tool you use in your school/district with the FEET. What are the similarities? What are the differences?

Community Engagement Opportunities

1. Present the FEET to your school community. Ask them to respond to the following:
   - Assess the strengths and weaknesses of the FEET.
   - Compare and contrast the FEET with the school/district evaluation tool.
   - Identify implications and next steps.
2. Meet with the members of a local community organization that advocate for historically marginalized Communities of Color. Ask them to respond to the following:
   - How does your organization help the community?
   - What makes a good teacher and/or school leader?
   - What resources can you provide for teachers to meet the needs of historically marginalized Communities of Color?
3. Attend a state or district school board meeting. When public comments are requested, share your perspective on CRTE and advocate for culturally responsive approaches in teacher evaluation.

References

ATLAS.ti (2015). (Version 8) [Software]. Retrieved from atlasti.com

Banks, J. A., & McGee Banks, C. A. (2010). *Multicultural education: Issues and perspectives* (7th ed.). Hoboken, NJ: John Wiley & Sons.

Baquedano-López, P., Alexander, R. A., & Hernandez, S. J. (2013). Equity issues in parental and community involvement in schools: What teacher educators need to know. *Review of Research in Education, 37*(1), 149–182.

Blank, R. K., Kim, J. J., & Smithson, J. (2000). *Survey results of urban school classroom practices in mathematics and science: 1999 report. Using the Survey of Enacted Curriculum conducted during four USI site visits. How reform works: An evaluative study of National Science Foundation's Urban Systemic Initiatives. Study monograph No. 2.* Norwood, MA: Systemic Research, Inc.

Cammarota, J. (2014). The social justice education project: Youth participatory action research in schools. In J. Cammarota & A. Romero (Eds.), *Raza Studies: The public option for educational revolution* (pp. 107–121). Tucson, AZ: University of Arizona Press.

Childre, A., Sands, J. R., & Pope, S. T. (2009). Backward design. *Teaching Exceptional Children, 41*(5), 6–14.

Cochran-Smith, M., Cummings Carney, M., Stringer Keefe, E., Burton, S., Chang, W., Fernandez, M. B., Miller, A. F., Sanchez, J. G., & Baker, M. (2018). *Reclaiming accountability in teacher education.* New York, NY: Teachers College Press.

Danielson, C. (2007). *Enhancing professional practice: A framework for teaching* (2nd ed.). Alexandria, VA: ASCD.

Danielson, C. (2013). *The Framework for Teaching: Evaluation instrument.* Princeton, NJ: The Danielson Group.

Darder, A., Baltodano, M., & Flores, R. D. (2003). *The critical pedagogy reader.* New York, NY: Routledge.

Darling-Hammond, L. (2012). *Creating a comprehensive system for evaluating and supporting effective teaching.* Stanford Center for Opportunity Policy in Education. Retrieved from https://edpolicy.stanford.edu/sites/default/files/publications/creating-comprehensive-system-evaluating-and-supporting-effective-teaching.pdf

Darling-Hammond, L., Wilhoit, G., & Pittenger, L. (2014). Accountability for college and career readiness: Developing a new paradigm. *Education Policy Analysis Archives, 22*(86), 1–38.

Delgado Bernal, D. (1998). Using a Chicana feminist epistemology in educational research. *Harvard Educational Review, 68*(4), 555–583.

Delpit, L. (2006). *Other people's children: Cultural conflict in the classroom.* New York, NY: The New Press.

Delpit, L. (2013). *"Multiplication is for white people": Raising expectations for other people's children.* New York, NY: The New Press.

Dever, B. V., Raines, T. C., & Barclay, C. M. (2012). Chasing the unicorn: Practical implementation of universal screening for behavioral and emotional risk. *School Psychology Forum, 6*(4), 108–118.

Duncan-Andrade, J. M. (2004). Toward teacher development for the urban in urban teaching. *Teaching Education, 15*(4), 339–350.

Duncan-Andrade, J. (2007). Gangstas, wankstas, and ridas: Defining, developing, and supporting effective teachers in urban schools. *International Journal of Qualitative Studies in Education, 20*(6), 617–638.

Farr, S. (2010). *Teaching as leadership: The highly effective teacher's guide to closing the achievement gap.* San Francisco, CA: Jossey-Bass.

Fine, M., Torre, M. E., Burns, A., & Payne, Y. A. (2007). How class matters: The geography of educational desire and despair in schools and courts. In L. Weis (Ed.), *The way class works: Readings on school, family, and the economy* (pp. 225–242). New York, NY: Routledge.

Ford, D. (2011). *Multicultural gifted education.* Austin, TX: Prufrock Press Inc.

Fránquiz, M. E., & Salinas, C. S. (2011). Newcomers developing English literacy through historical thinking and digitized primary sources. *Journal of Second Language Writing, 20*(3), 196–210.

Freire, P. (2000). *Pedagogy of the oppressed.* New York, NY: Bloomsbury Press.

Gay, G. (2010). *Culturally responsive teaching: Theory, research, and practice.* New York, NY: Teachers College Press.

Gay, G. (2013). Teaching to and through cultural diversity. *Curriculum Inquiry, 43*(1), 48–70.

Gay, G., & Howard, T. C. (2000). Multicultural teacher education for the 21st century. *The Teacher Educator, 36*(1), 1–16.

Gay, G., & Kirkland, K. (2003). Developing cultural critical consciousness and self-reflection in preservice teacher education. *Theory into Practice, 42*(3), 181–187.

Genesee, F., Lindholm-Leary, K., Christian, D., & Saunders, B. (2006). *Educating English language learners: A synthesis of research evidence.* New York, NY: Cambridge University Press.

Gorski, P. C. (2006). Complicity with conservatism: The de-politicizing of multicultural and intercultural education. *Intercultural Education, 17*(2), 163–177.

Grant, C. A., & Sleeter, C. E. (2011). *Doing multicultural education for achievement and equity.* New York, NY: Routledge.

Hollins, E. R. (2011). Teacher preparation for quality teaching. *Journal of Teacher Education, 62*(4), 395–407.

Hopson, R., & Kirkhart, K. (2012). *Strengthening evaluation through cultural relevance and cultural competence.* Retrieved from www.wcasa.org/file_open.php?id=869

Interstate Teacher Assessment and Support Consortium [InTASC] (2013). *InTASC Model Core Teaching Standards and Learning Progressions for Teachers 1.0.* Retrieved from www.ccsso.org/resources/programs/interstate_teacher_assessment_consortium_(intasc).html

Irvine, J. J. (2003). *Educating teachers for diversity: Seeing with a cultural eye* (Vol. 15). New York, NY: Teachers College Press.

Irvine, J. J., & Armento, B. J. (2001). *Culturally responsive teaching: Lesson planning for elementary and middle grades.* New York, NY: McGraw-Hill.

Jennings, J. L., & DiPrete, T. A. (2010). Teacher effects on social and behavioral skills in early elementary school. *Sociology of Education, 83*(2), 135–159.

Kumashiro, K. K. (2015). *Against common sense: Teaching and learning toward social justice.* New York, NY: Routledge.

Ladson-Billings, G. (1995). Toward a theory of culturally relevant pedagogy. *American Educational Research Journal, 32*(3), 465–491.

Ladson-Billings, G. (2014). Culturally relevant pedagogy 2.0: Aka the remix. *Harvard Educational Review, 84*(1), 74–84.

Linacre, J. M. (2013). *A user's guide to FACETS: Rasch measurement computer program* [Computer program manual]. Chicago, IL: MESA Press.

Lipka, J., & Ilutsik, E. (2014). *Transforming the culture of schools: Yupik Eskimo examples.* New York, NY: Routledge.

Lucas, T., & Villegas, A. M. (2013). Preparing linguistically responsive teachers: Laying the foundation in preservice teacher education. *Theory Into Practice, 52*(2), 98–109.

Matias, C. E. (2013). "Who you callin' white?!" A critical counter-story on coloring white identity. *Race Ethnicity and Education, 16*(3), 291–315.

McAllister, G., & Irvine, J. J. (2002). The role of empathy in teaching culturally diverse students: A qualitative study of teachers' beliefs. *Journal of Teacher Education, 53*(5), 433–443.

McCarty, T., & Lee, T. (2014). Critical culturally sustaining/revitalizing pedagogy and Indigenous education sovereignty. *Harvard Educational Review, 84*(1), 101–124.

McLaren, P. (2014). *Life in schools: An introduction to critical pedagogy in the foundations of education* (6th ed.). New York, NY: Routledge.

Milner, H. R., & Lomotey, K. (2013). *Handbook of urban education.* New York, NY: Routledge.

Moll, L. C. (2015). Tapping into the "hidden" home and community resources of students. *Kappa Delta Pi Record, 51*(3), 114–117.

Morrell, E. (2015). *Critical literacy and urban youth: Pedagogies of access, dissent, and liberation.* New York, NY: Routledge.

Morrell, E., & Duncan-Andrade, J. M. (2002). Promoting academic literacy with urban youth through engaging hip-hop culture. *English Journal, 91*(6), 88–92.

National Board for Professional Teaching Standards (n.d.). *Five core propositions.* Retrieved from www.nbpts.org/standards-five-core-propositions/

Nieto, S. (2017). *Language, culture, and teaching: Critical perspectives.* New York, NY: Routledge.

Oakes, J., Lipton, M., Anderson, L., & Stillman, J. (2015). *Teaching to change the world.* New York, NY: Routledge.

Pianta, R. C., La Paro, K., & Hamre, B. K. (2008). *Classroom Assessment Scoring System (CLASS).* Baltimore, MD: Paul H. Brookes.

Salazar, M. (2010). Pedagogical stances of high school ESL teachers: Huelgas in high school ESL classrooms. *Bilingual Research Journal, 33*(1), 111–124.

Salazar, M. (2013). A humanizing pedagogy: Reinventing the principles and practice of education as a journey toward liberation. *Review of Research in Education, 37*(1), 121–148.

Seidel, K., Green, K., & Briggs, D. (2011). *An exploration of novice teachers' core competencies: Impact on student achievement, and effectiveness of preparation.* U.S. Department of Education, Institute of Education Sciences award #R305A120233, Fiscal Year 2012. Retrieved from http://ies.ed.gov/funding/grantsearch/details.asp?ID=1274

Sleeter, C. E. (2017). Critical race theory and the whiteness of teacher education. *Urban Education, 52*(2), 155–169.

Sleeter, C., & Flores Carmona, J. (2016). Un-standardizing curriculum. *Multicultural teaching in the standards-based classroom* (2nd ed.). New York, NY: Teachers College Press.

Solórzano, D., & Yosso, T. (2002) A critical race counterstory of race, racism and affirmative action. *Equity and Excellence in Education, 35*(2), 155–168.

Stronge, J. H. (2007). *Qualities of effective teachers.* Alexandria, VA: ASCD.

Thomas, V. G., & Parsons, B. A. (2017). Culturally responsive evaluation meets systems-oriented evaluation. *American Journal of Evaluation, 38*(1), 1–22.

Villegas, A. M., & Irvine, J. J. (2010). Diversifying the teaching force: An examination of major arguments. *The Urban Review, 42*(3), 175–192.

Villegas, A. M., & Lucas, T. (2002). *Educating culturally responsive teachers: A coherent approach.* New York, NY: SUNY Press.

Walqui, A., & Van Lier, L. (2010). *Scaffolding the academic success of adolescent English language learners: A pedagogy of promise* (pp. 1–41). San Francisco, CA: WestEd.

Yamamura, E. K., Martinez, M. A., & Seanz, V. B. (2010). Moving beyond high school expectations: Examining stakeholders' responsibilities for increasing Latina/o students' college readiness. *The High School Journal, 93*(3), 126–148.

Yosso, T. J. (2005). Whose culture has capital? A critical race theory discussion of community cultural wealth. *Race Ethnicity and Education, 8*(1), 69–91.

Zamudio, M., Russell, C., Rios, F., & Bridgeman, J. L. (2011). *Critical race theory matters: Education and ideology.* New York, NY: Routledge.

5

DOCUMENTING CULTURALLY RESPONSIVE TEACHER EVALUATION THROUGH TEACHER NARRATIVES

Chapter Overview: This chapter offers narratives of five equitable and excellent in-service teachers that were prepared in pre-service with the FEET. The teachers share their perceptions of teaching and provide rich descriptions of their classroom practices. This chapter paints a vivid picture of the potential of culturally responsive teacher evaluation to develop equitable and excellent teaching.

Teachers of CLD Learners

According to the U.S. Department of Education (2016), the current U.S. teaching force includes 3.6 million elementary and secondary full-time-equivalent teachers. Of these, 76% are female, 44% are under the age of 40, and 82% are White. While the proportion of Teachers of Color has increased in the past decade, the proportion of Black teachers has decreased. Black/African American males make up less than 2% of the teaching force. This portrait of U.S. teachers is critical given that it is projected that Students of Color will make up 56% of public school enrollment by the year 2024. A comparison of teacher trends reveals inequities along color lines. For example, Teachers of Color are more likely to be employed in "high-poverty" schools. Further, Teachers of Color tend to leave the profession at a higher rate than other teachers. While Teachers of Color face unique challenges, all teachers face challenges and need support. In this chapter, we introduce you to five in-service teachers who were trained with the FEET in pre-service. Table 5.1 highlights their demographics and background.

TABLE 5.1 Teacher demographics and background

Name	No. of years teaching	Content area/grade	Race (self-described)
Brian	4	English High School	African American
Paulina	3	Second Grade Bilingual	Hispanic
Salvador	3	English High School	Mexican American
Aaron	4	Social Studies Middle School	Caucasian
Jennifer	5	Spanish High School	White

In the sections that follow, the aforementioned teachers describe why they teach and how they teach. They share rich descriptions of their lived experiences, classroom practices, and their perceptions of equity and excellence in education. Throughout their narratives, we italicize key words that signal the presence of culturally responsive pedagogy (CRP) in order to emphasize the potential of culturally responsive teacher evaluation (CRTE) to develop culturally responsive practices.

Brian

Background

Brian describes himself as African American. He is in his early thirties and has been teaching for four years. He completed his apprentice teaching in an elementary school in which the majority of students were Black or Latinx. He is currently teaching English Language Arts and English language development at a high school in a historically Black neighborhood where he grew up. Approximately 90% of the school's students qualify for free or reduced lunch. Brian has taught at the elementary, middle, and high school levels. Brian recently earned an overall rating of "effective" in the district evaluation tool for both professional practice and student growth. The following describes Brian's motivation for teaching.

Why I Teach

My own educational experiences helped shape what I think teaching should be. My third-grade teacher, a White woman, was one of the teachers that most impacted my life. She set *high academic standards* and *believed I was capable*. She *saw me as a person* and helped me develop *pride* for who I was. She led me to books about *African American history*. I saw her after I graduated from high school, and it was the most emotional reunion ever. She was in tears and it was humbling to see that someone *cared* about me that much.

Not all of my teachers believed in me or presented my ethnicity in a positive light. In fact, most of my educational experiences were negative.

I experienced a lot of discipline and redirection. It was almost like putting out a fire; like they wanted to extinguish something in me. Most of my teachers did not go above and beyond. They did what they were supposed to do. They did just enough.

After my first year of teaching in elementary school, I felt the calling to teach high school. I wanted to have conversations with my students about *real life* – about *race and equity* in America. My decision to teach high school was motivated by a trip I took to Chicago. I saw how violence is impacting the Black community, especially Black males. Then, the Trayvon Martin verdict came in. These experiences made me want to *change* things. I wanted to have a *voice* in the conversation. It was so personal that I really needed to make a move.

I currently teach high school English in the neighborhood where I grew up and my family still lives. I teach in a school that many consider to be the toughest and the highest need in the state. I am *committed* to my students, though the work is not easy. I find myself up at night thinking about my kids. I can't sleep. I feel like these kids face so many challenges in their personal lives. Those challenges get in the way of their dreams. Those challenges get in the way of their childhood. But, I feel like I have what it takes to *show them what is possible*. I don't know if my kids are aware of what they *can do*. It is *my responsibility* to show them.

Preparation for Equitable and Excellent Teaching

The following describes Brian's preparation for equitable and excellent teaching.

Readiness for Teaching

The FEET prepared me to set *positive rituals and routines* in my classroom. My students come from broken classroom environments. They enter classes late, leave their classrooms regularly, and are allowed to perform below their level or below expectation. They are told, "That's good enough for you." Their teachers often give up on them. That doesn't sit well with my *heart*. I want to be a *constant* so they can have some *peace* in their lives. I think my students feel like, "Our teacher is going to *be here every day*. I know he is going to *push* me. I know he is going to hold me *accountable*." My rituals and routines let my students know I *care* about them and their learning, I will keep them *safe*, and I will hold them to *high standards*.

The FEET gave me concrete guidance on how to *reach each student*. My supervisor in the program pushed me to provide *academic supports*. I learned to list my supports for each lesson, including *graphic organizers* and *technology applications* for reading support. I use writing *exemplars* and paragraph *outlines* with *sentence stems*. Using these *scaffolds*, students are able to use *receptive and productive language skills* to develop *academic language*.

I never felt like I was boxed in by the FEET. My supervisor encouraged me to look at my *strengths and areas for growth*. She told me I have what it takes to reach a *higher level*. I *reflect* on my practice, whether I'm looking at an evaluation tool, or just reflecting each day. It's how I strengthen my practice. The FEET helped me to be prepared to interact with my district's evaluation tool. It was very detailed and provided me with concrete examples of equitable and excellent teaching. I feel like the FEET actually goes further and takes me to the next level.

Equitable and Excellent Teaching

Brian is a constant and positive force in his students' lives. His affirming presence in their lives allows him to enact vital attributes of an equitable and excellent teacher.

Relationships with Students and Families

My teaching is built on *relationships* with students and their families. I gain their *trust* by *listening* and encouraging them to *share their lives*. My kids are always welcome to talk about their lives. It takes time to *listen* to your students and *understand what's going on in their lives*. I tell my students, "I'm not leaving, *I will be here* every day." I want to be a *life coach*: someone they *feel comfortable* with, can *ask questions*, and *helps them learn how to work problems out*. That is something I did not have, so I want to take that role on in my students' lives. I grew up without a father for most of my life. My father left the family when I was three years old. Other males were role models for me, including my brothers, uncles, grandfather, and coaches. I often wonder how my life would have been different if my father had been present. Ultimately, I want to provide my students with a *positive, ongoing relationship* with an adult.

Culturally Responsive Classroom Environment

Walking into my classroom, the first thing you might see are *pictures of People of Color* reading books. I have pictures of Kevin Hart, Martin Luther King Jr., and Sonia Sotomayor. I do that because I believe some of my students have never seen themselves just *reading*. I want them to *see themselves* on my wall reading books. I make sure my learning environment is *for my students*. *Music* is a big part of my environment. You might hear music in *multiple languages* like Spanish and Ethiopian. I tell my students, "This *classroom belongs to you.*"

High Academic Expectations with Support

I set *high expectations* for my students. I expect them to *work hard* and *excel academically*. My students know I am going *be there every day*. They know

I am going to *push them*. They know I am going to *hold them accountable*. I use many academic *supports* and *individualize* my instruction *to meet my students' needs*. Equitable teaching is all about *understanding your students' needs*. I analyze and use their assessment data to set *high expectations*.

I let my students know what *opportunities* are out there for them after high school. When my students share their life challenges with me, I help them think about how to make something out of this. One student shared how he protected his younger sister from harmful situations. I asked him, "Have you thought about becoming a lawyer and protecting people in similar situations?" We have been having ongoing conversations about careers in law and he has become very interested. I want my students to *see possible careers* after high school. I'm not sure my kids are always aware they *can do* this. I let my students know, "I am here to really *push you* so *you can perform at a college level*."

I am a *tough* teacher, but I am also *patient*. I can be *hard* on my kids because *I know they can handle it*. I don't look at whatever is going on at home is keeping them from performing at a high level. I look at it like whatever is going on at home is going to influence them to *perform at a high level*.

Social Justice Curricula

I make *connections* between the curriculum and my students' lives. That can look different for each student in the room. My students use their own experiences and interests to *make meaning* of the content. I encourage my students to *examine social issues* through writing, literature, and poetry.

I include *community resources* from the neighborhood by having my students visit local businesses and talk with community leaders. In one project, my students researched and wrote about *issues in the community* including the effects of neighborhood gentrification and the relationship between People of Color and the police.

I make sure that my students are exposed to literature that reflects them. Whether that's a character in a book or an author, I want my students to *see themselves* in the literature. The books include the same issues my students face. I want them to *see someone like them become something extraordinary*. For example, I include a book called *The Pact*, written by three Black male doctors from New Jersey. It is a story about three boys growing up in a Black neighborhood. It's a story about their journey, their good decisions, and their mistakes.

My students will become *agents of change* in their communities. Currently, we are focusing on the perception of beauty. We are reading poetry and prose that talks about how usually light skin is perceived as beautiful and dark skin is not beautiful. We've read articles that talk about Beyoncé and how she has become lighter over the years. We talk about *heavy topics* in my classroom, but I present it to my kids as a *liberating* element. I don't want to create an environment where my kids feel even more oppressed. I always want them to think, "Here's the information. How can I use it to *better who I am and better my community?*"

Aspirations

Brian recently started an educational leadership licensure and doctoral program. He adds, "With this, I will open a school to serve African American males with a focus on: careers, professional skills, literacy, community advocacy, and challenging negative portrayals of African American males." Brian wants to prepare these students to be insightful and impactful members of their communities.

Paulina

Background

Paulina is in her early thirties and identifies as Hispanic. She completed her apprentice teaching in a dual-language elementary school in which approximately 95% of the students were Latinx. She is now in her third year of teaching. She taught kindergarten in a bilingual Spanish/English classroom for two years and is now teaching in a second-grade bilingual classroom in a school in which approximately 90% of students are Black or Latinx.

Paulina's students have exceeded district expectations for academic growth. In her most recent evaluation, she was rated "distinguished," the highest score in the teacher evaluation framework used in her district. Paulina is a leader in her school community. She facilitates professional development for English language learners, provides demonstration lessons, and leads grade-level meetings. Paulina also works closely with parents and community members, providing training in English literacy. The following passages, in Paulina's own words, describe her background and motivation for teaching.

Why I Teach

I was born in the United States, but lived with my family in Juarez, Mexico during my early childhood. I came from a privileged family in Mexico. We had a chauffeur, a maid, and a nana (nanny). My parents got divorced when I was ten years old. My mom said I could not live in Juarez because it was too dangerous. So, she sent me to live with my grandma in the United States. It was horrible. I felt like I divorced my mom, dad, older brother, nana, teachers, and friends. It was a devastating time for me. I had everything and then I had nothing. A year later, my nana's daughter was killed in Juarez. My mom told me, "I am glad you are there. I know it is hard, but you are strong." But, I didn't feel strong.

I wanted desperately to go back to my family in Mexico. I was one of the few Students of Color in my school. My peers in the U.S. said things to me like, "Go back to your country wetback." I pretended I was not learning English, hoping that would be a reason to send me back. There was one gym teacher who did not like me at all. We were supposed to run laps, but I sprained my shoulder. She didn't care; she made me run. She said everyone must participate. But, there was another girl, with blonde hair and blue eyes who was complaining of a stomach ache. The teacher let her sit out. I was crying the whole time. She told me to read the gym rules, but I could not read them in English, so she sent me to the principal's office. They swatted me for not reading the rules. It was humiliating and heartbreaking.

Most of my teachers looked at everything about me as a deficit. But, my fifth-grade teacher was able to *see my potential*. Ms. Herrera worked hard to build a *relationship* with me and she *communicated her belief in me*. At first, I resisted her attempts to *get to know me*. I had built a wall around myself; I didn't want to be close to anyone. But, she tried to show an *understanding* of my family situation. She said, "I know you miss your mom, but remember why you are here. You are a very smart girl and you are learning, and you are shining." Little by little, I let her in. I remember I got 100% on a spelling test and she whispered in my ear, "I knew you were a shining star." I became a teacher because I want to be the one that believes in my students, just like Ms. Herrera believed in me.

Preparation for Equitable and Excellent Teaching

The following describes Paulina's preparation for equitable and excellent teaching.

Readiness for Teaching

The FEET really helped me to be prepared for my first year of teaching. I set everything up before my students walked in. I knew it was important for me to have a classroom management system up and running. In my pre-service year, I scored "approaching" on one of the FEET indicators for classroom environment. The comment on my evaluation was, "demonstrated loss of patience." During the lesson, I said to a student in frustration, "You are not doing this to me right now! Go sit down on the carpet." It was just like my elementary school gym teacher saying, "You will run those laps." I was that teacher! That evaluation experience forced me to *focus on the kids*. I realized that student was me. I learned to see my students through the lens of *"opportunity" instead of "gap."* An equitable teacher *sees students' strengths as a bridge and their weaknesses as potential and opportunity.*

The FEET helped me understand what it needs to look like for *every student to be engaged*. How would my classroom be set up so that I would be able to actively engage each student? What do I want them to learn and be able to do? How will I get every student there? How will I *draw on their diversity* to engage them?

The FEET prepared me for planning and designing *relevant* and *challenging* lessons. It also helped me learn how to *collect and analyze data and make adjustments based on my students' needs*. I would say, "Wait a minute, the data shows that was too easy for them. That group over here is going to need this. The other group is going to need me and another teacher. This group over there is going to need me, another teacher, their mom and the dad, and their grandma!"

Because of the FEET, I made a good transition to being evaluated when I started teaching. I wasn't afraid of evaluation. It was easy to understand the feedback I was getting and the rubrics. It helped me focus on improving.

Equitable and Excellent Teaching

Paulina is an affirming force in her students' lives. She enacts vital attributes of an equitable and excellent teacher.

Asset Orientation

At the beginning of my teaching career, I saw that sometimes my strategies were not working. Some of my students were not growing as quickly as the others. At the time, I was in crisis mode. It was easy to think that my students' deficiencies were the problem. But, I remembered how my own teacher, Ms. Herrera, insisted that I could do it. Today, I *see my students' potential*, what they *can do*. The students and families I serve are largely Hispanic and English language learners. Being an ELL myself, I believe it is essential to have *passionate, caring,* and *committed* teachers that help students *learn in their native language*, so they can *thrive socially, culturally, and academically*.

Relationships with Students and Families

I visit my students' homes before the first day of school. It's about getting to *know my students*. I get to *know their family's story and their own personal story*. For my students to understand the content, I have to *build relationships*. My first year, I visited every single one of the families. It was kindergarten and my home visits went so well. On the first day of school all the kids were so happy to see me. They shouted, "Hola!" Everything was great when they came in.

I *communicate regularly with parents and include them*. Every single one of my families has my cell phone number. They text me all the time. I send them parent letters every week that let them know what's going on. I *pump them up* about certain events that are happening in the school. For example, last month we had the read-a-thon. My students read a total of 7,448 minutes.

High Academic Expectations

I hold the kids to *high expectations*. I tell them, "Boys and girls, *we have to earn it. You can do this.*" Last night, I took a student to McDonald's because she improved her reading level. I told her, "You can do this. If you're reading every night, you are going to be able to see that you can do this." And she did it! She exceeded her goal. She bumped up 28 points. I *believe* in them and help my students *set goals to improve and get ready for college.*

Positive Classroom Community

We have a classroom president, vice president, and secretary. My tables are set up in a very specific way where students give each other rewards, and they give each other consequences if they are not following directions. It is about *student ownership.* The student ownership takes classroom management to a whole new level. My classroom environment is beautiful. It's a *joyful* place to be. If you come into my classroom, you'll see me *hugging them*, you'll see me *shaking their hand.* You'll see me *praising* them letting them know that *they can do better.* You'll see me using *supports* and helping them to *work independently and cooperatively.*

My classroom climate is all about *positive reinforcement and feedback.* Every Friday we have Choice Time. Some students join me in the "I need to make a better *choice*" group. We have a social contract too. The *students make the rules.* It's those positive things that I'm doing that are shaping their behavior. I am all about *incentives.* It makes them want to do a good job. It makes them want to become *leaders.*

Culturally Relevant Curricula

Finding *adequate materials and resources* for teaching in Spanish has been a challenge. Often, the materials are incomplete or difficult for my students to understand. For example, we were talking about monitoring our own reading. But, the translation to Spanish did not make sense to them. So, instead we talked about the word "supervising" our reading. We used "supervising" instead because we have moms that are supervisors. I have to *modify the curriculum to make sure that the students are understanding.*

I *connect the curriculum to my students' lives and to their families. I work with the parents* to help students understand the content. One time, a parent happened to be outside of the classroom and I said, "I need to do a math lesson and you build houses. Come on over!" I got him to talk about, when you build a house, is it important that you know how to measure? The dad was talking about framing and the wood and it just clicked with the kids. They saw a *real-life connection* about *why it is important to learn* how to measure.

Aspirations

Paulina is deeply committed to her students and aspires to become a leader in education. She states:

> It is my living passion to care about and *inspire my students, show them they matter, and that they can become someone in life because of all the circumstances and situations they face.* I want to attain a doctorate in education and become a principal in an elementary school. The daily challenges I face as a Spanish teacher bring me to the realization I cannot stop here; I want to *impact* the field of education.

Salvador

Background

Sal was born in the United States and his parents emigrated from Mexico. He describes himself as Mexican American. He is in his mid-twenties. He is now in his third year of teaching. His licensure area is secondary English Language Arts. He completed his apprentice teaching at the school where he is currently employed. Approximately 95% of the school's students are Latinx. He teaches social justice courses as electives in a charter high school. Sal initially started as an English Language Arts teacher; however, he felt he had limited opportunities to focus on equity. He felt pressured by policies, mandates, and standards that emphasized the Western canon and skill building for standardized test achievement. He felt these limitations did not allow him to teach his students in a way that felt authentic. Thus, he approached the school's administration about teaching social justice classes. He is consistently rated "proficient" on his school's evaluation framework. He facilitates professional development in his school on student voice and experiences as a primary source of knowledge. He also provides leadership on social change at the district level. In the passages that follow, Sal describes why he teaches.

Why I Teach

> Growing up, I was very aware of my surroundings and position in society. I knew what society expected of me as a Latino. I knew that my statistical destiny was to drop out of high school. I wanted to prove the system wrong. I wanted to do this for my family who made many sacrifices as immigrants from Mexico. I loved education, but I saw how the educational system criminalized us. I wanted to provide more opportunities for students that often get pushed out, students who look like me. There is not enough belief in them and they are not challenged.
>
> I was blessed with a lot of good teachers that helped me on my path. In fourth grade, I wrote in my journal that I was afraid I would not be able to

attend college because of the cost. My teacher responded that she would *do anything in her power* to help me pay for college. She *believed in me*, that was the biggest thing. My fifth-grade teacher had a reputation for being strict and mean, but she would challenge kids and that meant *she believed in them*. She expanded my learning beyond the classroom with field trips that helped me *explore real careers*. My twelfth-grade teacher spent time getting to *know me* as a person. She would play music I liked in class; that showed me she *listened* to me and *cared* about me. She *challenged and pushed me*, and she taught me to *question*. She also encouraged me to *aim high* in my choice of colleges, and this helped me to *believe in myself*. While my teachers *believed in my ability to succeed*, most of them did not nurture my cultural identity or help me question the systems of oppression I witnessed in my daily life.

I earned a full scholarship to attend a prestigious and predominately White university. I hated it when people would say I was lucky; it had nothing to do with luck. I worked my ass off to earn that. I majored in both English and Spanish. I was the model minority. I was able to get through, behave, and succeed in a White system. I learned not to question or try to change things. I was oblivious to the world around me as a Person of Color. I had a wake-up call once I got to college and it made college a lot more difficult because of that. The only reason I survived college was because I was able to *learn about my culture and social justice*.

I was telling my students just the other day, "We live our lives in discomfort all the time. But we're so used to it that we don't recognize it. It isn't until you get to a place that is so different than what you're used to that you realize how uncomfortable you've been living your life." And that's what I experienced in college, discomfort. I began to question if I really belonged there. I experienced culture shock. I felt the microaggressions, the stares. When I grew up, I went to school predominantly with Students of Color. I looked the same as them; I walked the same as them; I could communicate with them. Suddenly, I felt like I was on my own. It was difficult to survive.

The course content in my English classes was White and Eurocentric. I felt isolated. My Spanish courses focused on *culture* and *social justice*. Because of this, I found so much *power* in college. I felt fortunate to find professors that *supported* me, *challenged* me, and *opened my mind to systematic inequity*. *Connections with people of color* have helped me through oppressive systems. I want to live my life *liberated* from systems of oppression and inequality. I became a teacher because I want to give students an education grounded in *culture*, *liberation*, and *social justice*.

Preparation for Equitable and Excellent Teaching

The following describes Sal's preparation for equitable and excellent teaching.

Readiness for Teaching

One of the things the FEET does well is focus on the students themselves. The FEET prepared me to focus on the *rationale* for my lessons and *make connections to students' lives.* This was sometimes difficult in English class with books like *Huckleberry Finn* and *The Great Gatsby.* My students and I talked about why we were reading books by so many White authors. We talked about the *power of language* and the *power of culture.* In my practice now, I am very explicit with my students in every lesson. I tell them the reason we are learning the content is to give them the *power to create change.*

I think instructional coaching and teacher evaluation, like the FEET, can help teachers develop equitable practice. In schools with high percentages of Students of Color, administrators often assume teachers who choose to work there are committed to educational equity. This may lead administrators to focus on excellence and ignore equity. In reality, many teachers need intensive training and support in developing equitable teaching practice. My students tell me that they don't know how to *apply the social justice concepts* to other classes. They don't know how to talk about this in math or science. I think the teachers need support to be able to make those connections. If the teacher evaluation tool has *specific language about incorporating culture, connecting the lesson to students' lives,* and *social justice,* the coaching and supervising sessions could be a lot more *meaningful and authentic.*

Equitable and Excellent Teaching

Sal is a powerful force in his students' lives. He enacts vital attributes of an equitable and excellent teacher.

No Excellence Without Equity

Teachers cannot truly be excellent if they are not equitable. In my own experience as a student, many of my teachers fostered excellence, but they left out equity. Even those teachers who appeared to appreciate diversity tended to ignore *issues related to race, culture, and power dynamics.* Excellence is not enough. If you only focus on excellence you are missing a crucial part of education that People of Color need to survive in our country.

Equitable teaching is more than getting to know your students; it's about helping students *become aware of their position in society, explore their identity, resist internalizing microaggressions and stereotypes,* and *build consciousness of themselves and systems of oppression.*

As teachers, we hold the keys to that knowledge. We can limit them, or we can *open those boundaries.* Our students have to recognize that their discomfort is not coming from a place where they're not worthy enough, not smart enough, not White enough. My ultimate goal is to equip them with a *counternarrative.* "I'm *good enough.* There is something wrong with the system. How can I *change the system?*" I think that's the biggest goal that we should have for our students. And that's difficult because that would mean that they would directly *challenge White supremacy,* and the system doesn't want our students to do that.

Critical Consciousness

I believe an excellent teacher needs to be able to improve the academic *growth* of students no matter where they start. But I think that if you only do that, you are missing a crucial part of the education that Peoples of Color need to survive in our country. I think equitable teaching is *fighting for social justice.* Equitable teaching is being able to *open up boundaries* and have students *understand their positionality* in society and be able to *build consciousness of themselves and the systems of oppression* that they experience.

When students develop critical consciousness, they can *identify the systems that are blocking their ability to succeed.* They *open their eyes* and learn to *accept themselves.* They learn they are *smart and capable.* I want students to have the *culture of power,* but also the *power of culture.* You need *power to access systems,* so you can *implement change* and *create revolutionary spaces for your communities and for yourself.*

Helping White teachers develop critical consciousness can help them understand *White privilege.* They need to be *open* and *honest* in *questioning our educational system and how it upholds White supremacy.* I would ask them, "Do you truly *believe in our students* or are you just being a White savior?" I think people come with a good heart; but their intentions and their impact are really two different things. When teachers become White saviors, students depend on them. Our students can't depend on the system the way that it is; instead they should be *challenging* it and *revolutionizing* it.

Humanization

I think the system looks at numbers for success. I want success to look like acknowledging our students, their *humanity,* the issues they have to face, the systems around them. In order for them to challenge the system, I think students need to be brought into the conversation in terms of *what success means for them.* I think too often we get stuck in White values and don't consider what Students of Color and their families want and need.

Aspirations

Sal aspires to be a leader in education to extend his impact on systems that perpetuate oppression. He states:

When I think about my future, I go back to the foundation of who I am – my vision and purpose. My vision and purpose has always been clear and is rooted in this quote by an amazing Black queer scholar, Audre Lorde: "The master's tools will never dismantle the master's house." The knowledge and tools I was given throughout my K-12 experience were meant to keep me complacent and maintain the system. It wasn't until college that I encountered professors of color who finally gave me *knowledge and tools that were meant for my heart, my mind, and my hands.*

I continue to work toward *dismantling systems of oppression and breaking away from the mold of White supremacy* that is engrained in our education system. To do this, I need greater and more in-depth knowledge. I want to obtain a doctorate degree. Academic work will make my practice stronger, but it will also challenge the elitist, and often racist, ivory tower by adding another professor with a Latino surname and a Latino heritage. I see myself *challenging the system* from within by becoming a teacher of teachers – a professor. I hope that my work will help to equip future generations with the tools needed to finally help dismantle the master's house.

Aaron

Background

Aaron is in his mid-thirties and identifies as Caucasian. He completed his apprentice teaching in the dual-language school where he is currently employed. About 95% of the school's students are Latinx. He is in his fourth year of teaching middle school social studies. Aaron was rated "distinguished" on his most recent evaluation, the highest possible rating on his district's educator evaluation framework. Aaron is bilingual and teaches in both English and Spanish. He learned Spanish in school and by volunteering and working in Latin America. He developed an interest in the Spanish language in the small rural town where he grew up that had a small Latinx population.

Why I Teach

I went to school with Latino kids and I always wanted to know more about them. Then I went to Nicaragua; it was like I had another personality. My brain had made all these new connections and it was rewiring things. It just opened me so much.

My Spanish high school teacher also influenced me to learn Spanish. I was not good at Spanish – probably one of the worst students in the class. But, Mr. Sandoval was so *positive*; he taught me a lot about Latino *culture* and his own *background*. I went on a school trip to New Mexico and I saw where he grew up. I think that was one of the early experiences that started to connect me to a culture I didn't know a lot about. He was very influential.

After I returned from Latin America, I worked as a tutor in an after-school program in a dual-language immersion school in my home town. This experience convinced me teaching was right for me. My mom and dad were teachers; my sister is a teacher. I think that influenced me as well. My mom was a seventh-grade Language Arts teacher. In terms of lesson planning and pushing students to do their best, she was one of the best I've seen. My dad taught history by engaging students and my sister is considered one of the best teachers in the school district back home. They are all phenomenal teachers.

Preparation for Equitable and Excellent Teaching

The following describes Aaron's preparation for equitable and excellent teaching.

Readiness for Teaching

I think the FEET established my foundation. It's so much *more than teaching your content.* It's about *valuing students, their families, and cultures.*

The FEET set up a good foundation for my classroom management. I remember struggling with classroom management when I was a pre-service teacher. At first, I had low scores in classroom management on the FEET. My supervisor used the FEET to give me some concrete steps and that saved me. I started my first year of teaching with *routines* for classroom management. I also thought about *classroom management through the lens of their culture.* I think it's natural for White teachers, especially, to come into a classroom and be like, "Oh these poor kids." That is the "pobrecito syndrome" and that's not what they need. They need someone who really wants to *push them* and will *believe in them.*

The FEET helped me to focus on *engagement.* I routinely have students moving around, engaging in *kinesthetic* learning. We do a lot of *simulations.* It is challenging for the kids and they love it. Many say they want to do drama in high school.

It was also incredibly helpful to be evaluated using a rubric and being able to see your scores change. It helped me look at the areas I needed to work on. It helped me get used to the evaluation environment in schools today. The FEET broke up teaching into bite-size pieces that were digestible. It is important to prepare teachers for evaluation because they are going to be observed and evaluated a lot.

Equitable and Excellent Teaching

Aaron is a steadfast and devoted force in his students' lives. He enacts vital attributes of an equitable and excellent teacher.

Reflect on Biases

You have to *understand your own biases*. I've worked with Latinx populations for several years now and there are still certain things that, if I'm honest, I need to confront. I need to ask myself, why am I thinking about it this way? Why would the students be thinking about it this way? You have to keep finding ways to confront your own biases and help students see their own biases.

Know Your Students and Include Their Voices

You have to *know your students*. You can't just throw content at them. You have to *address cultural elements*. You have to consider race, socioeconomic status, gender, sexual preferences, learning styles, and personality. We have kids from Cuba, Honduras, Guatemala, and Mexico. How do they learn? How does their culture affect the way they learn?

There are times when the students need to *talk* about things. For instance, we talked a lot after the election last year and we continue to talk about things they see in the news. We talk about DACA and what that means. I want them to *know their rights* – whether they were born here or not. They have a *voice* and need to *express themselves*. They do this by *leading* conversations in the classroom.

High Expectations and Support

I have *high academic expectations* for my students. They need to state a claim and be able to back it up with sound reasoning and evidence. They need to be able to write a good summary with a main idea and supporting details. I provide them with *language supports*, like English and Spanish word walls, sentence frames, and kinesthetic movement to illustrate key vocabulary. They need to be able to use the *language of power* and the *power of their native language* to express themselves. They need to be *leaders* in our communities. They need these skills and the confidence to go to *college*.

Agents for Change

I *connect the curriculum to my students' lives.* I teach in a neighborhood that was once exclusively Latinx, but it is now facing overwhelming gentrification. In one unit, we relate Westward Expansion to gentrification in the area. It's not part of the curriculum, but we do a *simulation* relating gentrification to the experiences of Native Americans in the U.S. I teach them to confront and challenge injustice.

We talk about civics right now and laws and structures created by older White males. I showed the kids their representatives and two senators. We looked at pictures. Out of nine members of congress, one was female, and all were Caucasian. It's important for them to know. I tell them that they can be in these positions one day. They need to be part of the *change*. By 2050, they will be the majority. They'll be ready to take those *leadership* positions that a lot of people who look like them and talk like them don't have right now.

I encourage students to be *agents for change* though simulations. The school principal and I told the students they had to start paying for materials at school. I encouraged my students to exercise their *civic rights*. They made *protest* signs and went around the school and picketed. We hung the signs up in the hallway. They should not be afraid to *challenge the system*. It's their school; if there is something they don't like they can change it. I teach them not to just sit back and let things happen to them. They have that ability to *create change*.

Aspirations

Aaron will be taking on a new teaching position in the coming year in a magnet early college high school that is predominantly Latinx. Though Aaron has been recognized as an exemplary teacher, he is focused on continually improving his practice. He states:

> People often encourage me to begin the administration track to become a principal. I don't foresee this happening for many years, if at all. I do feel I would one day make a good mentor teacher or teacher leader. I have nearly completed four years of teaching and I feel I still have so much more room to grow to become the ideal teacher for students. In 10 years, I want to be considered a master teacher and someone students feel like they can connect with, who continually pushes them to think critically. I want to continue to have a strong focus on infusing literacy in social studies to help make high school students strong writers as they pursue a college education.

Jennifer

Background

Jenny is in her late twenties and identifies as White. She is now in her sixth year teaching high school Spanish. She completed her apprentice teaching in a high school that served predominantly Black and Latinx students. She currently teaches high school Spanish at one of the most diverse high schools in Denver, serving Black, Latinx, White, and international students. Jenny has been rated "distinguished" the past three years. This is the highest rating a teacher can receive in her district. Her students consistently pass the Advanced Placement Spanish exam at exceptionally high rates. In 2016, she won an award for excellence in teaching from her state's foreign language teaching association. She now designs professional development for all the language teachers in her school district and hosts lab classrooms.

Why I Teach

I was active in school growing up. I played sports and always knew I would attend college. I took Spanish in high school and I really enjoyed learning another language. After college, I had the opportunity to live in Chile and teach English. I made *connections* that would not have been possible without knowing another language. I started teaching because I enjoyed the Spanish language and I wanted my students to enjoy it too.

Preparation for Equitable and Excellent Teaching

The following describes Jenny's preparation for equitable and excellent teaching.

Readiness for Teaching

As a teacher education program, you want to model best practice, so you would never just throw all these expectations onto the student teachers without any context. You release them a little bit at a time. If you overload anyone, it will just feel overwhelming. It's like learning language through *comprehensible input.* You want to understand when you are ready for a little more. The FEET helped us to learn teaching skills a little at a time.

The FEET was a helpful tool that concretely told you what to do. The *positive feedback* from my supervisor was helpful. I remember my field supervisor telling me that I needed to keep it simple or I would burn out – totally true. I was not being clear in my planning and I was being hard on myself. I learned to be really *reflective* about what I can do to improve.

The FEET helped me to feel prepared for the evaluation process I would encounter as a teacher. I think it's about holding teachers accountable for good teaching and student learning. I feel fairly comfortable being evaluated and I have received strong evaluations throughout my years of teaching.

Equitable and Excellent Teaching

Jenny is an exemplary and dedicated force in her students' lives. She enacts vital attributes of an equitable and excellent teacher.

Relationships and Trust

I take time to build *trust* with my students. I show them that I *value them.* I believe communicating *respect* and value for my Students of Color is especially important. I *greet my students at the doorway*, which I think is a really powerful practice. Very few teachers at my school do it, but *seeing your students eye-to-eye* as they walk in, that might be the only *connection* they have with a teacher that day.

White students typically come to me. A White student, especially a girl, they may feel like, "I see you. You see me. I already know you. You look like all of the other teachers I've had. You look like me." Maybe they don't have questions about who I am.

For my Students of Color, they may question who I am and if they can *trust* me. It takes *patience*, and it takes me just *listening* to them. To connect with them I have to *be humble* and *check my own privilege and biases*. I have to acknowledge that I have benefitted so much from the system of education and all the opportunities I've had. If I don't have a certain sense of *humility* in who I am, then I can't connect with them. As my kids develop *trust* in me, they *open up. We learn a lot about each other. They teach me. I learn a lot from them.*

Language Is Power

Language is very much about power. It can reflect your level of education and belonging to a community. I think about this, especially teaching heritage speakers in Spanish. We talk about *code-switching*. We talk about how there's a reason for formal language norms. It is important to learn when to use a formal register in English and Spanish. However, they also need to maintain their home language and use this in powerful ways as well. They already have so many tools and skills. I ask myself, "How can I *build off of who they are and what they know, and give them the tools to be successful in all of their cultures?*"

Culturally Relevant Curricula

I make *content relevant* for students. Sometimes students are hesitant to share their cultural heritage, but I am *patient* with them. It is day by day, little by little. We *connect the content to bigger questions related to their lives*. We discuss why it is important that we know their own *traditions*.

It's like putting up a mirror in front of them. I make sure the *content reflects them*. I bring in *Chicano and Latino art*. I have posters and artifacts from *different cultures* on my classroom walls. We have virtual conversations with people from *different countries and cultures*. I teach about the iceberg model of culture and what is visible and invisible about *culture*. It is important to learn about cultures, more than food and celebrations. My students analyze Latino cultures and then compare them to their own.

Critical Consciousness

It's great that you can go to college, and go make money in a business or corporation, and keep moving in your world. It's great if you know how to think. But what can you do with that? I ask my students, "What does it mean for your *community* or for the people around you? How might you be an *agent of change* for your community? How can you develop *critical consciousness* and *take action?*" How can we, as teachers, help students act on their emerging consciousness? How can we help them to *act for social change?*

Aspirations

Jenny has recently accepted a position as a Spanish teacher, instructional coach, and teacher evaluator at a magnet secondary school with a diverse student population. While Jenny will spend part of her day as an instructional leader, she wants to stay connected to students. She states:

> I hope to continue teaching and coaching fellow teachers. Ideally, I will maintain a presence in the classroom in addition to leadership. I want to teach my students to develop a sense of empathy and tolerance, and a desire for change, while learning the skill of a new language. Language is a bridge and we need more bridges than ever.

Equitable and Excellent Teachers

Brian, Paulina, Sal, Aaron, and Jenny come from different backgrounds and are in different stages of their careers, but they express similar themes about what it means to be an equitable and excellent teacher. These teachers were trained with the FEET, which places a heavy emphasis on culturally responsive practices through a positive learning environment, culturally relevant curricula, teaching for social justice, and continuous reflection on their own practice.

Positive Learning Environment

All five teachers describe the importance of building a positive learning environment by: maintaining asset orientations; building relationships with students and families; and enacting student-centered approaches.

The teachers emphasize the importance of maintaining asset orientations of the students and families they serve. They value students, their families, and their cultures. Moreover, they look at their students from the perspective of "opportunity" versus "gap."

The teachers affirm the importance of establishing relationships with students and families. They believe that in order for students to learn, the teacher must build relationships with each child and her or his family. To build relationships they: listen; show patience, humility, and respect; build trust; and create connections. They also acknowledge students' humanity by giving them opportunities to explore their values, culture, and identities.

The teachers are student-centered. Students have ownership of the classroom. They express their voice through dialogue, meaning-making, and social justice pursuits. Moreover, the teachers acknowledge their students as individuals and members of groups.

Culturally Relevant Curricula

Each of the teachers explained how they connect their curricular content to their students' lives, interests, and cultures. The teachers stress the importance of knowing their students, not only to develop relationships, but also to connect content to their lives. To get to know their students, they: visit their homes; elicit their personal and family stories; include parents, families, and community; and encourage their voice in the classroom.

The teachers plan and enact curricula that build off of the curricula of students' lives. For example, they encourage dialogue and action that advances social justice issues that students care about. They modify the curricula so students access content concepts through their own lived experiences. Moreover, they include curricula that reflects the students' diversity through simulations, art, music, literature, and poetry. They also provide opportunities for students to question the Western canon and explore their own identities.

They enact culturally responsive curricula while setting high expectations. They encourage their students to hold "can-do attitudes" by emphasizing all that they are capable of, including: achieving academically, resisting inequity, and advocating for social justice. They emphasize literacy, high-order thinking skills, and interdisciplinary connections. They also offer supports for students such as scaffolds based on their language proficiency.

They use culturally responsive instructional strategies and assessments such as: collaborative work, music, kinesthetic movement, storytelling, multiple modalities, simulations, project-based learning, and authentic assessments, to name a few.

Teaching for Social Justice

The teachers described the importance of teaching for social justice. They desire to engage students in an education that is grounded in culture, liberation, and justice. They want their students to become aware of their positionality in society, explore their identities, resist internalizing stereotypes, see their value, and build consciousness of themselves and systems of oppression. They want students to believe in themselves, know their rights, challenge the system, advocate for social change, and create revolutionary spaces for their communities and themselves. They emphasize to students that they have the power to create change.

They include practices that promote social justice, such as: including materials that reflect their students' interests and community strengths and challenges;

including topics that represent diverse communities and students' own community; providing opportunities for students to examine content from multiple perspectives and challenge the Western canon; and engaging students in simulations that promote mobilization and action for social change.

Reflecting on Professional Practice

The teachers indicated that they strive for continuous improvement. They are committed to making a difference for their students, their families, and the field of education. They take on leadership roles in their schools and districts to advance equity and excellence. The Teachers of Color reflect on their own educational challenges and use this as fuel to provide their students with an empowering educational experience. The White teachers acknowledge their own bias and privileges, and express humility in the face of these. As the most experienced teacher of the five, Jenny shared sage advice: "You never really arrive at being excellent or equitable. I think there is always room to be more excellent and be more equitable, more aware, and more intentional with your practice. You have to have a personal mission or goal to be equitable and excellent."

Summary and Implications

It is not easy being an excellent and equitable teacher. It takes commitment, *ganas* (effort), patience with oneself and others, resiliency, humility, a sense of urgency, and the relentless pursuit of equity and justice. The five teachers highlighted in this chapter represent what is possible. They realize they are only just beginning and that the path toward equity and excellence is ongoing.

Critical Questions

The following critical questions are intended to extend your comprehension and help you relate the concepts to your own practice.

1. What makes these teachers equitable and excellent?
2. What differences do you note between the Teachers of Color and the White teachers?
3. What aspects of each teacher's background experiences do you feel contributed to the development of their critical consciousness and commitment to social justice?
4. What evidence did you see for the teachers' high expectations and support for students?
5. How do the classroom environments of these teachers differ from experiences you have had or observed in schools?

Resources for Further Reflection and Study

The following supplemental resources are intended to spur your personal and professional reflection, application of the concepts in your own context, and community outreach efforts.

Print

Blankstein, A., Noguera, P., & Kelly, L. (2016). *Excellence through equity: Five principles of courageous leadership to guide achievement for every student.* Alexandria, VA: ASCD.

Egalite, A. J., & Kisida, B. (2018). The effects of teacher match on students' academic perceptions and attitudes. *Educational Evaluation and Policy Analysis, 40*(1), 59–81.

Freire, P. (2005). *Teachers as cultural workers: Letters to those who dare to teach.* Boulder, CO: Westview Press.

Janks, H. (2010). *Literacy and power.* New York, NY: Routledge.

Web

- Edutopia
  Culturally responsive teaching
  www.edutopia.org/blogs/tag/culturally-responsive-teaching
- Edutopia
  Equity vs. equality: 6 steps toward equity
  www.edutopia.org/blog/equity-vs-equality-shane-safir

Media

- Brian Lozenski
  Bringing cultural context and self-identity into education
  www.youtube.com/watch?v=bX9vgD7iTqw
- Dorinda Carter Andrews
  The consciousness gap in education – an equity imperative
  www.youtube.com/watch?v=iOrgf3wTUbo
- Pedro Noguera
  Excellence through equity
  www.youtube.com/watch?v=fSQjenZAOvE

Learning Opportunities

1. Assess the curriculum you use for the inclusion of critical consciousness. Identify three ways to incorporate critical consciousness into the existing curriculum.
2. Select three practices discussed by the teachers in this chapter that you would like to implement in your classroom or school. Why did you select these three? What concrete actions will you take to enact these practices?

3. Write an email, Facebook post, or tweet to one of the teachers highlighted in this chapter, responding to the practices they enact that you believe are good for students. Give them concrete advice on how to improve.
4. Self-assess your equitable and excellent teaching using the FEET Observation Tool. Set three goals for improvement.
5. Write or perform a poem from the perspective of a student who is in one of the highlighted teacher's class.

Community Engagement Opportunities

1. Make a visual representation of your perception of critical consciousness in the community you serve. Ask your students to add to this representation. Take it to a community organization and ask them to add to this representation. Create a collaborative work of art that captures a collective sense of critical consciousness.
2. Ask a community organization to sponsor an event to engage community members in describing practices that they deem to be equitable and excellent. Create a digital story of their responses and share this with your colleagues.
3. Search social media sites for resources related to teaching for equity and social justice. Go further and add to, or create, a site to elicit examples of equitable and excellent teaching, and connect teachers to resources that support teaching for equity and social justice.

Reference

U.S. Department of Education (2016). *The state of racial diversity in the educator workforce.* Office of Planning, Evaluation and Policy Development. Retrieved from www2. ed.gov/rschstat/eval/highered/racial-diversity/state-racial-diversity-workforce.pdf

6

SUPPORTING CULTURALLY RESPONSIVE TEACHER EVALUATION THROUGH SCENARIOS

> **Chapter Overview:** This chapter delineates scenarios to help advance culturally responsive teacher evaluation (CRTE) in different educational contexts. The scenarios are based on actions that prospective and practicing teachers and school leaders can take to explore, assess, advocate, implement, and design CRTE.

Paulo Freire (1970) asserts that "thought has meaning only when generated by action upon the world" (p. 247). How can you act to improve the educational experience of students, particularly those in the margins? You can lead where you are. That is, lead within your current role in the educational system. For example, lead as a prospective teacher, a practicing teacher, or a school leader. You can lead in any role you are in.

If you are unsure where to start, we offer scenarios and practical advice for advancing culturally responsive teacher evaluation (CRTE) in your context. This chapter is organized into two sections. In the first section, we present three scenarios that describe concrete approaches to explore, assess, and advocate for CRTE. In the second section, we describe two scenarios that provide guidance on more complex practice related to implementation and design of CRTE. We encourage you to read all the scenarios regardless of your current role in the educational system. We want you to envision what is possible and help you prepare to lead now and in the future.

Explore, Assess, and Advocate for CRTE

The first three scenarios presented in this chapter describe concrete approaches to: (1) explore teacher evaluation as cultural practice and share this knowledge;

(2) assess teacher evaluation models for alignment with the tenets of CRTE; and (3) challenge current teacher evaluation practices and advocate for CRTE.

SCENARIO ONE: EXPLORE

I want to expand my knowledge about teacher evaluation as cultural practice by exploring teaching, teacher evaluation, and CRTE. I will reflect on this knowledge, take action to share my knowledge, and coalesce a critical mass of educators who are committed to advancing CRTE.

Explore Teaching and Teacher Evaluation

We acknowledge that teacher evaluation can be a divisive topic and can feel punitive as an accountability measure. To build a comprehensive and nuanced understanding of the issue, we recommend you approach the topic like a researcher by observing in various contexts and engaging in dialogue with a variety of stakeholders. Immerse yourself in exploring teacher evaluation on the ground.

Observe practices in different school and classroom contexts. Because educators are often isolated in their own settings, you may not have had the opportunity to witness the wide variability across schools and classrooms. Visit the same grade level in schools with contrasting socioeconomic status and cultural diversity. You can also observe different teachers and content areas in your own school building. Use the FEET to document your observations and reflect on the practices you observe. Do you see a pattern related to equitable and excellent teaching across contexts or within contexts? What are the strengths? What are the areas for growth? What goals for improvement would you set?

Dialogue with students and parents about their educational experiences. Do they describe a partnership between home and school? Are the students challenged and expected to succeed academically? Are there differences in student and family perceptions across educational settings or across different demographic variables such as race, gender, or class? What do students and parents think equitable and excellent teaching looks like?

Dialogue with teachers and administrators about teacher evaluation practices. From their perspective, what is the purpose of teacher evaluation? Does the evaluation model used in their current context capture what it means to be an equitable and excellent teacher? If they could change the current model used in their context, what would they suggest?

After exploring various contexts and dialoguing with stakeholders, reflect on what you learned. How do students' educational experiences vary across contexts? What are the opportunity gaps? What is required of a teacher evaluation model to improve outcomes for all students? How can teacher evaluation models be designed to develop equitable and excellent teaching?

Review the Tenets of CRTE

It is important for those engaged in this work to be knowledgeable about the theoretical and practical aspects of CRTE, including teacher evaluation reform, culturally responsive evaluation (CRE), and culturally responsive pedagogy (CRP). This knowledge is essential to fully understand the potential of CRTE and how it differs from existing approaches to teacher evaluation. Review Table 1.1, located in Chapter 1 of this book; it summarizes the tenets of each component and illustrates how they are synthesized into CRTE.

Reflect and Act

Reflect on the tenets of CRTE. How does CRTE differ from teacher evaluation reform? What are the strengths of the tenets of CRTE? What are the weaknesses? What is missing? How can the tenets be "remixed" (Ladson-Billings, 2014)? How do the tenets converge or diverge from the teacher evaluation model used in your context? How can the tenets push the boundaries of teacher education? What is the potential impact of CRTE on teaching and learning? Gather your reflections and act.

First, use the FEET Observation Tool to self-assess your instructional practice and set goals for improvement. This is an action step that can have an immediate impact on your practice. Identify your strengths and areas of growth and use the summative and formative observation tool to set two to three concrete goals for improvement. Ask a colleague to evaluate you using the FEET. Refine your goals or set new goals. Compare your results to your most recent formal evaluation. What pattern do you see? How does each of the evaluation models you compared support your growth and development as a teacher?

Second, take your knowledge of CRTE and the FEET and share it with your colleagues; teach them what CRTE is and why it matters. You will be one, then two, then more will join until you form a critical mass of educators who advocate for equity and social justice. Share your knowledge of CRTE with your school administrators and instructional coaches. Gather a professional learning community (PLC) to explore the topic of CRTE.

Third, ask questions in staff meetings and professional development trainings. Why are certain educational practices privileged? Who is included or excluded? Is assimilation the goal? What does good teaching look like for students that come from historically marginalized communities? How do we infuse every aspect of teaching and learning with equity and excellence? Challenge the status quo. Do not acquiesce to the culture of silence in schools. Be a relentless advocate for historically marginalized students and their families. Feel the urgency that so many

Teachers of Color experience as they witness generation upon generation of students who look like them being left behind.

Last, take the knowledge of CRTE and the content of this book and pass it forward as you work with a mentor teacher, work with pre-service teachers, collaborate in departmental or interdisciplinary teams, develop curriculum, coach your colleagues, receive coaching advice, serve on district committees, evaluate teachers, and/or develop policies.

SCENARIO TWO: ASSESS

I want to understand CRTE within my current context. I will assess the existing teacher evaluation model used in my school/district/state for alignment with the tenets of CRTE.

A main assertion in this book is that teacher evaluation models often lack a focus on CLD learners. We encourage you to assess the teacher evaluation model that is implemented in your context. This analysis should be based on the five tenets of CRTE. Here, we present guiding questions and points for consideration aligned to each of the categories used to illustrate the tenets of CRTE found in Chapter 1 (i.e., purpose, community engagement, content, technical properties, outcome). Use this information to guide your analysis of the current teacher evaluation model used in your context. We provide an assessment template in this section to help you capture and organize information about the teacher evaluation model implemented in your context.

Purpose

What is the stated purpose of the evaluation model used in your context? How does this compare with the purpose of CRTE? Teacher evaluation systems may have several objectives, including: make personnel decisions, improve teacher effectiveness, provide meaningful feedback on teacher performance, and boost student achievement. While CRTE concurs with those objectives, its primary purpose is to disrupt systematic inequity by developing equitable and excellent teaching.

Community Engagement

The process through which evaluation systems are developed varies widely depending on available resources, personnel expertise, and inclusion of diverse communities. Who was involved in the development of the evaluation model? Who collaborated in each phase of the model's development, including initial conceptualization, drafting, piloting, and implementation? To what extent was the model co-constructed by a diverse group of stakeholders (e.g., parents, students, teachers, and community members)? To what extent is the model supported by equity-focused scholarship and scholars from historically marginalized communities?

Content

Does the content of the evaluation model specifically address the needs of historically marginalized communities such as CLD and special needs learners? Examine the language the model employs to define effective teaching. Look for words related to culture, race, language, diversity, abilities, gender, sexual orientation, equity, social justice, community, and critical consciousness. Identify the teaching strategies that address the needs of diverse learners. Could an educator be highly rated using the evaluation tool without attending to the educational needs of diverse learners? Compare the content of the model to that of the FEET, described in Chapter 4. What are the similarities and differences between the content in the model used in your context and the FEET?

Technical Properties

What evidence exists of the validity and reliability of the evaluation model used in your context? To demonstrate reliability, teacher evaluation models should be fair and consistent. How have raters been trained to ensure inter-rater reliability? To demonstrate validity, models should show evidence that they measure what they intend to measure. How do evaluation scores correlate with student growth data, and specifically, diverse student growth? How do evaluation scores correlate with measures related to students' growth and development? Do diverse stakeholders concur that the model captures equitable and excellent teaching? How is multicultural validity established? If your model is based on a nationally implemented framework, validity and reliability studies may be available from the publisher.

Outcome

What student outcomes are expected as a result of the evaluation model? Ultimately, the goal of teacher evaluation is improved outcomes for students. How does the teacher evaluation model address or define student outcomes? What's missing? How are student outcomes measured? To what extent do the student outcomes measure students' full potential, as defined in your context?

Teacher Evaluation Assessment Template

The assessment template that follows is a tool to help your capture and organize information about existing teacher evaluation models. Use the template to gather and document evidence about a model's development and content. Information about nationally used frameworks is often posted on the developer's website. To gather information about state and district models, visit the corresponding website and/or contact the department responsible for educator accountability.

First, collect evidence. Examples of evidence include:

- policy language on website;
- model handbook or documents;
- list of contributors, role, and level of involvement;
- research or references from equity-based scholars and Scholars of Color from historically marginalized communities;
- language in the model related to diversity and equity;
- technical reports related to reliability and validity; and
- description of student measures used to support validity claims.

Next, document your findings on the CRTE Assessment Template in Table 6.1. Describe the evidence and your analysis of the evidence. How does the evidence demonstrate alignment to the tenets of CRTE? Circle your assessment of the alignment of the teacher evaluation model to the CRTE tenet: strong, moderate, weak. What are the implications for teaching, learning, and teacher evaluation?

SCENARIO THREE: CHALLENGE AND ADVOCATE

I want to question current teacher evaluation practices in my context. I will challenge current teacher evaluation practice and advocate for the implementation of CRTE.

We encourage you to challenge current teacher evaluation practices and advocate for CRTE. We recommend you start with scenarios one and two. Based on your growing knowledge of CRTE and the assessment of the teacher evaluation model used in your context, determine what your next steps will be. Here, we describe action steps aligned to each of the categories of the CRTE framework (i.e., purpose, community engagement, content, technical properties, outcome). Your professional role may dictate the extent to which you can influence changes to your evaluation system. The recommended action steps range from classroom and school-level initiatives to district-level advocacy.

Purpose

Stakeholders need to know the purpose of teacher evaluation. The purpose of CRTE is to develop equitable and excellent teaching to disrupt inequity and advocate for equity and social justice. CRTE contests the positioning of the dominant culture at the center of teacher evaluation; this reinforces systemic

TABLE 6.1 CRTE assessment template

	Culturally responsive teacher evaluation (CRTE) tenet	Alignment of teacher evaluation model to CRTE tenets		
Tenet 1	Develop equitable and excellent teaching to disrupt inequity and advocate for equity and social justice	Strong Alignment Evidence: Analysis:	Moderate Alignment	Weak Alignment
Tenet 2	Facilitate collaboration of diverse communities in co-construction of evaluation tools.	Strong Alignment Evidence: Analysis:	Moderate Alignment	Weak Alignment
Tenet 3	Incorporate targeted teacher competencies linked to student growth and development, particularly CLD learners	Strong Alignment Evidence: Analysis:	Moderate Alignment	Weak Alignment
Tenet 4	Establish and monitor reliability and validity within a cultural context	Strong Alignment Evidence: Analysis:	Moderate Alignment	Weak Alignment
Tenet 5	Advance equity and social justice in student outcomes	Strong Alignment Evidence: Analysis:	Moderate Alignment	Weak Alignment

educational inequities. CRTE advocates for moving the margins to the center as a disruptive force. If your current evaluation model's purpose is not clear, or if the stated purpose is not focused on educational equity, engage in the following action steps:

- Design a presentation on the educational needs of CLD learners and the importance of culturally responsive teaching practices. Present these findings to your colleagues, school, community advocacy organizations, school board meetings, and/or district leadership.
- Collect and document stakeholder perceptions about the model's purpose. How do teachers, administrators, parents, and students describe the purpose of the evaluation model? Do perceptions about the purpose align with the model's stated purpose? What do stakeholders think should be the aspirational purpose? Present these findings to your colleagues and/or school/district leadership team.

Community Engagement

CRTE calls for the co-construction of evaluation tools. This ensures that the development process, from start to end, is responsive to the needs of diverse communities. Stakeholders may include students, families, community organizations, higher education faculty, teachers, support staff, school counselors and psychologists, social workers, custodial staff, and district and school administrators. To ensure your current evaluation model is developed, or improved, in partnership with diverse communities, engage in the following actions:

- Engage parent and community groups in a discussion about effective teaching practices and share the results with your colleagues and school/district leadership team.
- Assemble a committee to review the evaluation model. Ensure the committee is diverse and represents multiple stakeholders. Use the results to advocate for the improvement of the evaluation model used in your context.
- Request that diverse stakeholders are included in the development, review, or revision of your current evaluation model. Depending on your role and context, this request may be made to school leadership, district personnel, state department of education leadership, or school board representatives.

Content

CRTE incorporates targeted teaching competencies that are linked to student growth and development, and particularly, the achievement of CLD learners. If the content of your current evaluation model does not include targeted teacher competencies that meet the needs of historically marginalized communities, engage in the following actions:

- Supplement the current model with strategies specific to historically marginalized learners. For example, if the model includes a competency related to the teacher's ability to establish positive relationships with students, add culturally responsive strategies as evidence (e.g., maintains asset orientation toward families, incorporates students' cultures).
- Share the FEET domains, competencies, and indicators with teachers, instructional coaches, and school leaders to advocate for the integration of CRTE within your school.
- Recommend specific changes related to content to school leaders, district leaders, school board members, policy makers, and state lawmakers.

Technical Properties

CRTE establishes and monitors validity and reliability in a cultural context. Inter-rater reliability should be established and continuously monitored. Validity should be continuously monitored using quantitative and qualitative methods, and include multicultural validity. If your current evaluation lacks evidence of reliability and validity, engage in the following actions:

- Analyze the teacher evaluation model's technical reports. For models implemented nationally, document the extent to which the published studies suggest validity in your district.
- If no validity or reliability studies are available, request that they be conducted. Your school, district, or state can partner with local universities.
- Advocate for the examination of multicultural validity (Hopson & Kirkhart, 2012) in the evaluation model used in your context.

Outcomes

CRTE advances equity and social justice in student outcomes as measured by assessments of students' full potential. To promote varied measures to assessing student outcomes, engage in the following:

- Challenge the sole use of narrow measures of achievement such as standardized tests. Use research to support your assertion that such measures provide a narrow view of students' capabilities.
- Advocate for a comprehensive student outcome measure which assesses students' full potential. This can be defined from the content of this book, the literature, and/or your local context.

- Develop or adapt teacher, student, and parent surveys with items specifically related to defining students' full potential.

Implement and Design CRTE

While the content of a teacher evaluation model may seem like one small component of educational policy, its implications are vast. Such models reflect what is valued and who is valued. They determine what we should teach and how we should teach it. They guide assessment of teaching, coaching, and professional development. Most importantly, teacher evaluation models determine a student's experience in the classroom. The two scenarios in the sections that follow press for systemic changes to current practice. Scenario four provides support for adopting the Salazar and Lerner Framework for Equitable and Excellent Teaching (FEET). Scenario five provides guidance for designing and implementing CRTE.

Managing Change

It is important to acknowledge that any shift in practice or policy can be challenging. We recommend thinking carefully about the change process. While a comprehensive discussion about organizational change is beyond the scope of this book, we find Knoster, Villa, and Thousand's framework for thinking about systems change helpful for avoiding potential pitfalls (Knoster et al., 2000). The authors provide a structured way of thinking about change in an educational context, particularly from a school leadership perspective. Knoster et al. contend that lasting change requires the presence of five elements: vision, skills, incentives, resources, and a plan. If one or more of these elements are missing, the process can be derailed. First, it is important to have a clearly articulated *vision* in order to avoid confusion. Second, participants tasked with designing and implementing the model need to have the requisite *skills* to accomplish the task; otherwise this may cause anxiety. Third, participants in the evaluation model need *incentives* to enact change; otherwise there may be resistance. Fourth, it is important to set aside time and provide *resources*; if not, participants may become frustrated. Last, it is important to have a well-articulated *plan* for implementation; in the absence of a plan, the participants may feel like the challenging work of teacher evaluation reform has no end. The following scenarios offer practical advice for adopting or designing CRTE systems. We encourage you approach this work with change theory in mind.

SCENARIO FOUR: IMPLEMENT

I want to implement CRTE. I will adopt the Salazar and Lerner Framework for Equitable and Excellent Teaching (FEET) in my context.

The FEET is a teacher evaluation framework developed in alignment with the tenets of CRTE. Successful implementation of the FEET in your context will require collaboration with local constituents and careful attention to process. In this section, we provide guidance for the adoption of the FEET based on the categories of CRTE (e.g., purpose, community engagement, content, technical properties, and outcome).

Purpose

Clearly articulate the purpose of revising or adopting the FEET. Community members need to know why it is important to adopt the FEET and how it will be used. The purpose of the FEET is to develop equitable and excellent teachers who disrupt inequity and advocate for equity and social justice. Take time to build consensus about the purpose of the FEET in your context. Identify how the FEET will be used, including: personnel decisions, improving teacher quality, providing meaningful feedback on instruction, and improving student outcomes.

Community Engagement

We recommend assembling a committee to gather input about the FEET evaluation model's content and make decisions about the process for implementation. Determine who will be involved in the FEET implementation in your context. Ensure the committee is diverse and represents multiple stakeholders (e.g., parents, students, teachers, staff, administrators, district leaders). Gather their feedback on the FEET and solicit their buy-in.

Content

Review the content of the FEET. It is important that all stakeholders have a common vision about equitable and excellent teaching practices. As a group, discuss each of the FEET competencies and how they align to, extend, or can change current practices. Ensure instructional coaches and school leaders have the knowledge, skills, and resources needed to support teacher development. This will require deep understanding, commitment, and professional development related to culturally responsive teaching practices.

Technical Properties

Because the FEET was developed in alignment with CRTE principles, evidence for reliability and validity has been established. However, it is important to continuously monitor inter-rater reliability and validity. To establish reliability, raters must be trained to use the evaluation framework. We provide a brief summary of the rater training guidance outlined in the text *Better Feedback for Better Teaching* (Archer et al., 2016). Guidelines from this resource can be applied to the adoption of the FEET. The following summary is intended to give a broad overview of the rater training process. We strongly encourage you to conduct a comprehensive review of this and other resources before implementing a new evaluation model. Well-trained raters are essential for fair and impactful teacher evaluation.

Laying the Foundation

You will need to determine how many raters will be needed and how they will be selected. Once raters are selected, rater training will require time and resources. Stakeholders should be included in discussions about the amount of training required, why it is necessary, and how it will be delivered. Archer et al. (2016) recommend first collecting survey data from teachers about current evaluation practices and their level of trust in the rating system. The authors also cite research studies suggesting that robust rater training improves teaching and learning.

Preparing Training Materials

The key to effective rater training is a catalog of pre-scored video aligned to each of the evaluation framework's competencies. Start with the MET project's policy brief on master coding to compile a video catalog. The policy brief provides detailed guidance on training master coders, selecting video, and building a video catalog (MET Project Policy and Practitioner Brief, 2013). Note that it can be challenging to find video clips of culturally responsive teaching. Video of classroom instruction should be rated by experts, or master coders. The master coders must agree on accurate scores and provide rationale based on the rubric language. Raters should demonstrate accuracy to a predetermined extent in order to be certified to conduct evaluations. We recommend new raters join more experienced raters during classroom observations before they engage in solo evaluations.

Training Raters

It is important that raters have the knowledge and skills to conduct high-quality evaluations. This requires intensive, ongoing training. Archer et al. (2016) recommend raters have prerequisite knowledge, including: (a) know the rubric; (b) collect evidence; (c) understand bias and develop core skills; (d) recognize evidence; (e) use criteria for rating; and (f) coach teachers.

Discuss the purpose of the rubric and its development. Then, review the rubric's structure and process for determining levels of performance. Start by looking closely at one competency. Examine the rubric language and allow raters to discuss their own experience in the classroom and their experiences working with other teachers. Progress through each of the competencies by viewing video clips and discussing evidence aligned to the rubric.

Discuss, model, and practice real-time data collection. Capturing data during a live observation requires practice. In the absence of a live observation, examine each of the competencies by viewing video clips and describing evidence aligned to the rubric. Decide what type of data raters should collect and document. We recommend documenting direct quotations from teachers and students and summarizing observed behaviors.

Each rater brings their own experience, values, and biases to this work. It is important to identify and discuss these biases. Research suggests that observer bias, left unchecked, can result in higher teacher evaluation scores for those who work with high-performing students (Whitehurst, Chingos, & Lindquist, 2015). In addition to bias related to students and teachers, raters may produce inaccurate evaluation scores based because of familiarity ("I know this teacher is capable of more"), halo (exceptional performance in one competency inflates other aspects), fatal flaw (low performance in one competency deflates other aspects), central tendency (over-use of the middle of the scale), consequence (inflated ratings due to possible consequences of low score), and drift (gradually produces higher or lower ratings over time). Discuss these sources of bias with raters and acknowledge that they are expected. Encourage raters to refer to the rubric language consistently and provide ongoing training and support.

Raters will need guidance and practice to accurately distinguish levels of performance within the rubric. In training sessions, practice interpreting evidence from video clips and provide feedback on ratings, evidence, and rationale. Focus on modeling, practice, and consistency.

Ongoing Support and Continuous Improvement

Plan to implement training sessions throughout the year. Depending on the level of experience of each rater on your team, you may need to differentiate training sessions. We recommend intensive training for new raters, and periodic and regular calibration with all raters through the year. Analyze evaluation scores to determine trends among competencies and among raters. For example, look for competencies that are consistently scored higher or lower than others. If the raters are accurate, lower-scoring competencies indicate a weakness in instruction for the evaluated population. Use this data to prioritize professional development and instructional coaching. Look for trends among raters. Some raters may be consistently severe, and others may be lenient. These raters will need additional calibration training.

Outcomes

The FEET promotes equitable and excellent teaching as a means of advancing equity and social justice in student outcomes. To determine how the evaluation model is affecting student success, select or design student outcome measures that assess students' full potential. Carefully consider the types of student outcomes that reflect your goals. Possible sources of data include: student test scores, measures of student engagement, cultural competence surveys, social justice indicators, authentic assessments, and student and family perception surveys.

SCENARIO FIVE: DESIGN

I want to design and use a CRTE model in my own context. I wil collaborate with others to develop and implement a CRTE model in my school/district/state.

Designing and implementing a new teacher evaluation model requires a process similar to the one outlined in scenario four, with the additional step of developing content for the evaluation framework. Here, we provide a brief summary of each component of CRTE that needs to be considered along with a more detailed discussion of content development.

Purpose

Clearly articulate the purpose of creating a new evaluation model. Take time to build consensus about the central purpose of your model, as it will guide important decisions throughout development and implementation. Write a purpose or mission statement for your evaluation model. In order to align with CRTE this must disrupt systemic inequities and promote equity.

Community Engagement

CRTE promotes collaboration with diverse communities. We recommend assembling a committee to gather input and make decisions about the evaluation model's content and process for implementation. Ensure the committee is diverse and represents diverse community members (e.g., parents, students, teachers, staff, administrators, district leaders, higher education faculty, community organizations). Make sure the members represent the demographics of the school or school system. Clearly articulate how decisions will be made, including input and voting procedures.

Content

There are several steps to consider when developing content for a teacher evaluation model. Take the following steps to develop the content:

Step 1: Review existing teacher evaluation models and discuss strengths and weaknesses related to structure, format, and content. Identify language that specifically addresses the needs of diverse learners. Examine the structure and content of models implemented nationally. Examine the structure and content of the FEET, and identify language related to equity and diversity.

Step 2: Review research that links teaching strategies to student outcomes, as defined in your context. Research syntheses and meta-analyses are particularly useful, though some research may include a narrow definition of student outcomes (e.g., test scores). Include research on culturally responsive practices and their association with a variety of student outcomes.

Step 3: Create a matrix that includes local, state, and national standards. As you develop content for your model, document its alignment to state, national, and international standards. We recommend alignment to the following national and international standards: InTASC Model Core Teaching Standards and Learning Progressions (2013), International Society for Technology in Education (ISTE) Standards (n.d.), and National Board for Professional Teaching Standards (NBPTS) Five Core Propositions (n.d.).

Step 4: Draft a framework that includes an organized hierarchy of teacher competencies (e.g., domains, competencies, and indicators). Begin with the "proficient" category. Gather feedback from diverse stakeholders. Be aware of your own personal and professional experiences and how they inform this work. Can a teacher still be effective if they do not demonstrate these competencies? Can a teacher be ineffective while demonstrating these competencies? Do the competencies meet the needs of historically marginalized communities?

Step 5: Create rubrics that describe performance at various levels of proficiency. Identify teaching strategies and teacher behaviors that align with the purpose of the model. When crafting rubric language, avoid relying on intensity or frequency adjectives (e.g., rarely, sometimes, often). Describe the differences in quality versus quantity. Field test the rubrics by conducting low-stakes observations. Encourage raters to be transparent about the process and ask teachers for feedback on the content of the framework. Compile feedback from evaluators and educators to revise the rubrics.

Step 6: Design evaluation protocols that include summative and formative assessment. Consider the logistical systems raters will use to document evidence and the structure of pre- and post-observation conversations.

Technical Properties

It is important to establish inter-rater reliability and continuously monitor validity based on quantitative and qualitative methods. To establish reliability, raters must be extensively trained to use the evaluation framework. We recommend the process for rater training outlined in the Gates Foundation 2012 Policy Report. Conduct ongoing validity assessments by testing the association between teachers' classroom observation ratings and student outcomes, as defined in your context.

Outcomes

To determine how the evaluation model is affecting student success, you must identify student outcome measures. Carefully consider the types of student outcomes that reflect the goals in your context. What does student success look like? What measures can capture success in meeting the needs of the whole child? What difference does difference make? How do diverse learners and their communities define success? How can we measure success according to their definitions?

Summary and Implications

In this chapter, we presented scenarios to offer practical advice for advancing CRTE in your context. Regardless of your role, you can lead meaningful change. Lead by example. You can make your own practice responsive to the educational needs of marginalized students. You can reflect and collaborate with peers to advocate for change in teacher evaluation. You can engage diverse community members in identifying high-quality instruction and advocate for the resources to implement a CRTE model. You can implement the FEET in your context, or you can design your own CRTE model. There are many ways you can make a difference through CRTE. Take the first step or many steps toward CRTE.

Critical Questions

The following critical questions are intended to extend your comprehension and help you relate the concepts to your own practice.

1. With what scenario did you most identify? How can you use your position to advocate for CRTE?
2. In your current position, how can you advance CRTE?
3. What may account for the absence of CRTE in your context?
4. Identify the vision, skills, incentives, resources, and/or action plan that would lay a foundation for the implementation of CRTE in your context.

Resources for Further Reflection and Study

The following supplemental resources are intended to spur your personal and professional reflection, application of the concepts in your own context, and community outreach efforts.

Print

Kirkhart, K. E. (2010). Eyes on the prize: Multicultural validity and evaluation theory. *American Journal of Evaluation, 31*(3), 400–413.

McMaster, H. (2010). Rethinking education as the practice of freedom: Paulo Freire and the promise of critical pedagogy. *Policy Futures in Education, 8*(6), 715–721.

Shor, I. (1987). *Freire for the classroom.* Portsmouth, NH: Boynton Cook.

Web

- Bill & Melinda Gates Foundation
- *Ensuring accurate feedback from observations*
  https://docs.gatesfoundation.org/documents/ensuring-accuracy-wp.pdf
- Centers for Disease Control and Prevention
  Developing an effective evaluation plan
  www.cdc.gov/obesity/downloads/cdc-evaluation-workbook-508.pdf
- The MET Project
  Gathering feedback for teaching
  http://files.eric.ed.gov/fulltext/ED540961.pdf

Media

- YouTube
  Freire Project versus YouTube
  Seeing through Paulo's glasses: Political clarity, courage and humility
  www.youtube.com/watch?v=U4jPZe-cZgc&t=102s

- MyM&E versus YouTube
  Cultural responsiveness in equity-focused evaluations
  www.youtube.com/watch?v=XJpACQjfluI

Learning Opportunities

1. Obtain a teacher evaluation framework from your local school district or state. What do you notice about the practices in comparison to CRTE and the FEET? In what ways would you change it? Identify which scenario would work best to help you change the framework used in your district.
2. Identify a scenario that you would like to pursue and set two to three concrete goals to help you get there.
3. Work with colleagues to develop a concept map of the ideas in this chapter. Use this map to set two to three goals to advance CRTE in your context.

Community Engagement Opportunities

1. Gather a team of colleagues. Make an action plan for CRTE based on one of the scenarios presented in this chapter.

2. Collaborate with colleagues with strong knowledge of assessment practices. Define students' full potential in your context. Identify ways you can assess a student's full potential, based on your definition.
3. Take one of the scenarios presented above and present it to a PTA, community organization, or your local school board. Solicit their feedback and set one to two goals to advance CRTE.

References

Archer, J., Cantrell, S., Holtzman, S. L., Joe, J. N., Tocci, C. M., & Wood, J. (2016). *Better feedback for better teaching: A practical guide to improving classroom observations.* Hoboken, NJ: John Wiley & Sons.

Freire, P. (1970). *Cultural action for freedom.* Boston, MA: Harvard Educational Review.

Hopson, R., & Kirkhart, K. (2012). *Strengthening evaluation through cultural relevance and cultural competence.* Retrieved from www.wcasa.org/file_open.php?id=869

International Society for Technology in Education (ISTE). (n.d.). *ISTE Standards* (n.d.). Retrieved from www.iste.org/standards

Interstate Teacher Assessment and Support Consortium [InTASC] (2013). *InTASC Model Core Teaching Standards and Learning Progressions.* Retrieved from www.ccsso.org/resources/programs/interstate_teacher_assessment_consortium_(intasc).html

Knoster, T. P., Villa, R. A., & Thousand, J. S. (2000). A framework for thinking about systems change. In R. A. Villa & J. S. Thousand (Eds.), *Restructuring for caring and effective education* (pp. 93–128). Baltimore, MD: Brookes.

Ladson-Billings, G. (2014). Culturally relevant pedagogy 2.0: Aka the remix. *Harvard Educational Review, 84*(1), 74–84.

MET Project Policy and Practitioner Brief (2013). *Ensuring fair and reliable measures of effective teaching.* Retrieved from www.edweek.org/media/17teach-met1.pdf

National Board for Professional Teaching Standards (NBPTS) (n.d.). *Five Core Propositions.* Retrieved from www.nbpts.org/standards-five-core-propositions/

Whitehurst, G., Chingos, M. M., & Lindquist, K. (2015). Getting classroom observations right. *Education Next, 15*(1), 62–68.

PART III

Moving Teacher Evaluation Beyond the Boundaries

Part III reviews the main points of the preceding chapters. Chapter 7 resurrects critical race theory (CRT) to interrogate teacher evaluation as a system that has the power to liberate and oppress CLD learners from historically marginalized communities. This chapter proposes a beginning, rather than an ending, by advocating for movement beyond the boundaries of teacher evaluation.

7

REFRAMING TEACHER EVALUATION AND PROPOSING A NEW BEGINNING AND WAY FORWARD

> **Chapter Overview:** This chapter recaps the main points of the preceding chapters and resurrects critical race theory (CRT) to interrogate teacher evaluation at the center, in the margins, and beyond. It poses critical questions of the role of teacher evaluation in reproducing or interrupting inequity. The authors advocate for approaches that move beyond the boundaries of teacher evaluation.

In this book, we have:

- explored the intersection between teacher evaluation reform, culturally responsive pedagogy and assessment, and culturally responsive evaluation;
- proposed five tenets for culturally responsive teacher evaluation (CRTE) and provided a sound exemplar;
- revealed that current teacher evaluation models center whiteness and the dominant culture, and exclude the resources of CLD learners;
- offered narratives of teacher practice fostered through CRTE;
- presented scenarios to advance CRTE; and
- posed critical questions and provided resources for practice and community engagement.

This final chapter is not an ending; it is a beginning. In the sections that follow, we resurrect critical race theory (CRT) to pose questions about teacher evaluation at the margins, the center, the boundaries, and beyond. Coates (2015) emphasizes that "the questions matter as much, perhaps more than, the answers" (p. 116).

Moving the Margins to the Center of Teacher Evaluation

hooks (1989) conceptualizes the margins from a vantage point of hope versus despair. She states, "I am located in the margin. I make a definite distinction between that marginality which is imposed by oppressive structures and that marginality one chooses as a site of resistance—as location of radical openness and possibility" (p. 53). hooks advocates for repositioning the margins to the center in order to disrupt oppressive conditions. However, she cautions that marginality should not be lost; rather, the margins must remain "a site one stays in, clings to even, because it nourishes one's capacity to resist" (p. 207).

We contend that the FEET fills a gap in teacher evaluation by providing a culturally responsive, theoretically and empirically based, and psychometrically sound teacher evaluation model strategically designed to move the margins to the center of teacher evaluation. We emphasize that marginality is not lost; instead, it is a source of power at the center.

We assert that the FEET is an important contribution to teacher evaluation reform. Ayers, Kumashiro, Meiners, Quinn, and Stovall (2016) state, "setting the frame turns out to be a particularly powerful piece of work—who names the world and who frames the issues matters" (p. 156). However, as CRT scholars, it is critical that we continuously interrogate the systems that have the power to liberate and oppress historically marginalized Communities of Color. Lawless (2003) declares, "Even those who are oppressed by the master narrative are complicit in its survival and effectiveness" (p. 61). Thus, in the spirit of CRT, we ask the question: Have we conceptualized the FEET in a way that promotes liberation or reifies the oppression of historically marginalized communities? In the sections that follow, we explore this question through a critical examination of the FEET and its aim to develop equitable and excellent teachers who provide access to the *culture of power*, sustain/ revitalize the *power of culture*, and advance the *power of change*.

The Culture of Power

The FEET includes knowledge and skills that emerge from the culture of power. This is a strategic decision on our part in order ensure teachers provide historically marginalized youth with access to the knowledge and skills that are prized by the dominant culture.

First, the FEET builds off of generalized teaching competencies that are regarded as best practice (Darling-Hammond, 2012), as stated in Chapter 4.

Second, the FEET promotes an empiricist model. Mirra, Garcia, and Morrell (2015) assert that empiricism advances the notion that "'true' knowledge can be gained only from particular kinds of inquiry in the world; namely, those based in science, with all of its attendant claims of objectivity" (p. 15). This approach is revered by the dominant culture as the method to uncover universal truths (Mirra, Garcia, & Morrell, 2015).

Third, the FEET is based on linear modes of expression that are typical of whitestream ways of knowing. A linear approach is evident in the organization of the FEET dimensions, competencies, and indicators, and the scoring rubrics. This approach aligns with teacher evaluation models that have been implemented nationally.

Fourth, while CRTE emphasizes including all stakeholders, the FEET was not developed based on feedback from CLD students and their parents. The reason for this was primarily logistical; it has been challenging for us to conduct research with students in the Western state where we are located due to student privacy laws.

Fifth, the FEET reifies "performativity," which positions teachers "as subjects judged by their ability to perform and produce measureable results…" (Fisher-Ari, Kavanagh, & Martin, 2017, p. 257). In taking this approach, only that which can be measured is considered.

The FEET provides access to the power prized by the dominant culture. In doing so, does the FEET reinforce what Coates (2015) describes as "the process of washing the disparate tribes white" (p. 8)? The process of "whitewashing" (Brown et al., 2003) is all too familiar to historically marginalized communities in the United States. Lorde (2003) describes what members of oppressed groups have done to survive in U.S. society:

> Traditionally, in American society, it is the members of oppressed, objecti-fied groups who are expected to stretch out and bridge the gap between the actualities of our lives and the consciousness of our oppressor. For in order to survive, those of us for whom oppression in America is as American as apple pie have always had to be watchers, to become familiar with the lan-guage and manners of the oppressor, even sometimes adopting them for some illusion of protection.
>
> *(p. 315)*

Does including the culture of power promote equity or reproduce inequity? Should we exclude the culture of power? What would be the consequences and advantages? Is it possible to simultaneously provide access to the culture of power and resist it?

The Power of Culture

The FEET is steeped in the power of culture. This is strategic on our part to ensure that the treasures of historically marginalized communities are sustained and revitalized, and the humanity of these communities is acknowledged, valued, and nurtured.

First, the FEET includes culturally responsive instructional practices, as described in Chapter 4. The FEET dimensions, competencies, and indicators teem with practices that include CLD learners' familial, linguistic, and cultural capital, and their ways of knowing. Moreover, the FEET aligns with the tenets of CRTE.

Second, the FEET positions CLD learners at the center of teacher evaluation, thus challenging structures that reinforce their positionality at the margins. We position CLD learners at the center through culturally responsive approaches to teaching and learning.

Third, the main developer of the FEET is a Woman of Color. I, Salazar, am Mexican, American, Latinx, bilingual, and bicultural. I have embodied the culture of power, power of culture, and power of change in order to "succeed" in U.S. society. We, Salazar and Lerner, used our cultural lenses from the margins and the center to develop the FEET.

Fourth, the methodology used to create the FEET is steeped in literature emerging from Scholars of Color and Communities of Color. This is evidenced in Chapter 4 and the references and resources found in each chapter. Moreover, the FEET was developed through qualitative and quantitative research methodology. This aligns with CRT; it is a problem-centered approach and thus the problem guides the methodology (Dixson & Rousseau, 2005). Lynn and Parker (2006) state that "Critical race scholars are committed to conducting both qualitative and quantitative research that exposes racist beliefs, practices, and structures in schools and the broader society" (p.282).

Fifth, the FEET was developed to advance equity and social justice in student outcomes as measured by assessments of students' full potential. This aim goes far beyond any existing teacher evaluation model in education, and it challenges notions of how success should be defined, not just for historically marginalized communities, but for all communities. Although these assessments have yet to be developed, our hope it that the content of this book will spur change in this direction.

We positioned the power of culture at the center. Will it be consumed by the power of the dominant culture? Will it be co-opted and morph into an unrecognizable mass that no longer resembles the resources of historically marginalized communities? Will its positionality at the center fuel liberation or oppression?

Power of Change

One of the most vital contributions of the FEET is the inclusion of critical consciousness; the inclusion of this concept sets the FEET apart from existing teacher evaluation models. Critical consciousness is the process of "learning to perceive social, political, and economic contradictions, and to take action against the oppressive elements of reality" (Freire, 1970, p. 17). This construct is vital for the success of CLD learners because it helps them to: see the relevance in their learning, explore their identities, engage their resources, and be a part of a collective struggle to survive and thrive (Salazar, 2013). Through the development of critical consciousness, students learn to think critically about their own contributions and the contributions of society to inequity, injustice, and oppression, and take up the power to create change.

Coates (2015) captures the concept of critical consciousness in his book, *Between the World and Me*. He recalls that his education was defined by compliance. He was expected to: discipline his body, walk in single file, practice writing between the lines, work quietly, memorize, pack an extra number 2 pencil, and make no mistakes. Coates came to the realization that "schools did not reveal truths, they concealed them" (p. 27). He felt that he had to leave the classroom to discover himself and "grow into consciousness" (p. 107). He gets to the core of critical consciousness through the following advice to his son: "Attack every day of your brief bright life in struggle… be a conscious citizen of this terrible and beautiful world" (pp. 107–108).

Some would say it is unrealistic to strive for critical consciousness in teaching and learning. Some say, it is difficult, and even impossible, to awaken those who uphold the "Dream of being white" (Coates, 2015, p. 111). Others would say critical consciousness is strangled in standardized approaches to schooling. We do not agree or disagree with the critics. It matters not; this is the struggle we must engage in for the benefit of CLD learners.

Working Within and Against the System

The FEET works "simultaneously within and against the system" (Cochran-Smith, 2010, p. 459). However, Lorde (2003) questions the notion of mounting a counterinsurgency using oppressive structures. She renounces the "tools of a racist patriarchy" that allow for "only the most narrow parameters of change" (p. 95). Lorde explains:

> We must root out internalized patterns of oppression within ourselves if we are to move beyond the most superficial aspects of social change… The old patterns, no matter how cleverly rearranged to imitate progress, still condemn us to cosmetically altered repetitions of the same old exchanges… For we have, built into all of us, old blueprints of expectation and response, old structures of oppression, and these must be altered… For the master's tools will never dismantle the master's house.
>
> *(p. 21)*

We have mounted a counterinsurgency by questioning the masternarrative of objectivity and neutrality in teacher evaluation, and unveiling whiteness at the center of teacher evaluation. Nevertheless, has our use of the master's tools stymied our aim to disrupt inequity?

Scholars dedicated to race-based scholarship have struggled to mount counterinsurgencies. Urrieta and Villenas (2013) contend that the legitimacy of scholars doing race-based work is often questioned because they are perceived as biased and unscholarly. Welch and Pollard (2006) state that: "Researchers from disenfranchised populations find themselves silenced, or only listened to if they frame their ideas in language that is familiar and comfortable for those in the center" (p. 2). They add that "when the work is acknowledged, it is frequently characterized as worthwhile only to the degree to which the research moves both the researcher and the population studied from the margins to the center" (p. 3).

Have we been pressured to move to the center? Have we used the tools of the center in a way that abandons the power of the margins? Have we maintained the marginalization of CLD communities?

We want our work to positively impact the learning and development of CLD learners, particularly those who are the most vulnerable and have been left behind. While emerging CRTE models have the potential to make a positive impact in the current educational context, it is important that we continue to challenge structures of racial domination and oppression, interrogate whiteness, reconceptualize the margins, and dismantle boundaries. We assert that the FEET is a better alternative to current approaches to teacher evaluation, but it is not our best answer.

Moving Beyond the Boundaries of Teacher Evaluation

Given that "formal teacher evaluation is in its infancy" (Shinkfield & Stufflebeam, 2012, p. 3), this creates an opportunity to move beyond our self-imposed boundaries. We must start first by asking the question: Who should be concerned about the issues we have posed in this chapter? Shinkfield and Stufflebeam (2012) indicate that the major stakeholders in teacher evaluation are teachers, administrators, school board members, and teachers' organizations. If we adhere to this perspective, given the demographics of educators in the United States, the major stakeholders are overwhelmingly representatives of the whitestream. We challenge Shinkfield and Stufflebeam; we assert that the major stakeholders in teacher evaluation are students and parents, particularly those whose survival depends on education to be the greatest equalizer, as promised by Horace Mann (1848). It is vital to include historically marginalized CLD communities in finding the answers to the greatest challenges we face in education. Educators must acknowledge and take ownership of the fact that Communities of Color are currently at the margins of teacher evaluation. This must change. We advocate for communal and egalitarian strategies for teacher evaluation; what follows are examples:

- Use a variety of tools to assess students' full potential, including, but not limited to: teacher-generated assessments; standardized tests; student-generated artifacts (e.g., spoken word poetry, plays, artistic and creative works); *testimonios*; performance assessments; social justice simulations and projects; and parent/community feedback.
- Engage youth and communities in participatory action research projects to define equitable and excellent teaching and develop alternative approaches to assessing teacher performance and student learning.
- Position students and families at the center of teacher evaluation activity by developing models that capture their voices and lived experiences.

- Engage students in developing surveys, and other alternatives, that yield data on teacher performance and student learning.
- Engage diverse teachers in envisioning novel approaches to teacher evaluation that develop teachers' and students' full potential.
- Advocate for teacher evaluation models that include the perspective of diverse stakeholders such as: students, families, community members, school leaders, teachers, counselors, support staff, custodial staff, and higher education faculty.
- Use alternative terms for teacher evaluation, such as: "teacher and student development," or "teaching and learning *colectivo*" (cooperative) to drive efforts for collaboration and support.

Our main objective in writing this book is to equip you with insights and questions to challenge educational systems that maintain inequality. Teacher evaluation can be a form of advocacy for historically marginalized communities, but we need a many-pronged approach to equity and excellence in education. We ask you to struggle with the following critical questions that emerge from the content of this book:

- Does the use of traditional paradigms fortify the dominant culture and instantiate hegemonic instruments of oppression?
- In moving the margins to the center, do those at the center become marginalized?
- Does moving the margins to the center result in positioning historically marginalized communities at the center of whiteness?
- How does educational reform create disruption as opposed to transformation?
- Do traditional paradigms reproduce rather than interrupt oppression?
- How do we acquiesce to the realities in education and yet imagine the possibilities?
- How can we move systems from the center to the margins?
- How can we move beyond the boundaries to envision approaches that foster transformation? Is this even possible?

We must go even further than reflection however. We must engage in praxis, or "reflection and action upon the world in order to transform it" (Freire, 1970, p. 36). Within this space, Lorde (2017) challenges us to consider that "the true focus of revolutionary change is never merely the oppressive situations which we seek to escape, but the piece of the oppressor which is planted deep within each of us, and which knows only the oppressor's tactics, the oppressor's relationships" (p. 22).

To pursue revolutionary change, we embrace the *radical imaginary*, a concept that emerges from the philosopher Castoriadis (1983). The radical imaginary represents the "human mind's capacity to create" (Tovar-Restrepo, 2012, p. 34). In the radical imaginary, creation is: a strategy of dissent; transgression of limits;

and a new space for thinking, feeling, acting, questioning, analyzing, and resisting (Ruiz, 1994). Creation is not imitative or reproductive, predetermined, or a logical consequence of an existing order (Tovar-Restrepo, 2012, p. 52). Societies must be wary of predetermined principles or standards that destroy creative imagination and close off the possibility of real change and revolution (Bilus Abaffy, 2012).

How can we infuse the radical imaginary into teacher evaluation when it is perceived as one of the master's tools? In discussing the contents of this book with scholars and educators, some outright rejected the notion of teacher evaluation because they believe it promotes uniformity, standardization, and whitification. We heard the following concerns:

- Standardized approaches cannot lead to substantive change because they are prescriptive and restrictive; limit teacher agency, individuality, and efficacy; and ultimately push good teachers out.
- It is not possible to create change in a system that standardizes inequity and resists equity and social justice.
- Even if you position CLD learners at the center of teacher evaluation, the system will ultimately resist change and revert to other mechanisms to maintain White power and privilege.

We hear you. We have more questions than answers. Yet, we strongly believe that teacher evaluation, or development, can foster equitable and excellent teaching for our nation's children. Rather than opting out, we must continue to grapple with the aforementioned challenges.

We acknowledge that the struggle for change is hard. Some opt out of the struggle, yet they consider themselves to be good intentioned. Coates (2015) sends this message to the good intentioned:

> It doesn't matter that the "intentions" of individual educators were noble. Forget about intentions. What any institution, or its agents, "intend" for you is secondary... A very large number of Americans will do all they can to preserve the Dream. No one directly proclaimed that schools were designed to sanctify failure and destruction. But a great number of educators spoke of "personal responsibility" in a country authored and sustained by a criminal irresponsibility. The point of this language of "intention" and "personal responsibility" is broad exoneration. Mistakes were made. Bodies were broken. People were enslaved. We meant well. We tried our best. "Good intention" is a hall pass through history, a sleeping pill that ensures the Dream.
>
> *(p. 33)*

Did we have good intentions in writing this book? Did we go far enough to challenge the status quo of teacher evaluation and agitate for change? We want you to answer that question. More importantly, we want you to ask and answer the question: What is the radical imaginary in teaching, learning, and teacher evaluation? It is our greatest desire that this chapter will provoke educators to collectively engage in dialogue that explores this essential question. We concur with Freire (1970): "Knowledge emerges only through invention and re-invention, through the restless, impatient, continuing, hopeful inquiry human beings pursue in the world, with the world, and with each other" (p. 244).

This book is not an end; it is a beginning. We ask you to begin the "remix" (Ladson-Billings, 2014), reimagine our ideas, and reinvent teacher evaluation. We call on those who experience the multiplicity, hybridity, and complexity of the liminal space between the margins, the center, and beyond. Such boundary spanners are aptly prepared to envisage the possible, and "seize the arrogance to create outrageously, *soñar* wildly, for the world becomes as we dream it" (Anzaldúa & Keating, 2002, p. 575). Let us move even beyond dreams. Let us embrace the struggle, collectively, and... transgress.

Summary and Implications

In this chapter, we engaged in a critical examination of teacher evaluation. We resurrected CRT to interrogate teacher evaluation. We advanced the notion that this book marks the beginning of critical questions about who is, and is not, being served by teacher evaluation. We ask you to consider what was, what is, and what can be in teacher evaluation. We encourage you to move beyond the boundaries to a radical imaginary. We call on you to struggle. We call on you to transgress.

Critical Questions

The following critical questions are intended to extend your comprehension and help you relate the concepts to your own practice.

1. Identify what aspects of CRT made an impact on you and describe why.
2. What ideas do you have to push teacher evaluation beyond the boundaries?
3. Brainstorm alternative ways to develop and assess equitable and excellent teaching.
4. Describe one way you can challenge the status quo of teacher evaluation.
5. Complete the following sentence stem: If I had a magic wand, I would make teacher evaluation _____.

Resources for Further Reflection and Study

The following supplemental resources are intended to spur your personal and professional reflection, application of the concepts in your own context, and community outreach efforts.

Print

Cochran-Smith, M. (2004). *Walking the road: Race diversity and social justice in teacher education.* New York: NY: Teachers College Press.

hooks, b. (2014). *Teaching to transgress.* New York, NY: Routledge.

Lorde, A. (2003). The master's tools will never dismantle the master's house. In R. Lewis & S. Mills (Eds.), *Feminist postcolonial theory: A reader* (pp. 25–28). New York, NY: Routledge.

Ovando, M. N. (2001). Teachers' perceptions of a learner-centered teacher evaluation system. *Journal of Personnel Evaluation in Education, 15*(3), 213–231.

Smith, L. T. (1999). *Decolonizing methodologies: Research and indigenous peoples.* New York, NY: Zed Books.

Tyack, D., & Cuban, L. (1995). *Tinkering toward utopia: A century of public school reform.* Cambridge, MA: Harvard University Press.

Web

- bell hooks
  Teaching to transgress
  Retrieved from https://academictrap.files.wordpress.com/2015/03/bell-hooks-teaching-to-transgress.pdf

- The University of Arizona Poetry Center
  An interview with Gloria Anzaldua
  https://poetry.arizona.edu/blog/interview-gloria-anzaldúa

- YPAR Hub
  Youth-led participatory action research
  http://yparhub.berkeley.edu

Media

- Charlie Rose
  bell hooks interview
  https://charlierose.com/videos/12053

- Get Inclusive
  There is no hierarchy of oppressions by Audre Lorde
  www.youtube.com/watch?v=i1pNsLsHsfs

- The Teaching Channel
  Multiple measures of effective teaching
  www.teachingchannel.org/videos/improving-teacher-performance

- U.S. Third World Feminism
  Nepantla: Mixing it up
  www.youtube.com/watch?v=zmiSaXbtPfk

Learning Opportunities

1. Create an emoji or bitmoji to illustrate the following:
    *   How does teacher evaluation make you feel?
    *   What is the impact of teacher evaluation on students?
    *   What is the impact of teacher evaluation on teachers?
    *   What is the future of teacher evaluation?
2. Create a meme for teacher evaluation.
3. Explore international examples of teacher evaluation models. What are their strengths and weaknesses? What can we learn from these examples to help us push the boundaries of teacher evaluation?
4. With your peers, brainstorm alternatives to teacher evaluation. Would you use a different term? What would be the components? What would be the process? Who would decide what is included?
5. Reflect on the statement by Lorde (2003): "For the master's tools will never dismantle the master's house. They may allow us to temporarily beat him at his own game, but they will never enable us to bring about genuine change." Do you agree or disagree with this statement?

Community Engagement Opportunities

1. Invite a diverse group of stakeholders to create an artistic representation of equitable and excellent teaching and display this in your school building.
2. Meet with members of community organizations that serve historically marginalized Communities of Color. Ask them to help you convene a diverse group of community members. Ask them to respond to the following questions:
    *   How should teachers be evaluated?
    *   What competencies should teachers demonstrate?
    *   Who should be included in the design of teacher evaluation models?
3. Gather a group of 10–15 diverse students. Ask them to create a method to assess good teaching. Pose the question: What does good teaching look like? How can we develop an assessment or test of good teaching? How should teachers be helped to develop good teaching skills?
4. Invite a diverse group of stakeholders, including educators, students, community members, politicians, and policy makers, to participate in a forum to interrogate teacher evaluation and identify solutions.

References

Anzaldúa, G., & Keating, A. (2002). *This bridge we call home*. New York, NY: Routledge.

Ayers, W., Kumashiro, K., Meiners, E., Quinn, T., & Stovall, D. (2016). *Teaching toward democracy 2e: Educators as agents of change*. New York, NY: Routledge.

Bilus Abaffy, N. (2012). The radical tragic imaginary: Castoriadis on Aeschylus & Sophocles. *Journal of Natural and Social Philosophy, 8*(2), 34–59.

Brown, M. K., Carnoy, M., Currie, E., Oppenheimer, D. B., Wellman, D., & Shultz, M. M. (2003). *Whitewashing race: The myth of a color-blind society*. Berkeley & Los Angeles, CA: University of California Press.

Castoriadis, C. (1983). The Greek polis and the creation of democracy. *Graduate Faculty Philosophy Journal, 9*(2), 79–115.

Coates, T. (2015). *Between the world and me*. New York, NY: Speigel & Grau.

Cochran-Smith, M. (2010). Toward a theory of teacher education for social justice. In A. Hargreaves, A. Lieberman, M. Fullan, & D. Hopkins (Eds.), *Second international handbook of educational change* (pp. 445–467). New York, NY: Springer International Handbooks of Education.

Darling-Hammond, L. (2012). *Creating a comprehensive system for evaluating and supporting effective teaching*. Stanford Center for Opportunity Policy in Education. Retrieved from https://edpolicy.stanford.edu/sites/default/files/publications/creating-comprehensive-system-evaluating-and-supporting-effective-teaching.pdf

Dixson, A., & Rousseau, C. K. (2005). And we are still not saved: Critical race theory in education ten years later. *Race, Ethnicity, and Education, 8*(1), 7–27

Fisher-Ari, T., Kavanagh, K. M., & Martin, A. (2017). Sisyphean neoliberal reforms: The intractable mythology of student growth and achievement master narratives within the testing and TFA era. *Journal of Education Policy, 32*(3), 255–280.

Freire, P. (1970). *Cultural action for freedom*. Boston, MA: Harvard Educational Review.

hooks, b. (1989). *Yearnings: Race, gender and cultural politics*. Brooklyn, NY: South End Press.

Ladson Billings, G. (2014). Culturally relevant pedagogy 2.0: Aka the remix. *Harvard Educational Review, 84*(1), 74–84.

Lawless, E. J. (2003). Transforming the master narrative: How women shift the religious subject. *Frontiers: A Journal of Women Studies, 24*(1), 61–75.

Lorde, A. (2003). The master's tools will never dismantle the master's house. In R. Lewis & S. Mills (Eds.), *Feminist postcolonial theory: A reader* (pp. 25–27). New York, NY: Routledge.

Lorde, A. (2017). Age, race, class, and sex: Women redefining difference. In B. Kime Scott, S. E. Cayleff, A. Donadey, & I. Lara (Eds.), *Women in culture: An intersectional anthology for gender and women's studies* (pp. 16–23). Oxford, UK: John Wiley & Sons, Ltd.

Lynn, M., & Parker, L. (2006). Critical race studies in education: Examining a decade of research on U.S. schools. *The Urban Review, 38*(4), 257–290.

Mann, H. (1848). *Report No. 12 of the Massachusetts Board*. Retrieved from https://usa.usembassy.de/etexts/democrac/16.htm

Mirra, N., Garcia, A., & Morrell, E. (2015). *Doing youth participatory action research: Transforming inquiry with researchers, educators, and students*. New York, NY: Routledge.

Ruiz, L. E. J. (1994). Toward a new radical imaginary: Constructing transformative cultural practices. *Alternatives, 19*, 247–261.

Salazar, M. (2013). A humanizing pedagogy: Reinventing the principles and practice of education as a journey toward liberation. *Review of Research in Education, 37*(1), 121–148.

Shinkfield, A. J., & Stufflebeam, D. L. (2012). *Teacher evaluation: Guide to effective practice*. Berlin, Germany: Springer Science & Business Media.

Tovar-Restrepo, M. (2012). *Castoriadis, Foucault, and autonomy: New approaches to subjectivity, society, and social change*. New York, NY: Bloomsbury.

Urrieta, L., & Villenas, S. A. (2013). The legacy of Derrick Bell and Latino/a education: A critical race testimonio. *Race Ethnicity and Education, 16*(4), 514–535.

Welch, O. M., & Pollard, D. S. (2006). Women researchers of color: Have we come a long way? In D. S. Pollard & O. M. Welch (Eds.), *From center to margins: The importance of self-definition in research* (pp. 1–6). Albany, NY: State University.

AUTHOR BIOS

María del Carmen Salazar is an Associate Professor of Curriculum and Instruction and Teacher Education in the Morgridge College of Education at the University of Denver. She is a former secondary social studies and bilingual education teacher. Her academic degrees include: Ph.D. in Social, Multicultural, and Bilingual Foundations of Education, M.A. in Curriculum and Instruction, teaching certificate in secondary Social Studies, and B.A. in Psychology. Salazar has authored numerous publications on humanizing pedagogy, equitable and excellent teaching, culturally responsive teaching, and college access and success for Latinx youth. She has given over 100 scholarly international, national, and regional presentations. Salazar served on the Colorado Quality Teachers Commission. She served on the Interstate Teacher Assessment and Support Consortium (InTASC), a national collaborative to revise standards for teacher licensure, assessment, and development. She was a key contributor in the development of the 2011 InTASC Model Core Teaching Standards and 2013 Learning Progressions. She currently serves on the Council for the Accreditation of Educator Preparation (CAEP) Board of Directors and the CAEP Equity and Diversity Committee. She also currently serves as an Associate Editor for the *Journal of Teacher Education*. She is the recipient of the 2018 American Educational Research Association (AERA) Division K Innovations in Research on Equity and Social Justice in Teacher Education award.

Jessica Lerner is an Assistant Professor of the Practice and the Director of Teacher Education in the Morgridge College of Education at the University of Denver. She is a former elementary school teacher, instructional coach, and teacher evaluator. Her professional interests include improving teacher effectiveness through pre-service preparation, coaching, and mentoring. Ms. Lerner's academic degrees include: EDS in Urban School Leadership, M.A. in Industrial & Organizational Psychology, and B.A. in Biology. She is currently a Ph.D candidate in Curriculum and Instruction at the University of Denver. Her areas of expertise include coaching, curriculum development, teacher evaluation, and teacher preparation.

APPENDICES

List of Appendices

Appendix A: FEET Equity-based Words
Appendix B: FEET Dimensions, Competencies, and Indicators
Appendix C: FEET Classroom Observation Instrument
Appendix D: FEET Supervisor Training Protocol
Appendix E: FEET Standards Matrix

Appendix A: FEET Equity-based Words

abilities	academic language	advocacy
agents of change	asset orientation	civil rights
class	codeswitch	college and career
community	critical	critical consciousness
cultural competence	culturally responsive	culture/cultural
diverse/diversity	eliminate bias	emergent bilingual (EB)
English language learner (ELL)	equity/equitable	ethnicity
gender	gifted	global
heritage language	home language	IEP
inclusive	language	oppression
race	religion	sexual orientation
social justice	special needs	stereotypes
student voice/choice	systemic change	vernaculars

Appendix B: FEET Dimensions, Competencies, and Indicators

Dimensions	Competencies	Indicators
Engage students in an inclusive and supportive learning community.	1.1 Develop affirming relationships with students and families.	E.1 Express value, respect, and asset perspectives of students' language(s), culture(s), and communities.
		E.2 Foster positive rapport (e.g., patience, caring) with students and facilitate positive interactions between students.
		E.3 Communicate belief in capacity of all learners to achieve at high levels (e.g., college and career readiness, high expectations, growth mindset).
		E.4 Collaborate with parents/guardians/ families to identify student interests and needs and set shared goals for student learning and development.
	1.2 Maintain an equitable classroom environment.	E.5 Facilitate classroom norms and routines, in collaboration with students/ families, that promote a positive learning community (e.g., clear expectations, positive reinforcement, individualized support).
		E.6 Guide student behaviors through teacher moves (e.g., tone, movement, positioning, cues, key phrases, direct speech) and a system of incentives that promotes student empowerment.
		E.7 Use predictable transition strategies to maintain students' focus on learning.
		E.8 Use a systematic process to ensure students have necessary materials for learning.

(continued)

(Cont.)

Dimensions	Competencies	Indicators
	1.3 Actively engage students in learning.	E.9 Use a variety of active engagement strategies to ensure each student participates through discussion and movement (e.g., interactive technology, assistive technology, total physical response, call-and-response, storytelling, props, simulations, scenarios, games, music/rhythm, arts integration, visual and performing arts).
		E.10 Incorporate modalities that facilitate content learning (e.g., auditory, visual, kinesthetic, tactile, and intra/ interpersonal, musical, naturalistic, logical, verbal, technological).
		E.11 Provide opportunities for students to experience joyful learning that includes discovery, application, collaboration, and/or advocacy for social justice issues.
		E.12 Demonstrate student-centered approach by consistently incorporating student voice, choice, teaching, and leadership.
Plan rigorous, culturally responsive, standards- and outcome-based lesson and unit plans.	2.1 Use culturally responsive backward design curriculum planning to develop units.	P.1 Identify big ideas, essential questions, enduring understandings, and social justice themes that are relevant to students' interests and diversity.
		P.2 Create engaging units of study that are aligned to relevant content, language, and college and career readiness standards.
		P.3 Supplement or adapt district-approved curriculum to reflect student diversity, and promote cultural competence and critical consciousness.
		P.4 Include materials and resources that reflect students' cultures and include a variety of cultures.

(Cont.)

Dimensions	Competencies	Indicators
	2.2 Design measurable, challenging, and culturally responsive lessons.	P.5 Design rigorous, relevant, and authentic unit performance tasks.
		P.6 Develop a sequence of lessons aligned to unit goals and social justice pursuits.
		P.7 Set clear, rigorous, measureable content and language objective (CLO) based on unit goals.
		P.8 Create a logical sequence with each lesson component aligning to objectives and assessments.
		P.9 Develop rationale that connects lesson objective with unit goals, students' lives, real-world application, and social justice pursuits.
		P.10 Incorporate topics that draw on student diversity (e.g., race, ethnicity, culture, gender, class, abilities, sexual orientation, religion) and include the contributions of diverse populations.
		P.11 Provide opportunities for students to identify oppression locally and globally, counteract stereotypes, develop critical consciousness, and see themselves as agents of change.
	2.3 Integrate culturally responsive assessment into planning.	P.12 Analyze assessments for validity, reliability, and bias (e.g., culture, language, gender, class, religion, etc.).
		P.13 Include a variety of assessment tools (e.g., formative, summative, authentic, project-based) to gather data on student learning.
		P.14 Analyze standardized and classroom-based student assessment data to set SMART learning targets.
		P.15 Use assessment data to identify individual and subgroup (e.g., EB/ELL, special needs, gifted) learning goals and design differentiated learning experiences.

(continued)

(Cont.)

Dimensions	Competencies	Indicators
		P.16 Use technology to collect, track, analyze, and share assessment data with students and families, and analyze trends in student progress to make planning decisions.
	2.4 Demonstrate knowledge of content and student development.	P.17 Analyze current research related to content pedagogy, and identify implications for teaching, learning, and equity. P.18 Understand how students' typical and atypical development (e.g., cognitive, socioemotional, linguistic) impacts learning. P.19 Identify prerequisite content and language knowledge and skills, and typical student errors, misconceptions, and challenges. P.20 Use knowledge of content to plan rigorous and relevant units and lessons that develop literacy and numeracy.
Teach equitably by setting high expectations and providing support for student growth and development.	3.1 Set context for lesson.	T.1 Post, preview, and review concise, rigorous, and measurable content and language objective (CLO). T.2 Engage students in discussing lesson rationale that connects content to students' diversity, prior content knowledge and skills, and interests. T.3 Promote real-world application of content in local, national, and global contexts. T.4 Clearly define performance expectations orally and in writing using student-friendly language.
	3.2 Facilitate clear and rigorous learning experiences.	T.5 Provide clear, concise, and relevant explanations of content (e.g., mental models, culturally responsive examples, accessible language). T.6 Use gradual release lesson cadence (I do, we do, you do) to scaffold students' independent application of learning. T.7 Align learning experiences to objectives.

Dimensions	Competencies	Indicators
		T.8 Adequately pace learning experiences by attending to student learning cues and progress on learning tasks.
	3.3 Promote rigorous academic talk.	T.9 Promote higher-order thinking skills by providing opportunities for students to use academic language, make claims, and articulate reasoning.
		T.10 Facilitate academic conversations by posing high-level questions, and asking students to pose questions and explain their thinking (e.g., elaborate, clarify, provide examples, build on or challenge ideas, paraphrase, synthesize).
		T.11 Set discussion norms with students and facilitate student conversations that foster critical consciousness (e.g., analyze multiple perspectives, ask critical questions, advocate for systemic change).
	3.4 Make content and language comprehensible for all learners.	T.12 Incorporate students' home language (e.g., heritage language, vernaculars, code-switching, translanguaging) into instruction and include materials in students' home language.
		T.13 Preview vocabulary to support understanding of concepts and context, and development of academic language.
		T.14 Incorporate sensory, graphic, and interactive supports (e.g., technology, visuals, manipulative/ realia, key vocabulary, graphic organizers, concept maps, sentence stems, total physical response, modeling, and cooperative learning).
	3.5 Use formal and informal assessment data to monitor student progress toward learning targets.	T.15 Collect data on individual student progress toward content and language objective and analyze data to adjust instruction for individuals and subgroups (e.g., EB/ELL, special needs, gifted).

(continued)

(Cont.)

Dimensions	Competencies	Indicators
		T.16 Engage students in continually assessing their own progress toward unit/lesson objectives and personal/ group goals.
		T.17 Provide students with frequent, timely, specific, and individual/ group feedback.
		T.18 Frequently check for understanding and adjust instruction according to evidence of student learning.
	3.6 Differentiate instruction to challenge students and meet diverse student needs.	T.19 Use assessment data to differentiate instruction according to student needs (e.g., language levels, special needs, socioemotional needs, learning modalities).
		T.20 Implement flexible grouping strategies to meet diverse student needs.
		T.21 Provide options for differentiated content, learning experiences, and/ or assessments that allow for student choice and expression of cultural ways of knowing.
		T.22 Collaborate with support specialists to develop and apply specific accommodations for individual students based on language needs, IEPs, and other legal requirements.
Lead by exemplifying professionalism and community advocacy.	4.1 Meet professional standards of practice.	L.1 Adhere to ethical and legal responsibilities for students' learning, behavior, safety, confidentiality, and civil rights as specified in local, state, and federal statutes.
		L.2 Maintain professional demeanor and communication in accordance with school, district, and/or university policy.

(Cont.)

Dimensions	Competencies	Indicators
		L.3 Collaborate with community and school partners to support students' needs (e.g., parents/guardians, community organizations, school psychologists, counselors, social workers, nurses).
	4.2 Demonstrate growth and commitment to students and communities.	L.4 Recognize own biases and how these affect teaching and learning, and take action to monitor and eliminate bias. L.5 Use feedback and data to set clear and measurable goals to improve instruction and promote student learning and development. L.6 Participate in school, district, and community initiatives and advocate for community needs (e.g., professional development opportunities, school events, community engagement).

Appendix C: FEET Classroom Observation Instrument

Apprentice teacher:	Supervisor/coach:	Date:	Grade/content:

Dimension	Competency and indicators	Feedback and evidence	Score (1–4)
ENGAGE Engage students in an inclusive and supportive learning community.	**1.1 Develop affirming relationships with students and families.** • Express value, respect, and asset perspectives of students' language(s), culture(s), and communities. • Foster positive rapport (e.g., patience, caring) with students and facilitate positive interactions between students. • Communicate belief in capacity of all learners to achieve at high levels (e.g., college and career readiness, high expectations, growth mindset). • Collaborate with parents/guardians/families to identify student interests and needs and set shared goals for student learning and development.	• Perspectives of students • Positive rapport • Belief in capacity • Collaborate with parents/guardians/families	
	1.2 Maintain an equitable classroom environment. • Facilitate classroom norms and routines, in collaboration with students/families, that promote a positive learning community (e.g., clear expectations, positive reinforcement, individualized support).	• Classroom norms and routines • Guide student behaviors	

(Cont.)

Apprentice teacher:	Supervisor/coach:	Date:	Grade/content:	
Dimension	Competency and indicators	Feedback and evidence	Score (1–4)	
	• Guide student behaviors through teacher moves (e.g., tone, movement, positioning, cues, key phrases, direct speech) and a system of incentives that promotes student empowerment.	• Transition strategies		
	• Use predictable transition strategies to maintain students' focus on learning. • Use a systematic process to ensure students have necessary materials for learning.	• Materials for learning		
	1.3 Actively engage students in learning. • Use a variety of active engagement strategies to ensure each student participates through discussion and movement (e.g., interactive technology, assistive technology, total physical response, call-and-response, storytelling, props, simulations, scenarios, games, music/rhythm, arts integration, visual and performing arts). • Incorporate modalities that facilitate content learning (e.g., auditory, visual, kinesthetic, tactile, and intra/interpersonal, musical, naturalistic, logical, verbal, technological).	• Engagement strategies • Modalities • Joyful learning		

(continued)

(Cont.)

Apprentice teacher:	Supervisor/coach:	Date:	Grade/content:	
Dimension	Competency and indicators	Feedback and evidence	Score (1–4)	
	• Provide opportunities for students to experience joyful learning that includes discovery, application, collaboration, and/ or advocacy for social justice issues. • Demonstrate student-centered approach by consistently incorporating student voice, choice, teaching, and leadership.	• Student-centered approaches	
TEACH Teach equitably by setting high expectations and providing support for student growth and development.	**3.1 Set context for lesson.** • Post, preview, and review concise, rigorous, and measurable content and language objective (CLO). • Engage students in discussing lesson rationale that connects content to students' diversity, prior content knowledge and skills, and interests. • Promote real-world application of content in local, national, and global contexts. • Clearly define performance expectations orally and in writing using student-friendly language.	• CLO • Rationale • Real-world application • Performance expectations	
	3.2 Facilitate clear and rigorous learning experiences. • Provide clear, concise, and relevant explanations of content (e.g., mental models, culturally responsive examples, accessible language).	• Explanation of content • Gradual release	

(Cont.)

Apprentice teacher: *Supervisor/coach:* *Date:* *Grade/content:*			
Dimension	*Competency and indicators*	*Feedback and evidence*	*Score (1–4)*
	• Use gradual release lesson cadence (I do, we do, you do) to scaffold students' independent application of learning. • Align learning experiences to objectives. • Adequately pace learning experiences by attending to student learning cues and progress on learning tasks.	• Alignment of objectives and experiences • Pacing	
	3.3 Promote rigorous academic talk. • Promote higher-order thinking skills by providing opportunities for students to use academic language, make claims, and articulate reasoning. • Facilitate academic conversations by posing high-level questions, and asking students to pose questions and explain their thinking (e.g., elaborate, clarify, provide examples, build on or challenge ideas, paraphrase, synthesize). • Set discussion norms with students and facilitate student conversations that foster critical consciousness (e.g., analyze multiple perspectives, ask critical questions, advocate for systemic change).	Higher-order thinking skills • Academic conversations • Critical conversations	

(*continued*)

(Cont.)

Apprentice teacher:	Supervisor/coach:	Date:	Grade/content:	
Dimension	Competency and indicators	Feedback and evidence	Score (1–4)	
	3.4 Make content and language comprehensible for all learners. • Incorporate students' home language (e.g., heritage language, vernaculars, code-switching, translanguaging) into instruction and include materials in students' home language. • Preview vocabulary to support understanding of concepts and context, and development of academic language.	• Home language • Vocabulary • Supports		
	• Incorporate sensory, graphic, and interactive supports (e.g., technology, visuals, manipulative/realia, key vocabulary, graphic organizers, concept maps, sentence stems, total physical response, modeling, and cooperative learning).			
	3.5 Use formal and informal assessment data to monitor student progress toward learning targets. • Collect data on individual student progress toward CLO and analyze data to adjust instruction for individuals and subgroups (e.g., EB/ELL, special needs, gifted).	• Use data to adjust instruction • Students assess own progress		

(Cont.)

Apprentice teacher:	Supervisor/coach:	Date:	Grade/content:
Dimension	Competency and indicators	Feedback and evidence	Score (1–4)
	• Engage students in continually assessing their own progress toward unit/lesson objectives and personal/group goals. • Provide students with frequent, timely, specific, and individual/group feedback. • Frequently check for understanding and adjust instruction according to evidence of student learning.	• Feedback • Checks for understanding	
	3.6 Differentiate instruction to challenge students and meet diverse student needs. • Use assessment data to differentiate instruction according to student needs (e.g., language levels, special needs, learning modalities, socioemotional).	• Use data to differentiate instruction • Flexible grouping strategies	
	• Implement flexible grouping strategies to meet diverse student needs. • Provide options for differentiated content, learning experiences, and/or assessments that allow for student choice and expression of cultural ways of knowing. • Collaborate with support specialists to develop and apply specific accommodations for individual students based on language needs, IEPs, and other legal requirements.	• Options, choice, expression • Accomodations	

(continued)

(Cont.)

Apprentice teacher:	Supervisor/coach:	Date:	Grade/content:

Dimension	Competency and indicators	Feedback and evidence	Score (1–4)
LEAD Lead by exemplifying professionalism and community advocacy.	**4.1 Meet professional standards of practice.** • Adhere to ethical and legal responsibilities for students' learning, behavior, safety, confidentiality, and civil rights as specified in local, state, and federal statutes. • Maintain professional demeanor and communication in accordance with school, district, and/or university policy. • Collaborate with community and school partners to support students' needs (e.g., parents/guardians, community organizations, school psychologists, counselors, social workers, nurses).	• Ethical and legal responsibilites • Professional demeanor and communication • Collaboration	
	4.2 Demonstrate growth and commitment to students and communities. • Recognize own biases and how these affect teaching and learning, and take action to monitor and eliminate bias. Use feedback and data to set clear and measurable goals to improve instruction and promote student learning and development. • Participate in school, district, and community initiatives and advocate for community needs (e.g., professional development opportunities, school events, community engagement).	• Biases • Goal-setting • Participation and advocacy	

Focus on student growth and development: What CLO did you target? What progress did students make toward meeting the CLO? How do you know?	Objective: Students' progress toward objective: Evidence:		
Strengths: What are your areas of strength?	Apprentice Teacher:		Supervisor/Coach:
Areas of growth: What are your areas of growth?	Apprentice Teacher:		Supervisor/Coach:
Interventions to next level of performance: What do you need to develop to the next level? What do your students need?			
Goals: What are three goals to improve your instruction and increase student growth and development?	Former Goals and Progress:		Goals:

Overall performance rating:	Unsatisfactory(1) 1 or more unsatisfactory	Developing (2) 1–11 developing 0–2 proficient or advanced	Proficient (3) 9–11 proficient or advanced 0–2 developing *must meet proficiency in 1.2 & 3.1	Advanced (4) 9–11 advanced 0–2 proficient 0 developing

Note. The Plan competencies are not included because they are not observable in a classroom observation. These competencies are assessed in the program curriculum.

Appendix D: FEET Supervisor Training Protocol

Supervisor Observation Protocols

The section that follows describes the procedures for implementing FEET classroom observation instruments in K–12 classrooms. The FEET requires that observers identify a score (1–4) for each of the competencies based on the degree to which apprentice teacher behaviors and apprentice teacher–student interactions are indicative of levels of performance identified as: unsatisfactory (1), developing (2), proficient (3), and advanced (4).

Each quarter (Fall, Winter, Spring), supervisors will complete a minimum of two formal evaluations, including:

- Observe a full lesson (30–90 minutes).
- Score each competency (1–unsatisfactory, 2–developing, 3–proficient, 4–advanced).
- Complete summative and formative parts of the observation instrument.
- Provide an overall performance rating (unsatisfactory, developing, proficient, advanced) using the following criteria:

Unsatisfactory (1)	Developing (2)	Proficient (3)	Advanced (4)
1 or more unsatisfactory	1–11 developing 0–2 proficient or advanced	9–11 proficient or advanced 0–2 developing *must reach 1.2 & 3.1	9–11 advanced 0–2 proficient 0 developing

- Use the FEET rubrics to distinguish levels of performance.
- Conduct a debrief session with the apprentice teacher (30–45 minutes).

Considerations:
- Focus on teacher behaviors, students' behaviors, evidence of students' progress toward meeting the content and language objective, and evidence of students' growth and development.
- Document specific evidence of indicators of performance. Script actual language. Be concise. Use bullet points. Start with verbs.

- It is not necessary to see all indicators of the competency to score at a particular range; however, the apprentice teacher should demonstrate behaviors that exemplify a majority of the indicators listed.
- Provide formative feedback that is explicit, targeted, and actionable.
- Set two to three specific, measureable, attainable, relevant, and timely (SMART) goals.
- Be aware of bias that may impact evaluations:
  - be cautious of overinflating ratings to adjust for classroom challenges;
  - avoid rating based on what apprentice teachers might have done and focus on what they actually did;
  - be conscious of bias based on personal values and prior experience with the candidate; and
  - be aware of evaluator drift, or the decline of rater scoring accuracy over time.
- The documentation of struggling students will be an important factor should we decide to "exit" a student from the program. Unsatisfactory scores on any fieldwork evaluation will result in specific intervention steps by the supervisor and the program coordinator.

Supervisor Reliability Training

Each quarter, supervisors meet for two to three hours to assess and discuss the FEET instruments, protocols, and procedures. Specifically, supervisors view three 20-minute videotaped segments of proficient scale level instruction to illustrate benchmark performance, and code the observation based on the FEET rubrics of performance. The segments are consensus coded by the two faculty experts. After practice scoring, the faculty experts provide rationales to describe specific evidence tied to scale-level indicators and give individualized feedback based on supervisor questions. The consensus ratings set a minimum threshold to establish the accuracy of ratings among observers. This practice ensures reliability of coding across supervisors, or inter-rater reliability. Inter-rater reliability is defined as "the extent to which two independent observers assign the same score or set of scores to the same classroom session" (National Governors Association, 2011, p. 9). If observers do not meet the reliability threshold (within one point of consensus codes) of 80%, additional training will be provided using targeted training materials.

Supervisor Feedback

Supervisors are encouraged to provide program faculty with regular feedback on the FEET evaluation model based on an evaluation rubric scorecard adapted from the TNTP (2011):

FEET evaluation model scorecard:		Points (1–3)
Covers essential performances that indicate equitable and excellent teaching 3=Meets, 2=Approaches, 1=Does not meet		
Sets high expectations for teacher apprentices and K-12 students 3=Meets, 2=Approaches, 1=Does not meet		
Includes a focus on evidence of K-12 student learning 3=Meets, 2=Approaches, 1=Does not meet		
Uses clear and precise language 3=Meets, 2=Approaches, 1=Does not meet		
Is concise and easy to use 3=Meets, 2=Approaches, 1=Does not meet		
Overall score		/15
Feedback:	*Areas of strength*	
	Areas of growth	
	Specific recommendations	

References

National Governors Association. Center for Best Practice (2011). *Issue brief: Teacher evaluator training and certification: Lessons learned from the Measures of Effective Teaching Project.* Washington DC: Author.

TNTP (2011). *Rating a teacher observation tool: Five ways to ensure classroom observations are focused and rigorous.* Retrieved from http://tntp.org/assets/documents/TNTP_RatingATeacherObservationTool_Feb2011.pdf?files/TNTP_RatingATeacherObservation Tool_Feb2011.pdf

Appendix E: FEET Standards Matrix

The FEET is aligned to the 2011 Interstate Teacher Assessment and Support Consortium (InTASC) Model Core Teaching Standards, the Colorado Teacher Quality Standards (CTQS), and the National Board of Professional Teaching Standards (NBPTS). The state standards may be substituted in this matrix.

Dimension	Competency	Indicator	
ENGAGE Engage students in an inclusive and supportive learning community. [InTASC 1, 2, 3; CTQS 2; NBPTS 1, 3]	1.1 Develop affirming relationships with students and families. [InTASC 2; CTQS 2; NBPTS 1, 3]	E.1	Express value, respect, and asset perspectives of students' language(s), culture(s), and communities. [InTASC 2e, 2i, 2k, 2m, 2o; CTQS 2c; NBPTS 1]
		E.2	Foster positive rapport (e.g., patience, caring) with students and facilitate positive interactions between students. [InTASC 2n; CTQS 2a; NBPTS 1]
		E.3	Communicate belief in capacity of all learners to achieve at high levels (e.g., college and career readiness, high expectations, growth mindset). [InTASC 2a, 2c; CTQS 2d; NBPTS 1, 3]
		E.4	Collaborate with parents/guardians/families to identify student interests and needs and set shared goals for student learning and development. [InTASC 2b, 2d, 2f; CTQS 2e; NBPTS 3]
	1.2 Maintain an equitable classroom environment. [InTASC 3; CTQS 2; NBPTS 1, 3]	E.5	Facilitate classroom norms and routines, in collaboration with students/families, that promote a positive learning community (e.g., clear expectations, positive reinforcement, individualized support). [InTASC 3a, 3c, 3k; CTQS 2a, 2f; NBPTS 3]
		E.6	Guide student behaviors through teacher moves (e.g., tone, movement, positioning, cues, key phrases, direct speech), and a system of incentives that promotes student empowerment. [InTASC 3k; CTQS 2f; NBPTS 3]
		E.7	Use predictable transition strategies to maintain students' focus on learning. [InTASC 3d, 3j; CTQS 2f; NBPTS 3]
		E.8	Use a systematic process to ensure students have necessary materials for learning. [InTASC 3b, 3d, 3g, 3h; CTQS 2f; NBPTS 3]
	1.3 Actively engage students in learning. [InTASC 1, 3; CTQS 2; NBPTS 1, 3]	E.9	Use a variety of active engagement strategies to ensure each student participates through discussion and movement (e.g., interactive technology, assistive technology, total physical response, call-and-response, storytelling, props, simulations, scenarios, games, music/rhythm, arts integration, visual and performing arts). [InTASC 1a, 1b, 1f, 1i; CTQS 2d; NBPTS 1, 3]
		E.10	Incorporate modalities that facilitate content learning (e.g., auditory, visual, kinesthetic, tactile, and intra/interpersonal, musical, naturalistic, logical, verbal, technological). [InTASC 1g, 1h; CTQS 2d; NBPTS 1, 3]
		E.11	Provide opportunities for students to experience joyful learning that includes discovery, application, collaboration, and/or advocacy for social justice issues. [InTASC 1c, 1d, 1j; CTQS 2c, 2d; NBPTS 1, 3]
		E.12	Demonstrate student-centered approach by consistently incorporating student voice, choice, teaching, and leadership. [InTASC 3e, 3f, 3l, 3m, 3o, 3p, 3q, 3r; CTQS 2fc, 2d; NBPTS 1, 3]

PLAN Plan rigorous, culturally responsive, standards- and outcome-based lesson and unit plans. [InTASC 4, 5, 6, 7; CTQS 1,3, 4; NBPTS 2, 4]	2.1 Use culturally responsive backward design curriculum planning to develop units. [InTASC 5; CTQS 1, 3; NBPTS 2]	P.1	Identify big ideas, essential questions, enduring understandings, and social justice themes that are relevant to students' interests and diversity. [InTASC 5a; CTQS 1d; NBPTS 2]
		P.2	Create engaging units of study that are aligned to relevant content, language, and college and career readiness standards. [InTASC 5h, 5j, 5e; CTQS 1a, 3e; NBPTS 2]
		P.3	Supplement or adapt district-approved curriculum to reflect student diversity, and promote cultural competence and critical consciousness. [InTASC 5i, 5k, 5s; CTQS 1a; NBPTS 2]
		P.4	Include materials and resources that reflect students' cultures and include a variety of cultures. [InTASC 5c, 5g, 5p, 5q; CTQS 1f; NBPTS 2]
		P.5	Design rigorous, relevant, and authentic unit performance tasks. [InTASC 5b, 5d, 5f, 5o; CTQS 1d, 1e, 1f, 3e; NBPTS 2]
		P.6	Develop a sequence of lessons aligned to unit goals and social justice pursuits. [InTASC 5n, 5m, 5l; CTQS 1e; NBPTS 2]
	2.2 Design measureable, challenging, and culturally responsive lessons. [InTASC 7; CTQS 1; NBPTS 2]	P.7	Set clear, rigorous, measureable content and language objective (CLO) based on unit goals. [InTASC 7a, 7d, 7f, 7g; CTQS 1e; NBPTS 2]
		P.8	Create a logical sequence with each lesson component aligning to objectives and assessments. [InTASC 7c, 7l, 7p; CTQS 1e; NBPTS 2]
		P.9	Develop rationale that connects lesson objective with unit goals, students' lives, real-world application, and social justice pursuits. [InTASC 7h, 7i, 7o; CTQS 1e; NBPTS 2]
		P.10	Incorporate topics that draw on student diversity (e.g., race, ethnicity, culture, gender, class, abilities, sexual orientation, religion) and include the contributions of diverse populations. [InTASC 7b, 7e, 7i, 7j, 7k, 7m, 7n, 7o, 7q; CTQS 1f; NBPTS 2]
		P.11	Provide opportunities for students to identify oppression locally and globally, counteract stereotypes, develop critical consciousness, and see themselves as agents of change. [InTASC 7h; CTQS 1f; NBPTS 2]

(continued)

(Cont.)

Dimension	Competency	Indicator	
	2.3 Integrate culturally responsive assessment into planning. [InTASC 6; CTQS 3, 4; NBPTS 2, 4]	P.12	Analyze assessments for validity, reliability, and bias (e.g., culture, language, gender, class, religion, etc.). [InTASC 6b, 6k, 6r; CTQS 3b, 3h, 4a, 4b; NBPTS 2, 4]
		P.13	Include a variety of assessment tools (e.g., formative, summative, authentic, project-based) to gather data on student learning. [InTASC 6a, 6c 6g, 6j, 6o, 6t; CTQS 3a, 4b; NBPTS 4]
		P.14	Analyze standardized and classroom-based student assessment data to set SMART learning targets. [InTASC 6m; CTQS 3b, 3c, 3e, 3h, 4a, 4b; NBPTS 2, 4]
		P.15	Use assessment data to identify individual and subgroup (e.g., EB/ELL, special needs, gifted) learning goals and design differentiated learning experiences. [InTASC 6e, 6g, 6h, 6i, 6p, 6u; CTQS 3b, 3e, 4a, 4b, 4c; NBPTS 2, 4]
		P.16	Use technology to collect, track, analyze, and share assessment data with students and families, and analyze trends in student progress to make planning decisions. [InTASC 6c, 6l, 6d, 6n, 6q, 6s, 6v; CTQS 3b, 4a; NBPTS 4]
	2.4 Demonstrate knowledge of content and student development. [InTASC 4; CTQS 1, 3; NBPTS 2, 4]	P.17	Analyze current research related to content pedagogy, and identify implications for teaching, learning, and equity. [InTASC 4a, 4j, 4c, 4o; CTQS 3c; NBPTS 2, 4]
		P.18	Understand how students' typical and atypical development (e.g., cognitive, socioemotional, linguistic) impacts learning. [InTASC 4f, 4m; CTQS 3a; NBPTS 2]
		P.19	Identify prerequisite content and language knowledge and skills, and typical student errors, misconceptions, and challenges. [InTASC 4d, 4e, 4k, 4l, 4p, 4q; CTQS 3b; NBPTS 2]
		P.20	Use knowledge of content to plan rigorous and relevant units and lessons that develop literacy and numeracy. [InTASC 4b, 4g, 4h, 4i, I4n, 4r; CTQS 1a, 1b; NBPTS 2]

TEACH Teach equitably by setting high expectations and providing support for student growth and development. [InTASC 2, 4, 7, 8; CTQS 1, 2, 3; NPBTS 1, 2, 4]	3.1 Set context for lesson. [InTASC 8, CTQS 1, 3; NBPTS 1, 2]	T.1	Post, preview, and review concise, rigorous, and measurable content and language objective (CLO). [InTASC 8k; CTQS 3g; NBPTS 1, 2]
		T.2	Engage students in discussing lesson rationale that connects content to students' diversity, prior content knowledge and skills, and interests. [InTASC 8p; CTQS 1e, 1f, 3g; NBPTS 1, 2]
		T.3	Promote real-world application of content in local, national, and global contexts. [InTASC 8g; CTQS 1e, 1f; NBPTS 1, 2]
		T.4	Clearly define performance expectations orally and in writing using student-friendly language. [InTASC 8m, 8g; CTQS 3g; NBPTS 1, 2]
	3.2 Facilitate clear and rigorous learning experiences. [InTASC 8; CTQS 1, 3; NBPTS 1, 2]	T.5	Provide clear, concise, and relevant explanations of content (e.g., mental models, culturally responsive examples, accessible language). [InTASC 4a; CTQS 1d; NBPTS 2]
		T.6	Use gradual release lesson cadence (I do, we do, you do) to scaffold students' independent application of learning. [InTASC 8d, 8s; CTQS 1d, 3a, 3c, 3e; NBPTS 1, 2]
		T.7	Align learning experiences to objectives. [InTASC 4b, 7a; CTQS 3b; NBPTS 2]
		T.8	Adequately pace learning experiences by attending to student learning cues and progress on learning tasks. [InTASC 8a, 8l; CTQS 1d, 3c; NBPTS 1, 2]
	3.3 Promote rigorous academic talk. [InTASC 8; CTQS 1, 3; NBPTS 2]	T.9	Promote higher-order thinking skills by providing opportunities for students to use academic language, make claims, and articulate reasoning. [InTASC 8f; CTQS 1b, 3c, 3e; NBPTS 2]
		T.10	Facilitate academic conversations by posing high-level questions, and asking students to pose questions and explain their thinking (e.g., elaborate, clarify, provide examples, build on or challenge ideas, paraphrase, synthesize). [InTASC 8i; CTQS 1b, 3c, 3e; NBPTS 2]
		T.11	Set discussion norms with students and facilitate student conversations that foster critical consciousness (e.g., analyze multiple perspectives, ask critical questions, advocate for systemic change). [InTASC 8g; CTQS 1b, 3e; NBPTS 2]

(continued)

(Cont.)

Dimension	Competency	Indicator	
	3.4 Make content and language comprehensible for all learners. [InTASC 2, 8; CTQS 1, 2, 3; NBPTS 2]	T.12	Incorporate students' home language (e.g., heritage language, vernaculars, code-switching, translanguaging) into instruction and include materials in students' home language. [InTASC 2e; CTQS 1b, 2a, 2b, 2c; NBPTS 2]
		T.13	Preview vocabulary to support understanding of concepts and context, and development of academic language. [InTASC 8e, 8h, 8q; CTQS 1b, 3a, 3c; NBPTS 2]
		T.14	Incorporate sensory, graphic, and interactive supports (e.g., technology, visuals, manipulative/realia, key vocabulary, graphic organizers, concept maps, sentence stems, total physical response, modeling, and cooperative learning). [InTASC 8i, 8h, 8m, 8r, 8o; CTQS 3a, 3c, 3d; NBPTS 2]
	3.5 Use formal and informal assessment data to monitor student progress toward learning targets. [InTASC 8; CTQS 2, 3, 4; NBPTS 4]	T.15	Collect data on individual student progress toward content and language objective and analyze data to adjust instruction for individuals and subgroups (e.g., EB/ELL, special needs, gifted). [InTASC 8b, 8l, 8s; CTQS 3h, 4a; NBPTS 4]
		T.16	Engage students in continually assessing their own progress toward unit/lesson objectives and personal/group goals. [InTASC 8c; CTQS 3b, 4a, 4b; NBPTS 4]
		T.17	Provide students with frequent, timely, specific, and individual/group feedback. [InTASC 6d; CTQS 2e, 3e, 4a; NBPTS 4]
		T.18	Frequently check for understanding and adjust instruction according to evidence of student learning. [InTASC 8b; CTQS 2d, 4a, 4c; NBPTS 4]
	3.6 Differentiate instruction to challenge students and meet diverse student needs. [InTASC 8; CTQS 2, 4; NBPTS 1, 2, 4]	T.19	Use assessment data to differentiate instruction according to student needs (e.g., language levels, special needs, learning modalities, socioemotional). [InTASC 8a, 8b, 8h, 8l, 8s; CTQS 4a; NBPTS 2, 4]
		T.20	Implement flexible grouping strategies to meet diverse student needs. [InTASC 8s; CTQS 4c; NBPTS 1, 2, 4]
		T.21	Provide options for differentiated content, learning experiences, and/or assessments that allow for student choice and expression of cultural ways of knowing. [InTASC 8e; CTQS 2c, 2d; NBPTS 1, 2, 4]

		T.22	Collaborate with support specialists to develop and apply specific accommodations for individual students based on language needs, IEPs, and other legal requirements. [InTASC 8p; CTQS 4c; NBPTS 1, 2, 4]
LEAD Lead by exemplifying professionalism and community advocacy. [InTASC 9, 10; CTQS 4, 5; NBTS 4, 5]	4.1 Meet professional standards of practice. [InTASC 9, 10; CTQS 4, 5; NBPTS 4, 5]	L.1	Adhere to ethical and legal responsibilities for students' learning, behavior, safety, confidentiality, and civil rights as specified in local, state, and federal statutes. [InTASC 9a, 9e, 9f, 9j, 9o; CTQS 5d; NBPTS 4]
		L.2	Maintain professional demeanor and communication in accordance with school, district, and/or university policy. [InTASC 9b, 9o, 10n; CTQS 5d; NBPTS 4]
		L.3	Collaborate with community and school partners to support students' needs (e.g., parents/guardians, community organizations, school psychologists, counselors, social workers, nurses) [InTASC 10d, 10m, 10q; CTQS 4c, 5b, 5c; NBPTS 4, 5]
	4.2 Demonstrate growth and commitment to students and communities. [InTASC 9, 10; CTQS 4, 5; NBPTS 4, 5]	L.4	Recognize own biases and how these affect teaching and learning, and take action to monitor and eliminate bias. [InTASC 9b, 9m, 9n, 10m, 10q; CTQS 4b, 4c, 5d; NBPTS 4]
		L.5	Use feedback and data to set clear and measurable goals to improve instruction and promote student learning and development. [InTASC 9c, 9g, 9k, 9m, 10b; CTQS 4b; NBPTS 4]
		L.6	Participate in school, district, and community initiatives and advocate for community needs (e.g., professional development opportunities, school events, community engagement). [InTASC 10f, 10h, 10j, 10k, 10p, 10r, 10s, 10t; CTQS 5a; NBPTS 5]

INDEX

Note: Page numbers in **bold** denote tables.

Angelou, M. 28
Anzaldúa, G. 47, 148
Askew, K. 11, 16
asset orientation 102, 114, 127, **154**
Ayers, W. 140

Banks, J. A. 13, 84, 91
Bonilla-Silva, E. 48, 49

Cammarota, J. 6, 85
Classroom Assessment Scoring System
  (CLASS) 5, 60, 62, 87
Coates, T. 33, 36, 48, 49–50, 139, 141,
  143, 146
Cochran-Smith, M. 85, 143
color-blind 38, 39, 49–50, 53, 79
community: Communities of Color 7,
  9, 41, 44, 48, 49–50, 63, 65, 79–80, 88,
  91, 140, 142, 144, 149; community
  engagement 10, **14**, 20, 44, 66, **79**,
  91, 118, 122–123, **124**, 126, 129, 132,
  135–136, 149, **161**, **168**, **179**
community cultural wealth 7, 35, 36, 50
counternarrative 7, 79–80, 107
critical consciousness 7–8, 10–11, **14**, 16,
  34, 36, 53, **54**, **75**, **77**, 84–85, 87, 107,
  113–114, 116–118, 123, 142–143, **154**,
  156, **157**, **159**, **165**, **175**, **177**
critical race theory (CRT) 47–51, 63, 65,
  79–80, 88, 139, 147; CRT methodology
  80, 142

cultural competence 6, 9, 11, **14**, 17, 19, **75**,
  90, 132, **154**, **156**, **175**
cultural intuition 80
culturally responsive assessment (CRA) 6,
  9–11, **76**, **157**, **176**
culturally responsive evaluation (CRE)
  6, 11–13, **14**, 15–20, 26–28, 88, 90,
  121, 139
culturally responsive pedagogy (CRP)
  6–10, 13, **14**, 16–20, 40, 82, 88, 96,
  121, 139
culturally responsive teacher evaluation
  (CRTE) 6, 13, **14**, 15–19, 26, 36, 40, 55,
  63, 73, 79–80, 85, 89, 91, 96, 119–122,
  124, **125**, 126–130, 132, 134–136, 139,
  141–142, 144
culturally sustaining pedagogy 7
culture of power 7–8, 10, 36, 53, 65, 83, 85,
  107, 140–142

Danielson, C. 5, 53, 55–58, 62, **63**,
  65, 80, 82
Danielson's Framework for Teaching 5, 53,
  55–58, 62
Darder, A. 7, 85
Darling-Hammond, L. 4–5, 27,
  51–52, 83–84
deficit orientation 50, 59
Delgado Bernal, D. 80
Delpit, L. 15, 84
Dixson, A. 142

dominant culture 1, 6, 7, 27, 41, 47, 49, 52, 53–56, 62–64, 73, 83, 85, 124, 139–142, 145
Du Bois, W. E. B. 28–29, 47
Duncan-Andrade, J. 36, 42, 84, 85
Dyer, R. 49

English Language Learner (ELL) 16, 43, 55, **76**, **77**, 84, 87, 100, 102, 110, 113, 115, **154**, **157**, **159**, **176**, **178**
Eurocentric 52, 105

Fine, M. 85
Framework for Equitable and Excellent Teaching (FEET) 55, 61–62, **62**, **63**, 73, **74–79**, 79–80, **81**, 82–91, 95, 97–98, 101–102, 106, 109, 112, 114, 118, 120–121, 123, 127–131, 133–135, 140–144, **154–179**
Franquiz, M. E. 49, 94
Freire, P. 7, 35, 94–95, 117, 119, 142, 145, 147
Frierson, H. T. 16, 19
funds of knowledge 35–36

Gay, G. 84, 85
Gonzalez, N. 35
Grande, S. 52
Grant, C. 84, 85

Hawley, W. D. 6, 16
historically marginalized communities 3, 13, 35, 41, 44, 50–51, 79–85, 89, 91, 121–124, 126, 133, 140–142, 144–147, 149
Hollins, E. R. 84
Hood, S. 11, 19
hooks, b. 35, 140, 148
Hopson, R. 11, 17, 19, 88
Howard, T. 42, 51, 84
humanity/humanization 31–36, 53, 64, 107, 114–115, 141–142

International Society for Technology in Education (ISTE) 133
Interstate Teacher Assessment and Support Consortium (InTASC) 15, 42, 80, 82–83, 133, 173, **174–179**
Irvine, J. J. 6, 16, 84

Kirkhart, K. 11, 17, 88, 127, 134
Kumashiro, K. 85, 140

Ladson-Billings, G. 4, 6–9, 17, 48–49, 82, 84, 131, 147
Lawless, E. 140
Lorde, A. 108, 141, 143, 145, 148, 149
Lucas, T. 84
Lynn, M. 48, 142

McGee Banks, C. A. 13, 84, 91
Marzano Teacher Evaluation Model 5, 53, 55, 58–60, 62–63
masternarratives 33–35, 49–50
Measure of Teacher Effectiveness (MET) 55–56, 60, 130, 135
Milner, H. R. 35, 48, 63, 84, 85
Moll, L. 35, 84
Morrell, E. 52, 84, 140
multicultural validity **14**, 17, 88, 123, 127, 134

National Board for Professional Teaching Standards (NBPTS) 15, 80, 133, 173, **174–179**
Nieto, S. 5, 6, 35, 49, 84, 85

Oakes, J. 84
Organisation for Economic Cooperation and Development (OECD) 3–4

Paris, D. 7
Parsons, B. A. 17, 27, 90
Pianta, R. C. 5, 60–61, 87
power of change 7–9, 51–53, 83–85, 140–143
power of culture 7–9, 51–53, 83–85, 106–107, 140–143
privilege 7–12, 16–17, 32, 40–41, 48–52, 64–65, 100, 113, 116, 121, 146

race 3, 43, 47–53, 65–66, **75**, 79–80, 85, 96–97, 106–108, 110, 149, **157**, **175**
racism 26–28, 33–40, 47–53, 143, 149
radical imaginary 145–147
reliability 13, **14**, 16–18, **76**, **81**, 85–87, 123–124, **125**, 127, 129–130, 133, **157**, 171, **176**
Rios, F. 48, 50, 79
Rousseau, C. K. 142

Salazar, M. **14**, 28–40, 42, 49, 53, 55, 57, 62, 73, 80, 84, 128, 142
Scholars of Color 82–83, 123–124, 142
Shakur, T. 28, 35–36, 43
Sleeter, C. E. 19, 84, 85

social justice 8, 10, 12–13, **14**, 17–18, 33–36, 40, 42–44, 48, 50–53, **54**, **74**, **75**, 79–80, 84–85, 88–89, 99–100, 104–107, 114–116, 118, 121, 123–124, **125**, 127, 129, 131–132, 142, 144–146, 148, **154**, **157**, **164**, **174**, **175**
sociocultural 6, 11–12, 18–19
sociopolitical 7–9, 12
Solorzano, D. 48
Stovall, D. 50, 140
Stronge, J. H. 84
student growth and development 13, **14**, 16, **76**, 83–85, **125**, 126–127, **158**, **164**, **168**, **169**, **177**
student outcomes 4, 13, **14**, 18, 88–89, 123, 125, 127–129, 131–134, 142
Students of Color 3, 34–35, 37–38, 48–50, 59, 63–64, 95, 100–101, 104–107, 112–113
subtractive schooling 35, 50

teacher evaluation: adopting 128–132; assessing 10, 13, 52, **54**, 56, 60–63, **75–78**, 83, 88–90, 123–124, **125**, 127–128, 144, 149, **159**, **167**, **178**; designing 56, 87, 102, 128, 132–134
teaching competencies: assessment 5–11, **14**, **54**, 56, 60–62, **75–76**, **78**, 90, 115, 122–128, 132–136, 142, 144, 149,

157–158, **159–160**, **166–167**, **175**, **178**; classroom management 8, 101–103, 109; scaffolding/differentiation 10, 52, **55**, 56, **77–78**, 99, **158**, **165**, **177**
The New Teacher Project (TNTP) 4, 51, **172**
Thomas, V. G. 17, 27, 90

Urrieta, L. 35, 52, 143
U.S. Department of Education 27, 95

Valencia, R. R. 35, 50
Valenzuela, A. 35
validity 13, **14**, 16–18, **76**, **81**, 83, 85, 87–89, 123–124, **125**, 127, 129–130, 133–134, **157**, **176**
Villegas, A. M. 84
Villenas, S. A. 143

Walqui, A. 84
White privilege 48, 49–50, 65, 106–107
White supremacy 106–108
Whitestream 35, 52–53, 57–63, 88–89, 141, 144–147

Yamamoto, E. K. 50
Yosso, T. 7, 35, 48, 50, 84

Zamudio, M. 79